DESCRIPTION OF THE CLERGY

IN RURAL RUSSIA

CONTENTS

[5]

Contents

I. S. BELLIUSTIN

DESCRIPTION OF THE CLERGY IN RURAL RUSSIA

THE MEMOIR OF A NINETEENTH-CENTURY PARISH PRIEST

TRANSLATED WITH AN INTERPRETIVE ESSAY BY
GREGORY L. FREEZE

CORNELL UNIVERSITY PRESS

ITHACA AND LONDON

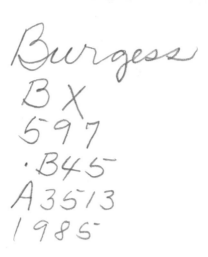

First published as *Opisanie sel'skogo
dukhovenstva* in Paris, 1858.

First published 1985 by Cornell University Press.

International Standard Book Number (cloth) 0-8014-1796-1
International Standard Book Number (paper) 0-8014-9335-8
Library of Congress Catalog Card Number 85-47699
Printed in the United States of America
*Librarians: Library of Congress cataloging information
appears on the last page of the book.*

*The paper in this book is acid-free and meets the guidelines for
permanence and durability of the Committee on Production Guidelines
for Book Longevity of the Council on Library Resources.*

PREFACE

Hardly any dimension of the ancien régime in Russia is more neglected and less understood than the Orthodox church and religious life. With the completion of Peter's synodal reform in 1721, the church silently vanishes from the standard histories and textbooks; what the church subsequently preached, what the clergy did, and what the people believed are all subjects about which we assume much and know little. This ignorance stands in marked contrast to the substantial literature on secular Russia. Historians have only begun to assemble elementary data, explore basic sources, and pose rudimentary questions about the fate of "Holy Rus' " in modern Russia. The present volume offers a famous exposé and reform memoir from the mid–nineteenth century which should give readers a fresh new perspective on the church—its problems at the grass-roots parish level, its prospects for reform in the last turbulent decades of the ancien régime.

Intended as a private memoir for the tsar but published without its author's knowledge or consent, I. S. Belliustin's *Opisanie sel'skogo dukhovenstva* (1858) has never been translated before and is a bibliographical rarity even in the Russian original. The present volume provides a full translation of the published text; all headings and ellipses in the text are Belliustin's. My notes provide some pertinent supplementary material, including explanations of obscure terms and references and the text of parts of the manuscript omitted from the published version. The translation itself seeks to reproduce the precise meaning of the original in idiomatic English; for the sake of readability and English convention, I have

[7]

divided some of Belliustin's paragraphs (which at times run on for several pages) and converted his first person plural ("we") to the singular ("I"). Some referents have been supplied to clarify the vague "this," which abounds in Belliustin's hasty prose. Transliteration follows the customary American practice, orthography has been modernized, and dates are given in accordance with the Old Style (Julian) calendar, which lagged twelve days behind that of the West in the nineteenth century. Belliustin's notes to the text are indicated by asterisks; my own follow the customary numerical form of notation.

Parts of the Introduction have appeared in different form in two of my earlier works: "Revolt from Below: A Priest's Manifesto on the Crisis in Russian Orthodoxy," in *Russian Orthodoxy under the Old Regime* (Minneapolis: University of Minnesota Press, 1978), pp. 90–124; and *The Parish Clergy in Nineteenth-Century Russia: Crisis, Reform, Counter-reform* (Princeton: Princeton University Press, 1983). I am grateful to both the University of Minnesota Press and Princeton University Press for permission to use, in revised form, this copyrighted material.

I also wish to acknowledge the support of various institutions and individuals in the preparation of this work. For material support and the opportunity to use Soviet archives I am much indebted to the International Research and Exchanges Board; a grant from the Alexander von Humboldt–Stiftung also made possible some final revisions in the translation and scholarly apparatus. And to Karen Freeze and Norman Naimark, who have read this work in various drafts and offered valuable criticisms on style and substance, I am very grateful indeed.

GREGORY L. FREEZE

Arlington, Massachusetts

ARCHIVAL ABBREVIATIONS

GAKO   Gosudarstvennyi arkhiv Kalininskoi oblasti
   f. 103   Tverskaia uchenaia arkhivnaia komissiia
   f. 160   Tverskaia dukhovnaia konsistoriia
IRLI   Institut russkoi literatury (Pushkinskii dom)
   f. 3   Aksakovy
   f. 34   S. O. Burachek
   f. 93   A. K. Korsak
   f. 274   M. I. Semevskii
   f. 319   P. S. Usov
   f. 616   A. D. Zheltukhin
LOII   Leningradskoe otdelenie instituta istorii
   f. 115   Kollektsiia rukopisnykh knig
OR GBL   Otdel rukopisei, Gosudarstvennaia biblioteka im. V. I. Lenina
   f. 120   M. N. Katkov
   f. 231   M. P. Pogodin
   f. 302   A. P. Tolstoi
   f. 316   Filaret (Drozdov)
   f. 327   Cherkasskie
   f. 344   P. P. Shibanov
OR GPB   Otdel rukopisei, Gosudarstvennaia publichnaia biblioteka im. M. E. Saltykova-Shchedrina
   f. 37   A. I. Artem'ev
   f. 52   Batiushkovy
   f. 377   I. P. Kornilov
   f. 391   A. A. Kraevskii
   f. 542   Oleniny
   f. 550   Osnovnoe sobranie rukopisnykh knig

Archival Abbreviations

TsGALI	Tsentral'nyi gosudarstvennyi arkhiv literatury i iskusstva
f. 275	N. S. Leskov
TsGAOR	Tsentral'nyi gosudarstvennyi arkhiv oktiabr'skoi revoliutsii
f. 109	Tret'e otdelenie
TsGIA SSSR	Tsentral'nyi gosudarstvennyi istoricheskii arkhiv SSSR
f. 776	Glavnoe upravlenie po delam pechati
f. 779	Tsentral'nyi komitet tsenzury inostrannoi
f. 796	Kantseliariia Sv. Sinoda
f. 797	Kantseliariia Ober-prokurora
f. 804	Osoboe prisutstvie po delam pravoslavnogo dukhovenstva
f. 807	S.-Peterburgskii dukhovnyi tsenzurnyi komitet
f. 832	Filaret (Drozdov)

The customary form of Soviet archival notation is observed here, with the following abbreviations:

ch.	*chast'* (part)
d.	*delo* (file)
f.	*fond* (collection)
g.	*god* (year)
k.	*karton* (carton)
l., ll.	*list, listy* (leaf, leaves)
ob.	*oborot* (verso)
op.	*opis'* (inventory)
otd.	*otdelenie* (department)
r.	*razdel* (division)
st.	*stol* (section)

DESCRIPTION OF THE CLERGY

IN RURAL RUSSIA

INTRODUCTION

Soon after Ioann Stefanovich Belliustin's *Description of the Clergy in Rural Russia* appeared in French bookstalls in 1858, it became a sensation in Russia.[1] It was a book without precedent: a rural priest in Russia had dared to denounce his superiors in print, exposed all the seamy sides of the ecclesiastical establishment, and summoned the state to impose reform on the church. For most laymen, even those closely associated with the church, it was their first inside view of the church and its clergy.[2] And what they found in Belliustin's slim volume was a shocking exposé of an institution in such disarray and so racked by evil and injustice that it simply could not perform its high mission to the world. On Belliustin's canvas the bishops appeared tyrannical and cruel, ecclesiastical administration venal and incompetent, seminaries ineffectual and misdirected, priests destitute and demoralized. Not surprisingly, government authorities prohibited public sale

---

1. The book was published anonymously under the title *Opisanie sel'skogo dukhovenstva* by a Paris publisher; the actual printing was done in Leipzig. The volume appeared as the fourth in the underground series Russkii zagranichnyi sbornik (A Russian miscellany abroad).
2. Thus even N. V. Gogol' candidly—and correctly—confessed that "in general we know the church poorly" (TsGIA SSSR, f. 797, op. 8, d. 37414, l. 7). The reason for such ignorance was in large part the vigilance of censorship in Nikolaevan Russia, which interdicted virtually all discussion of the church and religion, even of a conservative variety. For a good discussion of prereform ecclesiastical censorship, see A. Kotovich, *Dukhovnaia tsenzura v Rossii, 1799–1855 gg.* [St. Petersburg, 1909].

and circulation of the book—an act of repression that, naturally enough, guaranteed the widest possible interest and circulation.[3]

The volume was no passing fashion: it profoundly changed the politics and parameters of church reform in Russia. At the uppermost levels of the church and state, it significantly broadened the scope of reform, which, though previously under consideration, now acquired a new urgency and far wider dimensions. Still more dramatic was the book's impact on society, for Belliustin's poignant description of the "downtrodden parish clergy" won the sympathy of educated readers and their support for fundamental reform in the church.[4] Less visible but ultimately of still greater import was the book's impact on Belliustin's peers—the parish clergy. The passionate expression of their needs and interests, together with the apparent sympathy of the emperor and of educated society, served to swell the clergy's expectations that reform would be fundamental, swift, and munificent.[5] The book, quite naturally, had the contrary effect on its chief villains, the bishops, who were stunned by its vitriolic tone and aghast at its enormous popularity in high society and high circles. Suggestive, if apocryphal, was the purported reaction of the metropolitan of St. Petersburg, Grigorii (Postnikov), who was "so thunderstruck by the book's contents that it fell out of his hands."[6] Belliustin's book also had an enormous impact on the self-consciousness of the parish clergy, for it provided a manifesto against monastic control of the church, and penetrated the seminary as well, stirring discontent and even disorders.[7] With good reason, a prominent

3. In 1870 *Opisanie sel'skogo dukhovenstva* was still on the government's list of proscribed books; see *Alfavitnyi katalog knigam na russkom iazyke, zapreshchennym k obrashcheniiu i perepechataniiu v Rossii* [St. Petersburg, 1870], p. 12.
4. For the electrifying effect of Belliustin's book upon educated "society" (*obshchestvo*) in St. Petersburg, see the memoir of that well-informed racanteur A. V. Nikitenko, *Dnevnik*, 3 vols. (Moscow, 1955–56), 2:31.
5. For a typical comment on the response of parish clergy and seminarians to the book, see F. Dobroklonskii, "Vospominaniia o proidennoi zhizni," *Mirnyi trud*, 1909, no. 9, p. 63.
6. D. I. Rostislavov, *O chernom i belom pravoslavnom dukhovenstve*, 2 vols. (Leipzig, 1866), 1:22.
7. For evidence that Belliustin's volume was responsible for sparking student

newspaper in St. Petersburg recalled the book's sensational impact in 1858 and even compared it with that of Alexander Radishchev's *Journey from St. Petersburg to Moscow* in 1790.[8] Without question, Belliustin's volume presaged a whole new era in Russian church history.

CHURCH AND CLERGY IN RUSSIA, 1700–1855

When Peter the Great promulgated the church reform of 1721, he did a great deal more than simply replace the patriarchate with a collegial board of bishops known as the Holy Synod.[9] His primary aim was not to domesticate an obdurate patriarchate but to reconstruct the church's administration, to make the church a more effective institution. And for Peter that task required essentially a "regularized administration" like that established for the state—that is, a centralized, rationally structured organization operating in accordance with an explicit code of rules. Thus here, as in other domains, Peter's reform was fundamentally pragmatic; Peter sought not to "Westernize" the church, or to incorporate it into the state administration, but simply to superimpose the kind

---

disorders in the St. Petersburg Ecclesiastical Academy, see the letter from Metropolitan Isidor to Metropolitan Filaret in TsGIA SSSR, f. 832, op. 1, d. 15, ll. 121 ob.–122.

8. "Vnutrennee obozrenie o noveishikh reformakh dukhovenstva," *Nedelia*, 1868, no. 29, p. 898. For a similar assessment, though from a fiercely negative point of view, see N. V. Elagin, *Beloe dukhovenstvo i ego interesy* (St. Petersburg, 1881), p. 4.

9. The standard study of the Petrine reform is P. V. Verkhovskoi, *Uchrezhdenie Dukhovnoi Kollegii i dukhovnyi reglament*, 2 vols. (Rostov on Don, 1916). More recent literature has added little to this classic study: James Cracraft, *The Church Reforms of Peter the Great* (Stanford, 1971); G. L. Bissonnette, "Pufendorf and the Church Reforms of Peter the Great," Ph.D. dissertation, Columbia University, 1962; H. Fink, "Die Auswirkungen der Reform Peters des Grossen auf das Kirchenrecht der russischen orthodoxen Kirche, Juristische Dissertation, Erlangen, 1963; and O. F. Kozlov, "Tserkovnaia reforma pervoi chetverti XVIII v.," Candidate dissertation, Moscow State University, 1970.

of good order and good rules that he had already prescribed for secular administration.[10] The institutional charter for this new order was the Ecclesiastical Regulations of 1721, which adumbrated not only a new set of objectives for the church—such as improvement of clerical education, eradication of superstition, and conversion of schismatic dissidents—but also a whole new structure of church administration (see figure 1).[11]

The most visible change occurred at the top, where Peter replaced the patriarchate with a collegial board of bishops at first called the Ecclesiastical College. Though originally conceived as nothing more than another branch of the collegial administration, the new body almost immediately changed both its name (to Most Holy Governing Synod) and its status (becoming formal peer of the Senate, the supreme administrative body in secular administration). In 1722 Peter established the office of chief procurator (*ober-prokuror*) as lay overseer of the Synod, but did not alter its internal structure or legal status. The Petrine model thus established two parallel, nominally equal but separate domains—the "ecclesiastical domain" under the Synod and the "secular domain" under the Senate. Each was formally and directly subordinate to the emperor, but in routine matters was to operate with de facto autonomy in its particular domain. The chief procurator subsequently did augment his authority in the Synod (especially from the second quarter of the nineteenth century), but ultimate responsibility always rested with the Synod's clerical members; the chief procurator, no matter how influential he might become, never became a lay patriarch. But the most important effect of the synodal reform was to impose administrative unity on the

10. For penetrating critiques of the Westernization thesis, see such typical products of the Münster school as H.-J. Härtl, *Bysantinische Erbe und Orthodoxie bei Feofan Prokopovič* (Würzburg, 1970); Peter Hauptmann, *Die Katechismen der Russischen Orthodoxen Kirche. Entstehungsgeschichte und Lehrgehalt* (Göttingen, 1971); R. O. Stupperich, "Ursprung, Motive und Beurteilung der Kirchenreform unter Peter dem Grossen," *Kirche im Osten*, 17 (1974): 42–61. For a critique of the integration thesis, see G. L. Freeze, "Handmaiden of the State? The Church in Imperial Russia Reconsidered," *Journal of Ecclesiastical History*, 36 (1985): 82–102.
11. For a convenient English translation of the Ecclesiastical Regulations, see A. V. Muller, ed. and trans., *The Spiritual Regulations of Peter the Great* (Seattle, 1972).

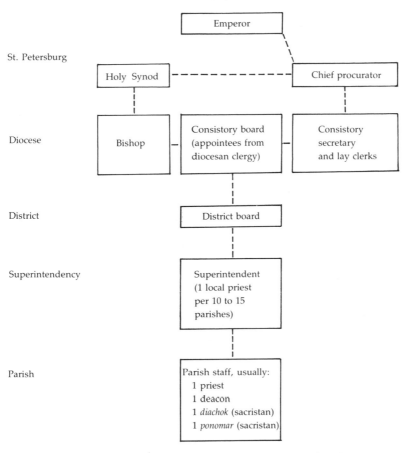

Figure 1. Structure of the Russian Orthodox Church

church: for the first time the church had a single, centralized system, with a supreme organ possessing not mere theoretical dominance but real administrative control over the subordinate dioceses.

Diocesan administration changed more slowly, but by the mid– or late eighteenth century had acquired the basic features that would last until the end of the imperial period. The diocese, though still the main administrative unit, became smaller and more manageable, and by the end of the century had been made

[17]

identical to a state province in most parts of the empire. As in earlier times, each diocese was governed by a bishop, who might hold one of three ascending personal ranks: bishop, archbishop, or metropolitan. The backbone of his administration was the consistory, a collegial board of five to seven clergy appointed from the ranks of local abbots, archpriests, and priests. For all the bishop's monocratic authority, it was actually the consistory that performed much of the day-to-day administrative toil—reviewing reports, investigating ecclesiastical crimes, and drafting resolutions for the bishop to approve, revise, or reject. At a lower level, each diocesan administration had several district boards, each responsible for two or three administrative districts (*uezdy*), and at the bottom, several score of ecclesiastical superintendents (*blagochinnye*), each responsible for ten to fifteen churches. By the late eighteenth century this pattern of organization existed in most dioceses, providing a uniform structure and integrated chain of command to execute the Synod's or bishop's will.

Whereas reform in the Synod or even diocesan administration proved relatively simple, it was far more difficult—both more complex and more costly—to impose changes at the parish level. The main task, as the authorities defined it, was to limit the numbers of churches and clergy to those genuinely needed and to place the parish on a firmer economic foundation. As Peter complained from the outset of his reign, the church had hitherto tolerated a senseless proliferation of churches and clergy, far in excess of either the parishioners' needs or their capacity to provide for them.[12] Beginning in the reign of Peter the Great, the state placed severe restrictions on the establishment of new parishes, requiring not only proof of real need but also the formal consent of the Synod.[13] To be sure, the state did not attempt a systematic

12. See, for example, Peter's decree in *Polnoe sobranie zakonov Rossiiskoi Imperii*, 1st ser. (hereafter cited as *PSZ*[1]), 45 vols. (St. Petersburg, 1830), vol. 5, no. 2985. Background data on the proliferation of churches and clergy in the eighteenth century are to be found in I. M. Pokrovskii, *Russkie eparkhii v XVI–XIX vv., ikh otkrytie i predely*, 2 vols. (Kazan, 1897–1913), 1:174–175, 234–235.
13. *PSZ(1)*, vol. 5, nos. 2985 and 3171; vol. 6, no. 3991; vol. 19, no. 13541.

reorganization of parishes into larger and more viable units, and
it did leave a loophole, permitting new parishes to be established
where real demographic need could be shown. Nevertheless, it
gradually achieved its principal goal: the elimination of tiny parishes and an increase in the number of parishioners ascribed to
each church.[14] To limit the number of clergymen in each parish,
in 1722 the Synod established the parish registry (*dukhovnyi shtat*),
a table of organization that fixed a numerical relationship between
the population of a parish and the size of the local clerical staff.[15]
Although cathedrals and more populous parishes might have larger
staffs, the typical rural or small-town parish had a staff of three
or four clerics—one priest assisted by two sacristans and often by
a deacon as well.[16] The fixed registry, together with the restrictions
on new parishes, brought a steady increase in the ratio of parishioners to clergy. That change, by increasing the lay population
that provided material support to the clergy, did promise to
improve their economic condition or at least to reduce the burden
on individual parishioners. Salutary as this change may have been
for parish economies, it had a deleterious effect on religious life
in the parish, for the individual clergyman now frequently had
to serve an exceedingly large population. And given the fact that
priests formed but a minority of the parish clergy (the bulk being
composed of deacons and sacristans), the ratio between parishioner and priest (not just clergyman) was extremely high—
among the highest in Europe, more like that of Protestant churches
than Catholic ones. But the Russian Orthodox clergy had to perform far more liturgical and sacramental duties (confession, prayer
services, masses, and a host of other rites) than the Protestant
clergy. As a consequence, a typical priest such as Belliustin found

14. For data showing an increase of 20 to 40 percent in central dioceses, see G. L.
Freeze, *The Russian Levites: Parish Clergy in the Eighteenth Century* (Cambridge,
Mass., 1977), p. 134.
15. *PSZ(1)*, vol. 6, no. 4035.
16. The two sacristans, who were not given rites of ordination but merely installed
in their positions, bore different titles (*diachok* and *ponomar*) but differed little in
education, status, or function.

it scarcely possible to perform traditional ritualistic functions effectively, much less assume such new ones as public education and catechization.

Despite Peter's imperious order for the establishment of seminaries, it was decades before the church could comply.[17] With virtually nothing to build on (ecclesiastical schools were virtually nonexistent in seventeenth-century Russia), the Russian church sought to model its schools on the Latin grammar school of the West, then still the model for elite education, adapted to include some specialized instruction in religion and theology. As the painful histories of individual seminaries abundantly demonstrate, the church had to overcome enormous barriers before it finally succeeded in establishing a stable educational order.

That success finally came after the mid–eighteenth century. Beginning in the 1750s and 1760s and continuing through the following decades, the schools recorded a steady upward spiral in enrollments, from 4,673 in 1766 to 20,397 in 1799.[18] In 1814 authorities reorganized this system into a four-tiered structure but essentially preserved the basic Latin curriculum.[19] Growth continued apace in the ensuing decades, with total enrollments rising to 61,798 pupils by the mid–nineteenth century.[20] Apart from producing more than an ample supply of ordinands, the church schools had a profound impact on the clergy's social and

17. Still the most detailed general treatment is the old classic by P. V. Znamenskii, *Dukhovnye shkoly v Rossii do reformy 1808 g.* (Kazan, 1881). For a more recent treatment, see Freeze, *Russian Levites*, chap. 4; Erich Bryner, *Der geistliche Stand in Russland: Sozialgeschichtliche Untersuchungen zu Episkopat und Gemeindegeistlichkeit der russischen orthodoxen Kirche im 18. Jahrhundert* (Göttingen, 1982); Christopher B. Becker, "The Church School in Tsarist Social and Educational Policy from Peter to the Great Reforms," Ph.D. dissertation, Harvard University, 1964.
18. TsGIA SSSR, f. 796, op. 51, g. 1770, d. 470, ll. 11–12; M. T. Beliavskii, "Shkola i obrazovanie v Rossii v kontse XVIII v.," *Vestnik MGU*, istoriko-filologicheskaia seriia, 1959, no. 2, pp. 105–120.
19. *PSZ(1)*, vol. 30, no. 23122; vol. 32, nos. 25673, 25674, 25676, 25678a. For a general overview with references to more specialized literature, see G. L. Freeze, *The Parish Clergy in Nineteenth-Century Russia: Crisis, Reform, Counter-reform* (Princeton, 1983), pp. 103–110.
20. B. V. Titlinov, *Dukhovnaia shkola v XIX v.*, 2 vols. (Vilna, 1908–9), 1:101.

service profile. Formal education of the clergy improved dramatically and soon became the primary determinant of career patterns. Whereas the ordinand in 1750 had little or no formal education, a candidate in 1800 had to demonstrate some study at the seminary, and within a few decades such aspirants had to possess a full seminary education to qualify for a position.[21] Although standards varied considerably from diocese to diocese, by the mid–nineteenth century a full seminary education had become the norm virtually everywhere—in striking contrast to the usual stereotype of illiterate, ignorant priests that has prevailed in most accounts.[22] Significantly, however, the radical improvement in formal education did *not* extend to the deacons and sacristans, who continued to hold only a modicum of formal education and almost never a seminary degree.[23] The difference in education created an enormous gap between the priest and his lesser colleagues, impelling many parish priests, such as Belliustin, to hold them in contempt and to demand their formal exclusion from the clerical estate.

The seminary, furthermore, proved a major dynamic in the transformation of the clergy, both monastic and secular, into a closed social estate. Although the signs of social separateness were visible earlier, it was only in the eighteenth century that the parish clergy became hermetically sealed off from the other social classes in Russian society. This social process accorded in every

---

21. In 1800 only 20 percent of priests had studied in the uppermost divisions of the seminary (the philosophy and theology divisions), but those standards underwent a revolutionary improvement in the next few decades: by 1835 some 43 percent of all priests held a seminary diploma, and by 1860 some 83 percent could claim this distinction. See TsGIA SSSR, f. 796, op. 107, g. 1826, d. 460, l. 29–29 ob; op. 117; g. 1836, d. 1210, ll. 3–6; op. 142, g. 1861, d. 2379.

22. For some data on the regional variations in clerical education, see Freeze, *Parish Clergy*, pp. 156–159. By mid-century, as the reports of the chief procurator demonstrate, virtually all new ordinands in the empire held a seminary diploma. See, for instance, the report in *Izvlecheniia iz otcheta po vedomstvu dukhovnykh del pravoslavnogo ispovedaniia za 1860 god* (St. Petersburg, 1862), p. 19.

23. In 1860, for example, only 16 percent of all deacons held a seminary degree; less than 1 percent of the sacristans could make this claim (TsGIA SSSR, f. 796, op. 142, g. 1861, d. 2379, unpaginated file).

way with the social policy of eighteenth-century Russian abso-
lutism, which not only built new institutions but also designated
specific hereditary groups in the population to provide the requisite manpower. Together with other pressures toward social
isolation (such as state laws that severely impeded the transfer
of peasants and townspeople into the clergy), the seminary—open
only to the clergy's sons—played a major role in closing the clergy
to men from other social estates.[24] By the late eighteenth century,
when formal study at the seminary had become a virtual *sine qua
non* for ordination, the seminary had thus become an insuperable
barrier to the ordination of outsiders. Paradoxically enough, the
school, an instrument of social mobility and change in the West,
functioned to freeze the social order in Russia and to consolidate
the estates into rigid hereditary orders.

That hereditary order was fraught with serious repercussions
for the church, which found its institutional structure increasingly
entangled with the special interests of the parish clergy. That
outcome was no accident: it was in fact a fundamental component
of the new Petrine system, which bound the institution to a particular estate by a set of mutual obligations and interests. While
that policy had the virtue of guaranteeing sufficient manpower
to the institution in question, each service estate had its own
special interests, not necessarily consonant with those of the institution. In the case of the church, it became common for a priest
to dispose of his position for money or to transfer it to a seminarian
willing to marry his daughter. Deplorable as they were, such
practices were necessitated by the dearth of church properties
and capital endowments: the church had little choice but to recognize such family claims and arrangements in order to provide
for retired clergy and their families. It did not totally disregard
educational qualifications; still, a candidate had only to satisfy the
minimum standards, not to demonstrate unusual promise on the
basis of his academic or moral record. In this most important

24. For a discussion of the processes leading to social closure, see Freeze, *Russian
Levites*, pp. 107–110; M. Vladimirskii-Budanov, *Gosudarstvo i narodnoe obrazovanie
XVIII v.* (Yaroslavl, 1874).

respect the Russian parish clergy were a phenomenon unique in modern Europe. Unlike the Catholic clergy (among whom celibacy ipso facto precluded such social exclusion) and the Protestant clergy (whose endogamous tendencies were weak and declining, with no more than 25 to 30 percent of pastors coming from clerical backgrounds),[25] the Russian parish clergy obtained virtually 100 percent of new recruits from its own estate. This wall of ingrown clannish ties had an enormous impact on the clergy, not only lowering professional standards but also segregating the group— culturally, socially, psychologically—from the lay groups in Russian society.

The seminary had equally profound effects on the celibate bishops of the Russian church, for they, too, had to have the formal education provided by the seminary and academy and hence had to come from clerical backgrounds. This new profile marked a significant break from earlier times, for even as late as the mid– eighteenth century the bishops counted a majority of outsiders in their midst, not only nonclerical in social origin but also non-Russian in nationality—men from the Ukraine, from the western borderlands, some even from foreign countries.[26] But as the Russian church began to require that candidates for the episcopacy be graduates of church schools, it limited itself socially to the clerical estate—that is, to the sons of parish clergy. As a result, by the late eighteenth century the episcopate had become strikingly homogeneous: Great Russian in nationality, elevated by elite education in the ecclesiastical academies, and experienced as teachers and administrators in the church schools. Though the reconstitution of the episcopate did isolate the group from lay society (with a corresponding erosion in its potential for direct

25. For pertinent data on Sweden, Norway, and Germany, see Ragnar Norrman, *Från Pråstoverflöd till prästbrist: Prästrykryteringen i Uppsala Ärkestift, 1786–1965* (Uppsala, 1970), p. 210; Dagfins Mannsåker, *Det norske presteskapet i det 19. Hundreåret* (Oslo, 1954), p. 144; K.-W. Dahm, *Beruf: Pfarrer: Empirische Aspekte* (Munich, 1971), pp. 86–88; A. Neher, *Die katholische und evangelische Geistlichkeit Württembergs, 1817–1901* (Ravensburg, 1904).
26. For a convenient compilation of data, see Bryner, *Der geistliche Stand*, pp. 30–31; still of value is K. V. Kharlampovich, *Malorossiiskoe vliianie na velikorusskuiu tserkovnuiu zhizn'* (Kazan, 1914).

[23]

influence and interaction), the change promised to create more effective administrators for the church: the modern bishop, knowledgeable and experienced, should have been able to govern more effectively the complex, bureaucratic organization that the church had now become.

Although the episcopate and parish clergy had a common social origin and common education, they formed not a unified "clerical estate" but rather two very distinct, often antagonistic social groups. Despite the superficial similarities, the bishops had an elite academy education (not a mere seminary diploma) and a career pattern utterly unlike that of the ordinary priest. But most important of all, the two had very different statuses: as a consequence of superior education, canon law, custom, and the norms that governed relationships between superiors and inferiors everywhere in prereform Russia, the bishop towered over the priest. It was thus perfectly natural for the bishop to drape himself in the imperious style of a ranking official. As Belliustin's writing demonstrates, the parish clergy perceived this change negatively, regarding it as a loss of paternalistic concern proper to the "spiritual father" of a diocese. Tensions between higher and lower clergy also existed in Western churches but did not become so intense as in Russia, where the two groups formed not separate levels in a single hierarchy but two distinct social populations, divided by custom and canon that effectively barred mobility and interchange between them.

By the first half of the nineteenth century, the Russian Orthodox Church faced mounting difficulties as fundamental disorders rent the Petrine system and authorities in St. Petersburg proved unable or unwilling to resolve them. To be sure, the state—under both Alexander I (1801–1825) and Nicholas I (1825–55)—took cognizance of the church's problems and periodically made an effort to address them. But neither the state nor the church dared embark on the basic structural reforms that were necessary if the ecclesiastical system constructed in the eighteenth century were to keep in step with the society of the nineteenth. By the mid-nineteenth century, when Belliustin sat down to write his memoir, the church faced widely recognized problems in four clearly defined

[24]

areas: administration, education, the system of parish service, and the hereditary clerical estate.

The disorders pervading ecclesiastical administration had become increasingly complex and multifaceted. Doubtless of greatest concern to the bishops was the recent augmentation of the chief procurator's role, mainly since 1836, when Count N. A. Protasov became chief procurator and gradually assumed an unprecedented role in church affairs. Although Protasov's power need not be exaggerated (ultimate decision making still rested with the Synod; such ranking prelates as Metropolitan Filaret remained influential; and the procurator had little control over diocesan administration), this procurator unquestionably exercised more authority than any of his predecessors had wielded.[27] For the parish clergy, however, it was not this "political" question of church–state relations but the venality and injustices of diocesan administration that were most important. The surfeit of red tape (synodal approval was required for even the most trivial matters), the corruption and incompetence of diocesan clerks, the exclusion of parish clergy from positions of influence and authority, the gross abuses and arbitrariness in ecclesiastical justice—all generated acute discontent among the parish clergy. Although similar problems existed in secular administration and justice, they seemed especially noxious in the church, not only because of the church's spiritual claims but also because a better-educated priesthood perceived its serflike status as intolerable, commensurate with neither its education nor its mission.

The seminary, another major innovation of the eighteenth century, was a second focus of concern. In part it was a victim of its own successful growth: the explosion in enrollments, especially from the late eighteenth century on, was not matched by a commensurate increase in financial resources. The new school statutes of 1814 attempted to finance the seminary through the sale of candles in parish churches, but the scheme did not work: the

27. The most systematic critique of Protasov's role was provided in a memorandum by a former synodal official, A. N. Murav'ev, who wrote almost concurrently with Belliustin ("O prichinakh bedstvennogo polozheniia pravoslavnoi katolicheskoi tserkvi v Rossii," OR GBL, f. 304, r. 2, d. 259, ll. 27–56).

original calculations proved overly optimistic, private vendors hawked candles on the streets, and peculation also took a toll. The result was unremitting penury that deprived the schools of adequate dormitories, qualified teachers, and sufficient books and teaching materials. Such problems were further aggravated by the maladministration of an educational bureaucracy that was too centralized and too remote to provide proper supervision and prompt decisions. Most fundamental of all, the whole learning process in the prereform seminary seemed increasingly unsatisfactory and misdirected: the outmoded pedagogy that put a premium on rote memorization, the suffocating predominance of the classical Latin curriculum, and the accumulation of numerous "practical subjects" such as agronomy and geodesy all combined to distract the seminarian from more professional preparation for pastoral service. Nor, as many critics complained, did the seminary even ensure proper moral training for these future men of the cloth: the church schools were in effect boarding schools, with no proper provisions either for housing or for proper moral supervision. Removed from their families and housed with poor townspeople or in overcrowded dormitories, the pupils could alternate between brutal discipline during the day and uncontrolled licentiousness at night.

A third set of issues concerned the system of parish service, especially the inadequacy of existing forms of material support for the priest and sacristans. In this respect, too, the Russian clergy formed a striking contrast to their peers in Western Europe: possessing neither the tithes, benefices, nor state salaries of the Western clergy, the Russian clergy had to subsist almost entirely on a combination of emoluments (voluntary gifts from parishioners for the performance of various rites, such as confession, marriage, burial) and the yield of the small plot of land belonging to the parish church. This system of economic support, as virtually all observers agreed, could scarcely have been less satisfactory. To cite only the main problems: it provided too little support; agriculture diverted the priest from his proper religious duties and lowered his social status; as the emoluments were voluntary and of unspecified amount, they generated incessant conflict with parishioners and left the priest highly dependent on their good-will, and hence reluctant to challenge their moral foibles and deviation from Orthodox canons and convictions. All of these problems were clearly perceived and abundantly aired from the time of Peter the Great but successfully eluded numerous attempts at reform.[28] The most significant plan for reform was adopted in 1842, when Nicholas' government sought to convert the traditional parish economy into a structure based on a combination of tithes, parsonages, parish labor, and state subsidies. But the reform was limited to a few dioceses, primarily those in the politically unstable western regions of the empire, and in any event failed to change the basic structure of the parish economy or the relations between priest and parishioners.[29]

A related problem concerned the composition of the parish clergy, which—in medieval Russia and in Petrine statute—consisted not only of the priests but also of the low-ranking deacons and sacristans. In pre-Petrine Russia this structure had some justification: the illiterate laity could not assist the priest in the conduct of church services, and service in the rank of deacon or sacristan provided valuable apprenticeship (often for kinsmen) in an age when formal education was still wanting even among the clergy. By the late eighteenth century, however, apprenticeship and subsequent rise to the priesthood had virtually disappeared. The reasons were many: official opposition to kinship ties within a single parish (apprenticeship had often been a device to train sons to succeed fathers), increased longevity of priests (which disrupted a natural "demographic" hierarchy), and, most important, the rise of the seminary (which obviated any need for informal apprenticeship). The result was a deep split within the parish clergy: on one side the priests, with a seminary degree and the spiritual authority to perform sacraments, on the other the deacons and sacristans, doomed by their minimal education to remain

28. For an official history of these efforts, see [E. Petrovskii], *Istoricheskaia spravka kasatel'no sposobov obespecheniia soderzhaniem pravoslavnogo dukhovenstva v Rossii za sinodal'nyi period upravleniia russkoiu tserkov'iu* (St. Petersburg, 1910). See also Freeze, *Russian Levites*, pp. 117–120, and Freeze, *Parish Clergy*, pp. 52–81.
29. Freeze, *Parish Clergy*, pp. 81–97, 200–205.

[27]

in inferior ranks. The gap between the two strata, educational as well as moral, widened considerably in the first half of the nineteenth century, and by the late 1840s had already provoked formal discussions in the Synod on what could and should be done with these lesser, ill-famed servitors of the church.[30] Although it was manifestly impossible, given the low literacy rates in preform Russia, to replace this service group with hired laymen or volunteers from the parish, church authorities were inclined to make drastic reductions in the number of sacristans and perhaps to modify their formal status within the clerical estate.

That policy derived, in large measure, from concern about a growing surfeit of clerical candidates.[31] The state had periodically complained about "uneducated and idle clerical youths" in the eighteenth century (and unceremoniously conscripted the excess into the army or consigned them to toil as factory serfs), but in the nineteenth century it eschewed such demeaning policies and, more important, faced an entirely different kind of problem. In the eighteenth century the problem had been a matter of uneducated youth; in the nineteenth century the surplus included numerous seminary *graduates* unable to find positions in the elastic system of parish churches. In 1849 the Synod established a secret committee to consider the issue, and two years later it resolved to set limits on seminary enrollments (commensurate only with the manpower needs of a particular diocese) and to encourage the transfer of clerical youths to the secular domain.[32]

The hereditary estate had, moreover, highly deleterious effects on clerical service. Of special concern to an ambitious and conscientious priest such as Belliustin was the growing contradiction

---

30. An early memorandum on the issue, circulated by the chief procurator and evidently enjoying his support, is in TsGIA SSSR, f. 797, op. 18, d. 41101, ll. 1–10 ob.

31. Complaints about this problem rang out in the annual reports of bishops in a number of dioceses (Vladimir, Saratov, Tambov, Viatka, Kursk, Penza, Nizhnii-Novgorod, St. Petersburg, and Kishinev): TsGIA SSSR, f. 796, op. 132, g. 1851, d. 2357, ll. 81–82, 128 ob., 149, 187–187 ob., 296–297, 305–305 ob., 347, 436 ob.–437.

32. TsGIA SSSR, f. 797, op. 19, otd. 1, st. 2, d. 42644; f. 796, op. 445, d. 354; f. 802, op. 5, d. 12977; f. 796, op. 132, g. 1851, d. 1181.

between the demands of the estate and those of professionalization: rather than select and promote the best clergy, the existing system sacrificed service and ability to family claims in the distribution of clerical positions. The discrepancy between estate and profession became increasingly apparent, for professional values had already begun (at least in theory) to modify such institutions as the civil service. The church itself had begun to redefine the tasks of clerical service, especially from the 1830s, demanding that priests not only perform liturgies and administer various sacraments but also teach in parish schools, provide rudimentary religious instruction for parishioners, catechize, and prepare simple sermons comprehensible to the uneducated rural parishioners. Moreover, the clergy's social isolation weakened their potential influence on the laity. Set apart from other social groups, high and low, the clergy lacked the close bonds of blood and mutual interest that would have served to reinforce their involvement in contemporary society and to strengthen the church's role in temporal matters.

Most of these problems were well known to high-ranking church and state officials (the glowing reports of the chief procurator notwithstanding) and elicited serious efforts by the Nikolaevan regime to resolve them. Thus the church, like many other institutions in Nikolaevan Russia, was a constant object of reform deliberations; at state or church behest, special committees were created to collect data, to ponder alternative measures, and to draft concrete proposals for the Synod or state to consider. But Petersburg had no fondness for far-reaching change; instead, it opted consistently for cautious, gradual reform—an approach wholly consonant with the Nikolaevan ideology of gradualism and the sheer lack of financial resources to attempt anything more ambitious.

But outside of tiny elite circles, knowledge of the church's problems was virtually nonexistent, even among those with an intense commitment to Orthodoxy and its interests. For most of its first readers, then, Belliustín's manuscript (or its published version) would provide their first real insight into the church and clergy.

[29]

I. S. BELLIUSTIN: PRIEST AND PUBLICIST

I. S. Belliustin's background and career were virtually archtypal for a Russian priest in the first half of the nineteenth century.[33] Born into the clerical estate, educated solely in church schools in his home diocese of Tver, married to a woman of the clerical estate, ordained to the position previously held by her father—such indeed were facts that could be found in the biography of nearly any priest in prereform Russia. But Belliustin did not remain long in this first position, in a rural parish populated by serfs and their noble master; after just four years he succeeded in transferring to the cathedral in a small district town, Kaliazin, where he earned an enviable reputation for his uncommon diligence and dedication.[34] In addition to performing his regular duties as priest, Belliustin served as the chief catechist for the town, as the official exhorter at the local prison, and as the teacher of religion in the local state school. For his toil he received various awards, had excellent relations with his parishioners, and by priestly standards enjoyed a very good income—nearly 400 rubles a year.[35]

33. Belliustin's legal name was Beliustin, the form he used in official documents. In most personal correspondence and published writings, however, he preferred the spelling Belliustin; as this is the form best known to his contemporaries, it will be used here.

34. According to Belliustin's own account, he enjoyed such extraordinarily good relations with his flock that "not a single family matter—from a son's marriage to a daughter's betrothal—took place without prior consultation with me" (Belliustin, "Iz zametok," GAKO, f. 103, op. 1, d. 1307, ll. 12 ob.–13). Testimonials from parishioners confirm this claim. A petition submitted in 1875 demanded that Belliustin be promoted from priest to archpriest (an honor he was in fact never to receive): "In the name of 200 peasant souls in the hamlet of Matveikovo [a small community just outside Kaliazin and formally attached to Belliustin's cathedral], I declare that our worthy pastor, Belliustin, without compensation, [over the years] has taught approximately 300 boys and girls to read and write as well as the fundamentals of the faith, and that to do this, he had to walk on foot to our hamlet, over two versts [1.2 miles] from town" (OR GBL, f. 344, k. 445, d. 10, l. 2). Similar petitions submitted in 1861, 1866, and 1879 may be found in TsGIA SSSR, f. 796, op. 160, g. 1879, d. 831, ll. 23–40.

35. In 1849 Belliustin received the *nabedrennik* (epigonation), in 1854 the *skuf'ia* (a kind of skullcap), and in 1855 a bronze cross (GAKO, f. 160, op. 1, d. 16298, ll. 4–6).

Appearances notwithstanding, Belliustin seethed with indignation and dissatisfaction. Anger pervades his private notes, letters, and diaries. His disaffection—by Belliustin's own account—began even in his student days in the seminary; although he later had praise for some of his teachers, he generally portrayed this early educational experience in the darkest of hues.[36] His early correspondence confirms this deep personal abhorrence of the seminary. To a friend, for example, he wrote that it was terrible "to see how, in the name of learning and education, wonderful boys (from the home of good parents) are made into moral and even physical freaks, and to know that my own children must follow this fateful path and not to see the means to give them an alternative."[37] Nor did the priest find much to praise in parish service. Recalling his first four years as priest in a serf parish, he flatly called these "the most difficult years of my life," a judgment he substantiated by a depressing account of endless physical toil, humiliating dependence on emoluments, and the arrogant condescension of country squires.[38] Nor could he find much solace or support in the famous "religiousness" of the Russian people: "My parishioners did not have the slightest conception of the most elementary truths of the Christian faith. They had heard of the Trinity, Christ, and the Holy Virgin, but all that was so dim, so incomprehensible, that not one of them (regardless of sex or age) could intelligently recount even a fragment from the life of Christ."[39] It proved impossible, even for such a zealous priest as he, to Christianize peasants living under the yoke of serfdom. As he later wrote, "the peasant works six days a week performing

---

36. I. S. Belliustin, "Iz zametok o perezhitom," *Tserkovno-obshchestvennyi vestnik,* 1882, nos. 18, 33, 36, 39, 43, 54, 59.
37. Belliustin to M. P. Pogodin, September 26, 1855, in OR GBL, f. 231/II, k. 3, d. 49/4, l. 1. Belliustin, especially in his private correspondence, was particularly concerned about the pernicious moral atmosphere of ecclesiastical schools. See, for instance, his comments on the case of two brothers from a good background who were corrupted by the seminary and even contracted syphilis (Belliustin to Pogodin, September 25, 1855, ibid., l. 3 ob.).
38. I. S. Belliustin, "Dnevnik i zametki," GAKO, f. 103, op. 1, d. 1291, l. 149 ob.
39. Belliustin, "Iz zametok," GAKO, f. 103, op. 1, d. 1307, l. 2 ob.

barshchina [corvée or labor dues] for his master, devotes the seventh day to his own plot, and hence visits the church only on the most important religious holidays. . . . When and how can one teach [the faith] to the peasant if, from early morning to late at night, all year round, he works for his master?"[40] Although the move to Kaliazin brought some amenities and freed Belliustin from the drudgery of field toil, it did not solve his economic problems (he had a large family to support, his sons requiring education and his daughters dowries), and in fact made him totally dependent on the degrading emoluments for various rites.[41] But Belliustin held only a seminary degree, never having studied at an advanced academy, and hence lacked the credentials for a better position; as priest in a poor district town, he had reached the ceiling in his career potential.[42] Belliustin endeavored to compensate for his deficiencies in formal education by publishing learned articles, but in vain: his efforts were foiled by vigilant church censorship and the skeptical condescension of various bishops—all "learned monks" in charge of the church and its institutions.[43]

40. Belliustin to S. O. Burachek, March 20, 1858, IRLI, f. 34, op. 1, d. 62, ll. 3 ob.–4.

41. His frustration and intense concern that his children should be properly provided for are seen in his letters to M. P. Pogodin, such as that of September 25, 1855, in OR GBL, f. 231/II, k. 3, d. 49/4, l. 4.

42. The very best positions—priest in Moscow, St. Petersburg, and the diocesan capital—normally were given to the relatively few priests with academy degrees, who received these posts without regard to age, experience, or practical service as clergymen. As Belliustin complained:

> I cannot obtain [a position in one of the capitals]—I do not hold either a master's or candidate's degree. . . . Even if one graduated from the seminary as the best student and did not enter the academy for family and extremely important reasons, even if one served more than sixteen years irreproachably (and not just irreproachably—but with a certain distinction: two years ago I received an award for my efforts, which have been quite onerous)—all that does not mean a thing. [Belliustin to M. P. Pogodin, November 26, 1855, OR GBL, f. 231/II, k. 3, d. 49/4, l. 1 ob.]

43. For an account of Belliustin's early literary efforts, including his embitterment over encounters with Grigorii (Postnikov) and Filaret (Drozdov), see Freeze, "Revolt from Below: A Priest's Manifesto on the Crisis in Russian Orthodoxy," in *Russian Orthodoxy under the Old Regime,* ed. Theofanis Stavrou and Robert Nichols (Minneapolis, 1978), pp. 94–95.

Frustrated in his hopes for promotion, Belliustin directed his animus primarily at these learned monks who held power and blocked all his efforts, no matter how well intentioned.[44] He wrote in his diary in 1848:

O monks, an evil greater than any other, Pharisees and hypocrites: *quousque tandem abutere* [how long will you perpetrate abuse] with your rights? *Quousque tandem* will you trample law and justice? You promote and award honors to those who have the means to feed you, like oxen; you reward those who can pay; you persecute and destroy the poor. . . . *Quousque tandem?*

And one can well imagine a bishop's reaction had he read Belliustin's list of "canons" for the behavior of a learned monk:

1. A diocese or monastery is an estate from which one can take everything that is good and valuable.

2. Because it is impossible to have one wife, one may have two or three "nieces," as one likes.

3. To avoid unnecessary efforts in running the diocese, turn over everything to a petty clerk or, in the case of monasteries, to a nephew.

4. For a true monk everything is permissible, but if he should do something really horrendous (such as strangle or stab his mistress), then keep everything as secret as possible and use all your powers to defend him before the courts.

5. Persecute and destroy any who have the insolence not to live by these rules.

6. Spare no money to rise from archimandrite to bishop, and then to become a member of the Synod.

7. For this purpose one can become a Freemason or a Communist—anything you like, just so you achieve this [promotion to bishop] as soon as possible.[45]

---

44. The phenomenon of "learned monasticism" is discussed in Igor Smolitsch, *Geschichte der russischen Kirche* (Leiden, 1964), pp. 392–398, and *Russisches Mönchtum: Entstehung, Entwicklung und Wesen, 988–1917* (Würzburg, 1953), pp. 427–451.
45. Belliustin, "Dnevnik," GAKO, f. 103, op. 1, d. 1291, ll. 108–109.

Introduction

It was hardly surprising, complained Belliustin, that such prelates were incapable of understanding the priests' needs and problems, meted out draconian punishments for minor misdeeds, ignored genuine achievement in parish service, and tolerated venality in diocesan administration. Typical of such prelates was his own superior, Archbishop Grigorii (Postnikov): "Oh, God alone knows how many priests, honest and worthy, perished under the rule of Grigorii—and for no reason at all."[46]

Not that he was an uncritical defender of his own class, the "white" or parish clergy, as distinguished from the "black" or monastic clergy. On the contrary, he castigated his fellow priests relentlessly for their various foibles and, in one unpublished note, asserted that the work of many parish priests—especially those of the older generation—had little in common with true pastorship. Recalling his first years in the countryside, he wrote that "it was impossible to draw close [to the neighboring priests], for they were utterly alien to everything called scholarship and literature, even of a spiritual sort. Moreover, acquaintance with them was inconceivable without the maximum use of stupefying drink."[47] These were the priests, he argued, who ultimately bore responsibility for the "darkness" of the Russian peasantry. "Just as most squires are guilty of causing the peasants' material poverty," he wrote, "so too are all priests [popy, a pejorative term] guilty of causing their spiritual poverty."[48] Believing that the clergy's decline commenced with Peter the Great, Belliustin argued that they had lost all vitality and become a mere "shadow, an apparition. . . . Humiliated, oppressed, downtrodden, they

46. From an unpublished section of the original manuscript that eventually became *Description of Clergy in Rural Russia,* in OR GBL, f. 231/III, k. 1, d. 66, ll. 2 ob.–3. Belliustin's hatred of Grigorii knew no bounds; hence the priest gleefully disseminated rumors that Grigorii preyed upon young boys at the seminary (Belliustin to Pogodin, January 6, 1859, in OR GBL, f. 231/II, k. 3, d. 50/2, l. 2). For reports of Grigorii's ill repute as a harsh bishop in Riazan diocese, see N. A. Dubrovin, ed., "Materialy dlia istorii pravoslaviia v tsarstvovanie Imp. Nikolaia I-go," *Sbornik Imperatorskogo istoricheskogo obshchestva,* vol. 113 (St. Petersburg, 1902), pp. 70–71.
47. Belliustin, "Iz zametok," GAKO, f. 103, op. 1, d. 1291, l. 34 ob.
48. Belliustin to A. D. Zheltukhin, June 21, 1858, IRLI, f. 616, op. 1, d. 6, l. 9.

themselves have already lost consciousness of their own significance."⁴⁹

As the criticism of Peter the Great suggests, in these years Belliustin considered himself a Slavophile, professed openly to be "a Slavophile with my whole heart," and caustically denounced the "Europeanism" of the enemy camp.⁵⁰ But Belliustin's Slavophilism was permeated by profound despair, for his experience in the village permitted no delusions—such as those common in Moscow salons—about the religious state of the people:

> Out of one hundred male peasants, a maximum of ten can read the creed and two or three short prayers (naturally, without the slightest idea or comprehension of what they have read). Out of one thousand men, at most two or three know the Ten Commandments; so far as the women are concerned, nothing even needs to be said here. And this is Orthodox Rus'!⁵¹ What a shame and disgrace! And our pharisees dare to shout for everyone to hear that only in Russia has the faith been preserved undefiled, in Rus', where two-thirds of the people have not the slightest conception of the faith!⁵²

The parish clergy—as guardians of religious tradition, a potential social and intellectual base for a broad Slavophile movement—were simply too close to the harsh realities of the village to accept the fantasies concocted from the romantic idealism and wishful thinking of Slavophiles in the capital.

49. Belliustin, "Dnevnik," GAKO, f. 103, op. 1, d. 1291, l. 34 ob.
50. Belliustin to I. S. Aksakov, January 18, 1858, IRLI, f. 3, op. 4, d. 35, l. 1. Belliustin derided such famous Westerners as V. G. Belinskii and N. A. Nekrasov, and deplored the dissemination of the "destructive ideas" of Hegel and Humboldt in Russia (Belliustin, "Dnevnik," GAKO, f. 103, op. 1, d. 1291, ll. 8 ob.–11). He was particularly vitriolic in his attack on a journal published by A. A. Kraevskii: "May the Lord give just deserts to Kraevskii & Co. Many are the souls they have corrupted with their quasi-philosophical teachings! Many are the harmful ideas they have cast upon Russian soil" (Belliustin to Pogodin, September 25, 1853, OR GBL, f. 231/II, k. 3, d. 49/2, l. 7).
51. "Rus'," an archaic term for "Russia," occurs often in Belliustin's prose and reflects his early Slavophile sympathies, particularly his devotion to pre-Petrine Muscovy.
52. Belliustin to Pogodin, May 22, 1857, OR GBL, f. 231/II, k. 3, d. 49/6, l. 1.

[35]

For all the peasants' failings, however, Belliustin sided whole-heartedly with them against the serf-owning nobility. That attitude derives, at least in part, from the clergy's resentment of the nobility's occasional abuse of priests and failure to pay due respect to their special status and education.[53] But Belliustin was also sensitive to the injustices of serfdom. One diary entry reads:

> The peasants complained repeatedly of [their squire's] misdeeds to the district and provincial marshals of the nobility, and informed the local police of murders that he had committed. But what effect did all their complaints have? The marshals and officials are all squires; each is more or less the same as Iakov Vasil'evich [the squire in question]. Hence their complaints not only brought no relief but even served as a source of harm: they were flogged in the local court for daring to seek protection and defense![54]

In desperation they eventually murdered their master and had to face justice at the hands of local authorites. The result, in Belliustin's opinion, was predictable: "The entire case was investigated and decided by the squires: can one expect any mercy from these scourges of mankind, these predatory beasts, these incurable ulcers that afflict every state?"[55] With that experience in mind, Belliustin saw virtually no prospect for a peaceful, voluntary emancipation, despite all the humanitarian sentiments expressed by some members of the serf-owning gentry. After recounting the misdeeds perpetrated by a local squire (who demanded that a peasant surrender his daughter for the master's "innocent amusement"), Belliustin rejected any hope of appealing to the gentry's "higher" motives: "Just try to awaken in these people a feeling of humanity, when they are imbued with the notion that

53. For the traditional tenor of squire–priest relations, see the Senate's decree in 1769 admonishing the nobility not to subject the clergy to corporal punishment: *PSZ(1)*, vol. 12, no. 9079.
54. Belliustin, "Dnevnik," GAKO, f. 103, op. 1, d. 1291, ll. 7 ob.–8.
55. Ibid., l. 8.

everything is permissible and possible for them, and their unbridled will, their most absurd caprice, is law for everyone else."[56]

Although Belliustin naturally enough supported the emancipation of serfs, he was still more interested in "improving the *spiritual* life of the peasants."[57] That concern was hardly surprising, given his profession and his practical experience with rural parishioners. The primary task, he averred, was to introduce a fundamental reorientation in Russian Orthodoxy, to replace traditional "ritualistic" Byzantinism with a more conscious piety, to raise Christianity from mere custom and routine, and to make Christ's teachings an integral part of the people's life and consciousness. The first step was simply to make the faith directly accessible. The literate and educated were most in need of a new, readable Bible. The old Slavonic Bible was virtually incomprehensible, in language and script, to the modern layman; it needed to be replaced by a Bible translated into the vernacular and made available in inexpensive editions. Belliustin also urged a major reform in liturgical practices, such as the inclusion of modern church music and especially the introduction of simpler, more comprehensible sermons.[58] Historically, the sermon had developed in Russia as a literary genre and not as a means of communication with the popular classes; by the nineteenth century, however, church authorities were urging as strongly as Belliustin that "learned sermons" be replaced by informal talks comprehensible to simple, uneducated parishioners.[59] Whereas European clergy had long since made that transition and already used the sermon as a key instrument in their mission, the Russian clergy

56. Belliustin to Zheltukhin, April 25, 1858, IRLI, f. 616, op. 1, d. 6, l. 5 ob.

57. Belliustin to Zheltukhin, June 21, 1858, ibid., l. 9–9 ob.

58. Belliustin, "Pravoslavnaia Rus'," an unpublished section of the manuscript that was eventually published as *Description of the Clergy in Rural Russia*, in OR GBL, f. 231/III, k. 1, d. 66, ll. 36 ob.–44. For published examples of Belliustin's own sermons, see *Zhurnal 112-ogo zasedaniia Tverskoi uchenoi arkhivnoi komissii* (Tver, 1912), pp. 61–109.

59. Such demands were commonplace by the mid–nineteenth century; see, for example, the report by the bishop of Iaroslavl in 1850 in TsGIA SSSR, f. 796, op. 132, g. 1851, d. 2357, l. 113.

had only begun to do so, and indeed most of them still delivered only a few sermons each year.[60] To supplement these talks and to teach basic religious truths to the people, Belliustin stressed that the clergy must play a major role in public education and ensure that it instill morality and Christianity, not mere literacy.[61] Such a program, he hoped, would achieve a veritable reformation in popular religion. Such a basic "reformation" in Orthodoxy, however, presupposed a truly effective clergy, and it was this concern that eventually impelled him to write the memoir later published as *Description of the Clergy in Rural Russia*.

The initial impetus for this work came from M. P. Pogodin, a conservative publicist and historian, who shared Belliustin's concern about the dismal plight of the church.[62] Pogodin himself had once inspected a seminary on behalf of the chief procurator and thus had a far better notion of the church's staggering problems than did most laymen of his time.[63] The two discussed these matters early in 1855, and with Pogodin's encouragement Belliustin began to prepare a memoir (*zapiska*) on the clergy's condition and needs, primarily with the intent of using Pogodin's connections with high-ranking officials and with the emperor himself. The priest consulted a number of fellow clergy for ideas and information, and two years later, in April 1857, sent Pogodin the main body of the text. Belliustin continued to write, however,

60. For the infrequency of sermons, see the annual service lists of clergy, such as those for Belliustin's home diocese, Tver (GAKO, f. 160, op. 1, d. 16272 and 16298). For the development of sermons in England, see Brian Heeney, *A Different Kind of Gentleman: The Parish Clergy as Professional Men in Early and Mid-Victorian England* (Hamden, Conn., 1976), pp. 40–41; Dianna McClatchey, *Oxfordshire Clergy, 1777–1869* (Oxford, 1960), p. 82; and Anthony Russell, *The Clerical Profession* (London, 1980), pp. 85–99.
61. For a discussion of Belliustin's work on the educational question and a list of his publications in *Zhurnal ministerstva narodnogo prosveshcheniia*, see *Arkhiv K. D. Ushinskogo*, 1 (Moscow, 1959): 85, 88–89.
62. Details of the relationship between Belliustin and Pogodin, which commenced with Belliustin's desire to write for Pogodin's paper and encompassed as well their common interests in old Russian manuscripts, may be found in Freeze, "Revolt from Below," pp. 97–98.
63. M. P. Pogodin, "Ob"iasnenie," *Russkii vestnik*, 21 (1859): 45–46.

and in December of the same year sent Pogodin a set of appendixes to complete the work.[64] Structured as a chronological account of a priest's life and career, from early schooling to daily service, the memoir itemized virtually all the problems that would preoccupy reformers during the final decades of the old regime—ecclesiastical schools, the parish economy, diocesan administration, and the social structure of the clerical estate.

But Belliustin's memoir, like all such *zapiski* intended for the tsar, sought not only to describe problems but also to prescribe solutions. The first part, a detailed account of ecclesiastical schools, adumbrates numerous shortcomings and concludes that such institutions simply could not produce good pastors—men with sound moral training and practical preparation for effective pastorship. The solution, argued Belliustin, was to construct suitable dormitories (to ensure close supervision over the students' moral development), fundamental changes in curriculum (elimination of Latin and other "useless" courses to allow more practical training for the priesthood), and improvements in pedagogy and methods of teacher selection. A second major focus is the traditional structure and economy of parish service. Emphasizing the gravity of the crisis here, Belliustin warned that the church must carry out a fundamental transformation: make clerical appointments on the basis of education and merit (not mere family claims), remove the ill-famed deacons and sacristans from the clerical estate, and—perhaps most essential of all—replace emoluments and agriculture with a regular state salary. A third focus is diocesan administration, which, as Belliustin graphically shows, was rent by endemic corruption, venality, and injustice. To eliminate such evils he proposed to give the diocesan clerks a sufficient salary

64. Belliustin to Pogodin, April 2 and December 26, 1857, OR GBL, f.231/II, k. 3, d. 49/6, ll. 5, 13 ob. This supplementary section, however, arrived too late for inclusion in the manuscript that Pogodin had already transmitted abroad for publication as *Opisanie sel'skogo dukhovenstva*; the omitted segments treat such issues as the problem of clerical widows and orphans, voluntary defrocking, and the religious condition of "Orthodox Rus'." This unpublished manuscript, "Zapiska o dukhovenstve," is in OR GBL, f. 231/III, k. 1, d. 66, ll. 30–44 ob.

and, at the lower echelon, to permit the local clergy to elect the local superintendent.

Still more radical was a proposal, implied throughout the memoir but made explicit only at the end: the transfer of dominance in the church from the "learned monks" to the parish clergy. In addition to appeals to the early church, where dominance by the black clergy was unknown and the distance between bishop and priest nonexistent, Belliustin adduced a strictly practical argument to justify a transfer of power from monks to priests: monks lacked real worldly experience, and indeed, given their ascetic vows, should not be burdened with such onerous temporal responsibilities. That argument was neither original nor unreasonable; it had been expressed before and would be reiterated often in the coming decades.[65] What made Belliustin's argument so extraordinary was the fact that he buttressed it within the inflammatory— and unfair—assertion that the bishops did not *want* to assist the parish clergy, that they desired to hold the parish clergy in servile bondage, and that they saw the priests' demoralization as a useful device for preserving their own hegemony in the church. In large measure Belliustin sought to determine not only what was wrong with the church but also who was to blame for the deplorable state of affairs. On the first page of his memoir, in fact, he asks outright: "What is the cause of all this?" and by the end his answer is unmistakable: the bishops.

It is therefore hardly surprising that Belliustin looked not to the bishops but to the state, and specifically the tsar, to realize his ambitious scheme for church reform. Even so, his reliance on the state, and especially his exaggerated notion of the state's magnanimity, are really quite extraordinary. Whether it was a matter of funds for schools, salaries for priests, or other essential needs of the church, Belliustin was confident that the church had but

65. For the most famous earlier articulation of this argument, see the essay of Archpriest Petr Alekseev, "Rassuzhdenie na vopros: Mozhno li dostoinomu sviashchenniku, minovav monashestvo, proizvedenu byt' vo episkopa?" *Chteniia v Obshchestve istorii i drevnostei rossiiskikh,* 1867, kniga 3, otd. 5: 17–26; and V. I. Savva, ed., *Sochineniia protiv episkopov XVIII v.* (St. Petersburg, 1910).

to ask and the state would give. That notion was not without precedent; the state *had* given subsidies to clergy in some dioceses, increased the budget for diocesan administration, and sponsored the first diocesan schools for women in the clerical estate. Belliustin's faith in the tsar's munificence perhaps derived as well from the traditional myth of a just and pious tsar, a notion no doubt quite congenial to a self-professed Slavophile such as Belliustin. It is also striking that Belliustin felt no compunction about requesting various state medals and awards for the clergy, even though such honors would implicitly transform them into state employees. More concerned with practicality than precept, Belliustin simply accorded due recognition to the high status of the civil servants, whose prestige and perquisites made them the natural reference group for the rest of Russian society, the clergy included.[66]

Invaluable for its portrait of the church from below, Belliustin's manuscript is remarkably taciturn and even ill informed in its treatment of the upper reaches of the church. Whether from sheer ignorance of contemporary synodal politics or from a desire to solicit state support, Belliustin paid no attention to the issue of greatest concern to bishops and conservative churchmen: the recent encroachment of the state on ecclesiastical authority and prerogatives. More important, Belliustin even misrepresented the views of bishops on various issues, asserting, for instance, that the prelates opposed state salaries for the parish clergy.[67] As the archives of the Synod plainly show, however, the problem lay not in the bishops' indifference (still less in their desire to keep the parish clergy enslaved) but in the state's refusal to allocate the vast sums

66. It bears noting that this was not simply a bizarre proposal conceived by Belliustin; such proposals were still being made in the early 1860s, even in official church documents, such as the report of a diocesan committee in Kiev in 1863 (TsGIA SSSR, f. 804, op. 1, r. 1, d. 59, ll. 54–55 ob.)

67. Though the published work provided no concrete evidence in support of Belliustin's views, his private correspondence contains the assertion that a former metropolitan of St. Petersburg, Serafim, once declared: "No salary is needed. If the clergy are given a salary, they will cease to bow down before us" (Belliustin to Pogodin, May 26, 1859, OR GBL, f. 231/II, k. 3, d. 50/2, l. 20 ob.).

[41]

needed to renovate the church's various institutions. Still, the very fact that Belliustin could make such insinuations is significant, testifying to the enormous political distance between the capital and the provinces, even for one who, like Belliustin, had good contacts in St. Petersburg. This gap, in fact, formed a crucial element in the myth of the tsar, permitting the presumption of the tsar's ignorance and hence his freedom from culpability. Characteristically, rumors would later circulate that the tsar had praised Belliustin's work for providing "true" and "completely new" information.[68]

Such notions, in fact, underlay the very genre of Belliustin's work—a memoir intended to open the eyes of ranking officials and especially of the tsar. The memoir was actually a key institution in nineteenth-century Russia: it reified the myth of personal autocracy and the just tsar and, in effect, provided a substitute for the reformist institutions that were so manifestly lacking in the prerevolutionary bureaucracy. It is to this genre that Belliustin's memoir belongs. In the first instance it sought to arouse the sympathy and interest of responsible authorities in St. Petersburg. In contrast to the usual type of memoir, which originated within the depths of the bureaucracy and bore the arid, matter-of-fact tone of an official document, Belliustin's memoir sought not only to convince but to capture attention; it was a cry of despair meant to be heard all the way to St. Petersburg. Thus it combines at once two styles—that of the memoir and that of the traditional supplication, with the hyperbole characteristic of the latter's desperate appeals for the tsar's clemency.

The style itself is a remarkably discordant mixture of classicisms and colloquialisms. It was doubtless the author's intention to impress the educated layman—ordinarily inclined to regard the clergy as boorish, ignorant, and even illiterate—by citations in Greek and Latin, references to the "newest" pedagogical literature, and allusions to classical authors and figures in Greek mythology.. Although in itself unobjectionable, Belliustin's use of

68. I. V. Kalachov to Belliustin, January 10, 1859, GAKO, f. 103, op. 1, d. 1333, ll. 3 ob.–4.

such material (especially for the lay audience he was addressing) has the distinct ring of affected erudition and seems hardly appropriate for a book of this sort, an exposé permeated with shocking anecdotes and written in a colloquial idiom. The explanation for such affectation rests partly in the shortcomings of the seminary (where good writing skills, especially in Russian, were neglected) and partly in the author's biography: it was important to him to demonstrate his erudition.

Another salient element of the memoir is its worldly pragmatism: Belliustin's arguments rely little on canon, tradition, history, or even Scripture, and rest instead chiefly on common sense and mundane practicality. That emphasis is apparent, for example, in his treatment of such matters as monastic domination, clerical salaries, ecclesiastical justice, and voluntary defrocking by parish clergy. His pragmatism and indifference to tradition reflected both his antipathy to "Byzantinism" and his desire to make the church fit to function effectively in contemporary society, a concern one might well expect from a secular priest. Practicality, moreover, was more likely to convince the bureaucrats and tsar to whom the memoir was implicitly addressed; not esoterica from canon law or ecclesiastical history but functionality seemed likely to be persuasive. Striking, too, are Belliustin's inexact quotations from the Bible. Startling as these liberties may now seem, they testify both to the limited role of the Bible in the traditional religious life of Russia and to the author's apparent belief that his free play with Holy Writ would not unduly offend his readers' sensibilities.

Hastily drafted and submitted in separate chunks, the memoir also contains a variety of oversights and contradictions. One is the tendency to pronounce one or another measure "the single most important reform," whether it be the construction of dormitories, establishment of salaries, or expulsion of sacristans from the clerical estate. Given the complex, interlocking problems then confronting the church, it was evidently difficult for Belliustin—and all of his contemporaries, for that matter—to determine precisely where one should begin in reconstructing the church. The text also contains some contradictions, such as the argument that bishops are unfit to rule because they are too remote from the

[43]

world *and* because are they too worldly, career-minded, and materialistic. But the most substantive contradition is to be found in Belliustin's treatment of the white clergy. For all his antipathy toward the hereditary order and its baneful effect on parish service, Belliustin does not urge its abolition and transformation into an open social group (as reformers would demand in the coming decade). Whether from loyalty to his own estate or from doubts that educated candidates would voluntarily enter the clergy from other social groups, Belliustin eschewed such radical changes as abolition of the estate. Instead, he sought only to uplift the estate by giving assistance to the present stratum of priests' families, even making the allocation of salaries contingent upon the number of children and other family members the priest had to support. Though Belliustin desired to professionalize clerical service, he hoped to do so without the kinds of changes that would undermine the traditional estate system.

How reliable is Belliustin's picture of the church and clergy? Although its sarcastic and polemical style may suggest a distorted and one-sided account, the substance of the description is essentially accurate, conforming to that given not only by other well-informed observers but also to the data and conclusions of numerous official commissions in the late 1850s and early 1860s. Like Belliustin, a committee on seminary reform in 1860–1862 found the seminary in a shambles, suffering from an overloaded and misdirected curriculum, inadequate moral training, antiquated pedagogy, and maladministration.[69] The pernicious effect of the hereditary estate likewise became a commonplace in the official investigations and journalistic commentaries of the 1860s.[70] Nor were Belliustin's demands for a state salary unusual; when polled

---

69. See the data compiled from diocesan schools and the formal minutes of the committee in TsGIA SSSR, f. 796, op. 141, g. 1860, d. 367, ll. 1–593.

70. For two early critiques, both by fairly prominent state officials, see the memoranda by P. N. Batiushkov and P. A. Valuev in, respectively, OR GBL, f. 316, k. 65, d. 22, and TsGIA SSSR, f. 1284, op. 241, d. 30, ll. 66–80. Still more impressive is the critique of the hereditary order contained in the "considerations" (*soobrazheniia*) of diocesan authorities in 1863 on the problem of the juridical status of the clergy. For a brief overview, see G. L. Freeze, "Caste and Emancipation: The Changing Status of Clerical Families in the Great Reforms," in *The Family in Imperial Russia*, ed. David L. Ransel (Urbana, Ill., 1978), pp. 124–150.

for their opinion on the economic issue in 1863, parish clergy all over the empire voiced an overwhelming desire to convert the traditional emoluments and agriculture into a regular, reliable salary from the state. Their aspiration was tersely summed up in the response of a priest from Vladimir diocese: "To improve the clergy's condition in a material sense, there is no other means than a sufficient [state] salary. The clergy have but one desire: Salary! Salary!! Salary!!!"[71] Belliustin's denunciation of diocesan administration, shocking as it was in 1858, had become routine within a few years, appearing not only in muckraking anticlerical organs but in conservative Slavophile papers as well.[72]

Significantly, Belliustin's first readers, especially those well informed on conditions in the church, found little to fault in his description. Pogodin himself was delighted by the piece, and when he showed the manuscript to clerical acquaintances, they corroborated its grim account.[73] A knowledgable archpriest wrote that the work "realistically describes the pathetic condition of the clergy," and the future metropolitan of Moscow declared that "the most earnest defenders of the existing [seminary order] find little that is exaggerated" in Belliustin's description.[74] Perhaps most telling of all, even the chief procurator of the Synod, A. P. Tolstoi—who was more conservative than most prelates in the Synod—accepted the basic veracity of Belliustin's account. The marginalia on his personal copy of the manuscript (his comments are reproduced in the footnotes to the present translation) make it clear that Tolstoi found much to laud in the piece. He wrote "True!" alongside many shocking passages and added anecdotes from his own knowledge of church affairs to confirm Belliustin's horrifying description.

Though intended as a memorandum for the emperor and first circulated as a manuscript inside Russia, the work was soon

71. TsGIA SSSR, f. 804, op. 1, r. 3, d. 13, l. 148 ob.
72. See, for instance, "Koe-chto po voprosu ob uluchshenii byta dukhovenstva," *Den'*, 1863, no. 13, pp. 1–2; no. 17, pp. 11–14.
73. Pogodin, "Ob"iasnenie," pp. 47–48.
74. V. Pevnitskii, "Zapiski," *Russkaia starina*, 123 (1905): 541; I. Barsukov, ed., *Pis'ma Innokentiia, Mitropolita Moskovskogo i Kolomenskogo*, 2 vols. (St. Petersburg, 1897–98), 2:168.

published abroad at the behest of Pogodin, without the author's prior knowledge or consent.[75] When apprised of what Pogodin had done, Belliustin was positively petrified with fear. "There is now such chaos in my head," he wrote, "that I cannot put two ideas together sensibly."[76] He had good reason to quake in terror: however accurate the book's factual basis, it was offensive in style if not in content. As Belliustin himself observed, "this was originally a private work [not intended for publication], and I did not deem it necessary to indulge in sly circumlocutions."[77] Still more dangerous was the foreign publication of the volume; as Belliustin later learned, "my guilt, in their words, consists not in writing the book but in [permitting] all Europe to know what is going on here."[78] Apart from embarrassing the church in Western eyes, the book also provided ammunition for Catholic propagandists, especially the Russian Jesuits in Paris, who were already a source of growing anxiety for state and church authorities in Russia.[79]

The authorities' search to uncover the identity of the author did not take long: within a few months synodal investigators began to close in on Belliustin, and by January 1859 he was summoned to explain why he had written the book and how he had managed to publish it abroad. Belliustin flatly denied any culpability; seizing upon the technicality that he had written an untitled *zapiska*, he swore that he had not written, or even seen, a book titled *Description of the Clergy in Rural Russia*.[80] Church authorities paid no heed to such denials and prepared to sentence

---

75. Pogodin explains his decision to publish the manuscript abroad in "Ob"iasnenie," pp. 47–48; cf. the account in Freeze, "Revolt from Below," pp. 103–104.
76. Belliustin to Pogodin, February 22, 1858, OR GBL, f. 231/II, k. 3, d. 50./1, l. 5–5 ob.
77. Belliustin to P. I. Mel'nikov-Pecherskii, 1859, OR GPB, f. 37, d. 703, l. 2–2 ob.
78. Belliustin to Pogodin, May 26, 1859, OR GBL, f. 231/II, k. 3, d. 50/2, l. 19–19 ob.
79. To add insult to injury, Belliustin's book even bore an epigraph from I. S. Gagarin, the most renowned Jesuit of them all. The censors' fight against Catholic propaganda is exemplified by the banning of a book containing an essay by Gagarin, whose attack was (in the censors' words) "aimed at our Holy Synod" (TsGIA SSSR, f. 779, op. 4, g. 1858, d. 38, l. 107 ob).
80. Belliustin to Pogodin, October 24, 1858, and January 14, 1859, OR GBL, f. 231/II, k. 3, d. 50/1, l. 20; d. 50/2, l. 3–3 ob.

him to permanent exile in the forbidding Solovetskii Monastery, in the far north.[81]

Just as it prepared to do so, however, the priest was miraculously saved by the personal intervention of the emperor, Alexander II, who acted to quash the Synod's decision. As early as 10 January 1859, a friend in St. Petersburg wrote to inform Belliustin of the latest rumor in high society: "There are some good people who have taken your side, including (so it is said) the imperial family, which has read your work and found much in it that is true and completely new."[82] In some accounts, indeed, the emperor's intervention was nothing less than high drama: "The Synod had resolved to send you [Belliustin] to Solovki [Solovetskii Monastery], but before the session adjourned, the chief procurator received a note bearing the Sovereign's seal. The seal expressed His Imperial Majesty's and the imperial family's gratitude for the informative account of your book, and added that the author deserves recognition for the truth [contained in his work]."[83] Whatever the veracity of such stories, they achieved wide circulation (within a few months even the Russian Jesuits in Paris were repeating them)[84] and testified to the popular identification of the emperor with the cause of church reform.

The book—and perhaps still more, rumors about the sensational denouement in the Synod—precipitated a furious debate in the press about the "clerical question," and fueled hopes that

81. Belliustin to Pogodin, January 27, 1859, ibid., d. 50/2, l. 7 ob. With venomous sarcasm Belliustin later wrote that "the *Most Holy* Synod ordered that I be exiled permanently to Solovki [Solovetskii Monastery]—without a trial, without any refutation of my testimony" (Belliustin to Mel'nikov-Pecherskii, 1859, OR GPB, f. 37, d. 703, l. 2 ob.).
82. N. V. Kalachov to Belliustin, January 10, 1859, GAKO, f. 103, op. 1, d. 1333, ll. 3 ob.–4.
83. Unidentified source, quoted in Belliustin to Zheltukhin, January 27, 1859, IRLI, f. 616, op. 1, d. 6, l. 44 ob. Curiously, the church archives of the Synod, chief procurator, and various censorship organs show no trace of the entire Belliustin case; mention of it is even missing from the volumes of "secret resolutions" of the Synod (*Knigi dlia zapisyvaniia protokolov na sekretnoi ekspeditsii II-go otdeleniia Sinodal'noi kantseliarii* for 1857–60 in TsGIA SSSR, f. 796, op., 449, dd. 166–170). Evidently, once the emperor had intervened, the chief procurator and Synod destroyed whatever file had been assembled on the case.
84. I. Martynov to I. S. Gagarin, April 15, 1859, Bibliothèque slave (Paris), Archive Gagarine, no. 70.2 (unpaginated).

far-reaching changes were imminent.[85] The well-connected Belliustin spread rumors himself—from "one of the members of the Synod"—that the emperor had cast his support for radical church reform: "From the top [the emperor] came the following proposal in His [Majesty's] own hand: 'Consider: (1) It is not useful to convert monasteries into hospitals and monks into feldshers [paramedics] and doctors? (2) Is it not useful to remove the white clergy from the influence of the black clergy? (3) Is it not useful to make sacristans into hired laymen? (4) Present a report on the progress made in improving the condition of the rural clergy.' "[86] Characteristically, he was adamant that the reform process be removed from the bishops' control and that priests like himself be placed in charge. To Pogodin, who continued to relay his views and writings to the court, he wrote: "Now one must communicate to the very top this idea: 'These questions must not be decided by the Synod, which definitely thinks and acts contrary to the ideas of the Tsar and defends the monks' authority. Rather, as in the peasant question, experts from all corners of Russia should be chosen.' "[87] Rumors of the wildest sort spread through society, high and low, and Belliustin himself remained a tireless disseminator of such talk. In early 1860, in fact, he seemed close to realizing the goal articulated in his memoir when he reported new rumors that "V. B. Bazhanov [the tsar's personal confessor and Belliustin's patron] will soon become metropolitan of the entire white clergy."[88]

85. The debate over Belliustin's book commenced with an essay in the journal *Dukhovnaia beseda*, republished with the approval of church censors as a small pamphlet, *Mysli svetskogo cheloveka o knige "Opisanie sel'skogo dukhoventva"* (St. Petersburg, 1859). The anonymous author was A. N. Murav'ev, and the essay was allegedly edited by Metropolitan Filaret (Drozdov) of Moscow; see "Tekushchaia khronika i osobye proizshestviia: Dnevnik V. F. Odoevskogo, 1858–1859 gg.," *Literaturnoe nasledstvo*, 22–24 (Moscow, 1935): 94. The ensuing debate in the contemporary press, which included a rebuttal to Belliustin in the conservatives' own "underground book" (*Russkoe dukhovenstvo* [Berlin, 1859]), is surveyed in Freeze, "Revolt from Below," pp. 109–112.
86. Belliustin to Pogodin, October 6, 1859, OR GBL, f. 231/II, k. 3, d. 50/2, l. 25 ob.
87. Ibid., ll. 25 ob.–26.
88. Belliustin to Pogodin, January 8, 1860, OR GBL, f. 231/II, k. 3, d. 51/1, l. 2.

A CHURCH BETWEEN REFORMATION
AND REVOLUTION

Even as Belliustin placed the final touches on his manuscript in late 1857, his superiors in the church—the prelates he so mercilessly attacked in the memoir—were in fact making preparations for reform. To be sure, their plans did not include such radical ideas as the consecration of ordinary priests into the episcopate. But the ranking prelates, no less than Belliustin, understood the gravity of the church's problems and the urgent necessity of reform, especially in the system of clerical economic support and in ecclesiastical schools. By 1860 the Synod had created special committees to assemble data and to draft proposals for reform.[89] Widely publicized in the contemporary press, these activities reinforced expectations—among clergy and laymen alike—that the "Great Reforms" in the Orthodox church were imminent and that they would be no less fundamental than those that were already recasting other institutions in society and state.

To the disappointment of all concerned, however, these first efforts invariably ended in failure, with no tangible results. The failure of the reform efforts was due in part to the specific character of ecclesiastical politics: the resistance of ranking prelates to radical reform, their abiding distrust of state intrusion into ecclesiastical affairs, and disagreement—between bishops and bureaucrats and among the bishops themselves—as to how best to renovate the church and revitalize Orthodoxy. But most fundamental and insuperable was the financial problem: where was one to find the *means* to finance such improvements as the construction of dormitories, elimination of administrative corruption, and more honorable support for the parish clergy? The Church was loath to embark on draconian solutions, such as sharp reductions in parish staffs or seminary enrollments. Though such

89. For a recent account of these reform activities, see Freeze, *Parish Clergy*, chaps. 5–7. Older accounts may be found in A. A. Papkov, *Tserkovno-obshchestvennye voprosy v epokhu Tsaria-Osvoboditelia (1855–1870 gg.)* (St. Petersburg, 1902), and N. Runovskii, *Tserkovno-grazhdanskoe zakonopolozhenie otnositel'no pravoslavnogo dukhovenstva v tsarstvovanie Imp. Aleksandra II* (Kazan, 1898).

[49]

Introduction

measures would mean considerable economies (and eliminate the need for additional resources), they would also weaken the church's parish infrastructure and diminish its pool of future ordinands. The state, for its part, was already hard-pressed by fiscal problems and committed to finance a host of other governmental and social reforms; it simply refused to consider the kind of massive allocation that would have been required for fundamental restructuring of the church and its institutions. In desperation authorities made an effort to enlist the voluntary cooperation of society—a tactic entirely consistent with the prevailing spirit of the Great Reforms. In this case the government hoped to liberate the "creative energies" of society by establishing new organs of self-government, which would arouse popular interest and serve to mobilize voluntary assistance for an attack on the church's problems. But none of these new institutions—neither the parish council nor the zemstvo—evinced any serious interest in improving the clergy's material condition or even in the development of parish schools.

This stalemate in reform, especially amidst the changes already adopted in the secular domain, had a profound effect on the outlook of the rank-and-file clergy. Just as some cautious officials had warned,[90] an "open" reform process was certain to have a profound effect on the clergy's political and social consciousness, perhaps in an undesired fashion. The unprecedented "publicity" (*glasnost'*) of reform, the candid discussions in the contemporary press, the formation of a Special Commission on the Affairs of Orthodox Clergy under the personal supervision of the emperor— all combined to fuel the clergy's expectations of imminent, munificent reform. The subsequent failure, especially against the backdrop of reform elsewhere in the old order, quite naturally left many parish clergymen utterly disillusioned and disaffected. That new tone became increasingly audible in the contemporary press,

90. Grand Duke Konstantin Nikolaevich, normally a strong supporter of reform and experienced in the use of "publicity" to advance its cause, had raised doubts about the wisdom of this tactic in the clergy's case for fear it would only raise expectations that could never be fulfilled. See the conversations reported in P. A. Valuev, *Dnevnik*, 2 vols. (Moscow, 1961), 1:131–132.

censorship notwithstanding, and some clerics even argued that
their condition had positively deteriorated since the onset of
reform.[91] Hence in a few brief years the naive belief that the
emperor would come to their rescue—would gladly provide the
requisite funds for dormitories, better clerks and teachers, priests'
salaries, and the like—turned into despair and even disillusion-
ment with the emperor himself.

Belliustin's own writing in the 1860s exemplified this shift.
Indeed, even as the Special Commission commenced its work,
he sensed that reform had taken the wrong course: it remained
in the purview of bishops and bureaucrats, with no provision for
the direct participation of priests such as himself.[92] In despair he
wrote that the church could survive only if it were subjected to
fundamental reform, and predicted that such a transformation
probably could not be achieved by a commission, but only by "la
revolution du peuple."[93] That kind of idea, expressed in private
letters that the police subjected to routine inspection, soon earned
him official disfavor, reflected initially in an increasing disappearance of his mail and then in his failure to obtain a better
position.[94] Then, in 1864, the emperor issued a secret instruction

91. See, for example, the essay by A. Baratynskii, *O postepennom ukhudshenii byta
dukhovenstva i o sovremennykh ego nadezhdakh* (Kharkov, 1865).
92. Belliustin to his son, N. I. Belliustin, May 24, 1863, in LOII, f. 115, op. 1,
d. 1217 (unpaginated). Even as early as April 1862 Belliustin warned that the
reform was going awry: "[The Synod] discussed it all at length, but not the slightest
good came of it, because which of these gentlemen know the clergy the way it
does them? Fools, fools! Belliustin is before their very eyes, but they do not want
to ask him what to do. The devil with them!" (I. S. Belliustin to N. I. Belliustin,
April 17, 1862, ibid.).
93. Belliustin to A. K. Meiendorf, January 1, 1863, OR GPB, f. 542, op. 1, d. 900,
l. 1 ob.
94. Riding high on public sympathy after publication of his book, Belliustin sought
a better priestly appointment in such elite quarters as the estate of Grand Duchess
Elena Pavlovna, a member of the imperial family and renowned supporter of the
Great Reforms. Despite a personal interview, the endeavor failed—according to
Belliustin, because of calumny about his alleged alcoholism and contumacy. See
I. S. Belliustin to N. I. Belliustin, May 9, 1862, LOII, f. 115, d. 1217, unpaginated;
and Belliustin to A. K. Korsak, December 2, 1862, IRLI, f. 93, d. 72, l. 4. For
complaints about the disappearance of his mail, see Belliustin to Pogodin, April 2,
1860, OR GBL, f. 231/II, k. 3, d. 51/1, l. 10–10 ob.; and Belliustin to E. A. Cher-
kasskaia, August 1, 1860, OR GBL, f. 327/II, k. 31, l. 4.

that Belliustin be prevented altogether from visiting St. Petersburg. The order was easily implemented: priests, like peasants,
required "passports" to travel inside the empire, and the local
bishop was simply directed to withhold the necessary documents
from Belliustin. As the chief procurator explained in a private
letter to Belliustin's bishop, "the government [had] become
apprised that Belliustin [permitted] himself inappropriate comments on various subjects," and it was therefore incumbent on
the bishop to see that he not be "released to visit the capital
without [good] cause and without prior consultation with me."[95]
Such harassment, however, only made the priest more irascible,
even to the point of labeling the emperor as the bishop's sworn
ally. In one letter, for instance, he asserted that the emperor had
instructed his new appointee as chief procurator, Count D. A.
Tolstoi, to conserve the old order: "Into your hands," Alexander
is alleged to have said, "I am entrusting the entire future of Russia,
and you will doubtless fulfill your duties in such a manner that
Russia is not torn from the path of Byzantium, along which she
has so blissfully trod."[96]

But such assertions could hardly have been more erroneous:
Tolstoi, in fact, soon engineered the reforms that had been so
long demanded and deferred. To be sure, not after the model of
Byzantium or Belliustin; Tolstoi's reforms aimed to modernize the
church, principally by realigning it with the new norms in parallel
state institutions (in education, censorship, and justice, for example) and by transforming the clergy from a hereditary estate into
a professional service class. Fundamentally, his aim was to advance
the institutional interests of the church, not the special interests
of its servitors; confronting the traditional interpenetration of estate
and institution, Tolstoi sought to disentangle the two and to give
unequivocal priority to the institution. As a *gosudarstvennik* (state-
minded bureaucrat) committed to the larger interests of state, not
to the narrow, selfish concerns of his own noble estate and still

95. TsGIA SSSR, f. 797, op. 34, otd. 1, d. 89, ll. 1–6.
96. Belliustin to A. A. Kraevskii, June 3, 1866, OR GPB, f. 391, d. 188, l. 10 ob.

less to those of other estates, Tolstoi sought to rebuild and improve the institution, even at the expense of the traditional estate that had served it.[97]

This aspiration was most systematically and explicitly apparent in the first major reform of his tenure, the ecclesiastical school reforms of 1867–1869.[98] To overcome the financial problems that afflicted ecclesiastical schools, Tolstoi turned to a host of devices, including a substantial allocation of direct state aid. But his primary strategy involved a reduction in expenditures (through strict limits on seminary enrollments) and an increase in revenues from the sale of church candles (through direct participation of parish clergy in the management and supervision of such collections). In curricular matters the classicist Tolstoi proved less innovative; he retained most of the old Latin core. Still, the new statutes did adopt some curricular proposals of the 1860s, including the deletion of superfluous courses and redirection of studies toward a more practical preparation of future village priests. No less significant were the reforms promulgated after 1867 to dismantle the hereditary clerical estate. A reform *not* espoused in Belliustin's book, it had subsequently acquired considerable support, chiefly in the government and the liberal press. The seminary reform itself abetted this change: though anticipating that most of the clergy's sons would still prefer a clerical career, the new statutes explicitly annulled all formal barriers to the matriculation of outsiders and permitted any qualified student, regardless of social origin, to enroll in a church school. Tolstoi, in fact, justified preservation of the classical curriculum partly in the name of social mobility, since a common curriculum in ecclesiastical and state schools would facilitate transfer between the two systems, as the students' inclinations and aspirations dictated. Of more direct and immediate import was a synodal resolution of 1867, which formally abolished family claims to clerical positions and forbade

97. See Freeze, *Parish Clergy*, pp. 298–347.
98. See Titlinov, *Dukhovnaia shkola*, 2:300–420; Freeze, *Parish Clergy*, pp. 319–329; and the main archival file, TsGIA SSSR, f. 797, op. 36, otd. 1, st. 2, d. 395, ch. 1–6.

bishops to take "family needs" into consideration when they made appointments.[99] Two years later the emperor signed into law a piece of legislation legally separating the clergy's children from formal membership in the clerical estate. As a result, they no longer held their father's clerical status but acquired a secular social status of their own (personal noble or honored citizen, depending on their father's rank in the church). At least in law, the reform knocked out the legal underpinnings of the hereditary order, both facilitating the exit of the clergy's sons to lay careers and the admission of "vital new forces" from the outside.

More intractable proved the economic and social problems of parish service, which Belliustin had so graphically described and which had been the primary object of reform, especially among the parish clergy themselves. With no auxiliary resources forthcoming from the church, state, or local community, the reform act of 16 April 1869 perforce had to rely on some other means of solving the problem of the parish economy. Its solution was bureaucratic: rationalization of the traditional service structure, primarily by reducing the number of clerical positions and by merging small parishes into larger, more economically viable units. That tactic, designed to increase the proportion of parishioners to clergy, assumed that a larger parish could provide sufficient voluntary contributions and still be able to satisfy the spiritual needs of the laity. The reform sought in addition to improve the quality of the parish clergy, with particular focus on the dismal state of deacons and sacristans, which Belliustin and others had so vehemently criticized. Thus deacons were to be eliminated altogether (except in wealthy urban parishes and cathedrals), and the customary pair of sacristans was to be reduced to one. And those sacristans who remained were to be of an entirely different breed: they were to have a seminary diploma, to bear a new title ("psalmist"), and to regard their service in this rank as a temporary apprenticeship for subsequent promotion to the rank of priest. The reform of 1869 also promised to raise the clergy's legal status,

99. *Polnoe sobranie zakonov Rossiiskoi Imperii,* 2d ser. (hereafter cited as *PSZ[2]*), 55 vols. (St. Petersburg, 1830–84), vol. 42, no. 44610.

abolishing various restrictions on their civil rights (such as the right to preach and to publish in secular periodicals without prior censorship) and holding out the prospect of the awards and medals that Belliustin had urged. In short, although the reform conferred no salaries, it did bestow new rights and foresaw a gradual improvement in the clergy's economic status as bishops gradually implemented the new rules in their dioceses.

But in one important area, that of ecclesiastical administration, Tolstoi achieved precious little. Finances, as ever, provided one basic reason for the stalemate, but were by no means the chief obstacle to reform. More important was the resilient opposition of the bishops, who were amenable to reform that would improve the lot of parish clergy and their performance but not to changes that would contravene canon law or infringe on traditional episcopal prerogatives. They did make certain concessions, to be sure; in some dioceses, for example, the bishops voluntarily experimented in the election of local superintendents, as Belliustin and others had demanded. But the prelates eschewed more fundamental reform in administration, censorship, or justice. Most indicative of their attitude—and indeed of the changing atmosphere that had once been so propitious to reform—was their categorical rejection of Tolstoi's plan to modernize ecclesiastical justice. Seeking to apply the liberal, Western principles that underlay the 1864 reform in secular justice, Tolstoi proposed to introduce modern judicial procedures, to reduce the bishop's role, and to permit parish clergy to elect ecclesiastical judges. But the plan foundered on the uncompromising opposition of the bishops, who regarded the whole scheme as a crass violation of their authority and the precepts of tradition and canon.[100] Thus the prereform administrative order in the church remained intact, at least in principle and in statute, and any modifications in

---

100. The commentaries by diocesan bishops on the planned reform were published for internal use under the title *Mneniia preosviashchennykh eparkhial'nykh arkhiereev otnositel'no proekta dukhovno-sudebnoi chasti*, 2 vols. (St. Petersburg, 1874–76); the main archival file on the planned reform is in TsGIA SSSR, f. 797, op. 39, otd. 1, st. 1, d. 295. For a summary account, see Freeze, *Parish Clergy*, pp. 340–345, 401–404.

practice—such as the election of superintendents by the local clergy—could easily be retracted in a less favorable political climate.

Not surprisingly, the parish clergy responded negatively to Tolstoi's "Great Reforms," finding them even more anathema than the nonreforms of the early 1860s. The cause is not far to seek: Tolstoi aimed to serve the interests of the *church*, not those of its clergy, who indeed suffered serious losses as a result of the reform. The seminary reform, for example, deprived their sons of free, automatic education by the church and made the parish clergy primarily responsible for improving the schools' economic conditions. As Tolstoi himself candidly admitted in a memorandum to the emperor: "Before the new statutes had reached the dioceses, false rumors about them had succeeded in arousing debates among the clergy in some areas (and they bordered on outright discontent in the diocese of Nizhnii Novgorod) toward the impending reform."[101] Nor did the abolition of the clerical estate give the parish clergy any more cause to rejoice. As they soon realized, the reform simply abrogated their traditional right to social welfare from the church, made no provision for clerical pensions, and meant that "now the priest is obliged to hand over his daughter to the lowliest peasant."[102] Still more vehement opposition was provoked by the plans for parish reform and reduction in clerical positions; though scheduled for gradual implementation, the new order threatened all with forcible relocation and other hardships. The clergy's response to the reform was understandably negative; as the Third Section reported, "all the provincial clergy share the fear of being deprived of their livelihood."[103] A priest in Vladimir summed up the mood well when he declared that "the tsar is generous [to the rest of you], but he's not worth a brass farthing

101. Tolstoi to Alexander II, November 28, 1867, in TsGIA SSSR, f. 797, op. 36, otd. 1, st. 2, d. 395, ch. 1, ll. 343 ob.–344.

102. F. Vinogradov, "Delo uluchsheniia byta dukhovenstva," *Sovremennyi listok,* 1870, no. 17.

103. TsGAOR, f. 109, op. 223, g. 1869, d. 34, ll. 83 ob.–84. The Third Section was a division of the emperor's personal chancellery which performed the basic functions of the secret police until 1880.

to us: he gave you medals, but he's taking away everything we had left."[104]

Belliustin reflected this mood in ever more radical, uncompromising writings of the 1870s and 1880s. In 1872 he summed up his thoroughly negative assessment of the reforms in an inflammatory essay that, predictably, soon came to the attention of the censors. In their apt summary of the piece: "The article, deeming all measures taken hitherto to be palliatives and merely superficial, turns attention to the clergy's moral level and, in a whole series of exceedingly acerbic assertions and facts, accuses various people in the clerical estate of deviating from the order of church canons and of conduct unbecoming the clerical rank."[105] Disappointed by the failure of *church* reform, Belliustin turned his attention increasingly to *religious* reform, elaborating—and radicalizing—his earlier ideas about the need for a fundamental reformation in Russian spiritual life and religious practice. The most essential task, in his view, was to extirpate "the terrible Byzantinism" that had reduced Orthodoxy to a hollow ritualism, distracted the people from a true perception of Christ's teachings and meaning, and even caused the schism that had done such harm to the vitality of Orthodoxy in Russia.[106] Antipathy to ritualism permeated much of his writing, even a book nominally about the parish clergy in France; as the censors complained, "it is impossible to overlook the author's general view that the ritualistic aspect of the church is superfluous and even harmful."[107]

104. Ibid., ll. 36 ob.–37.
105. TsGIA SSSR, f, 797, op. 41, otd. 2, st. 3, d. 235, l. 1–1 ob. The essay in question was "Chto sdelano po voprosu o dukhovenstve," *Beseda*, 1871, no. 3, pp. 134–157; no. 11, pp. 61–82; 1872, no. 2, pp. 179–210.
106. For a characteristic attack on Byzantinism, see Belliustin to M. N. Katkov, March 19, 1866, OR GBL, f. 120, d. 22, l. 187–187 ob. His views on such matters became increasingly radical in the following decade and finally led him to publish a notorious essay on the Old Belief that very nearly ended in his defrocking. The essay, "K voprosu o raskole" (*Tserkovno-obshchestvennyi vestnik*, 1879, nos. 43–44), depicted the official church and the Old Belief as two "parties," each the victim of a blind, Byzantine ritualism. The long synodal file on the case, revealing just how close the priest came to being defrocked, is in TsGIA SSSR, f. 796, op. 160, g. 1879, d. 831.
107. TsGIA SSSR, f. 796, op. 2, d. 1478, l. 52. The censors were not imagining things; Belliustin himself, in private correspondence, boasted of this hidden message

In lieu of Byzantine ritualism Belliustin proposed to instill a more conscious, participatory Christianity, and to that end he urged a number of fundamental changes in Russian religious life: the replacement of Church Slavonic by vernacular Russian, an abridgment of the overlong liturgy, the adoption of more harmonious and appealing church music, and the establishment of Sunday "readings" for the edification of adult peasants.[108] The last few years before his death, in 1890, Belliustin became still more radical in his antiritualism, and indeed seemed quasi-Protestant in his vision of the reforms required to revitalize Orthodoxy.[109]

The conservative atmosphere and repressive policies of the 1880s and 1890s effectively drove such dissent underground but could hardly eradicate the dissatisfaction that surged among bishops and priests. The prelates, appalled first by the reforms of Tolstoi and then by the importunities of his successor, K. P. Pobedonostsev, profoundly resented the blatant violation of ecclesiastical privilege and grew sympathetic toward fundamental changes in the church's relationship to the state, favoring, in particular, restoration of the patriarchate. Nor did the parish clergy have more cause to be satisfied with either Tolstoi's reforms or Pobedonostsev's countermeasures designed to nullify them: in the end the church still suffered from the same complex of debilitating problems in administration, education, and parish service.

It was hardly surprising that when revolution violently shook the empire in the early decades of the twentieth century, the church and clergy did *not* emerge as the pillars of conservatism that both autocracy and its opponents had expected them to be.

---

in the book (Belliustin to N. S. Leskov, July 20, 1876, TsGALI, f. 275, op. 4, d. 12, l. 9–9 ob.) The book in question was Belliustin's *Sel'skoe dukhovenstvo vo Frantsii* (St. Petersburg, 1871).

108. See, in particular, the series of essays "K redaktoru *Russkogo*," OR GBL, f.231/ III, k. 1, dd. 59 and 59a; and "Voskresnye chteniia," ibid., d. 56.

109. In one private letter, for instance, Belliustin directly pronounced the Lutheran clergy superior to both Catholic and Orthodox priests: "At least [the Lutheran clergy] do not conspire to suppress the intellectual development of their flock, and to hoodwink mankind with the miracles of a Madonna, relics, and similar nonsense" (I. S. Belliustin to N. I. Belliustin, November 12, 1884, LOII, f. 115, d. 1220, letter no. 703).

Even the bishops, including the most conservative in their midst, grew restless and began to press their demands upon a shaken autocracy.[110] In February 1905—when the uproar over Bloody Sunday had scarcely subsided—the moderate metropolitan of St. Petersburg, Antonii (Vadkovskii), formally raised the question "whether now is not the proper time to abolish (or at least to moderate) the constant tutelage and all the vigilant control exercised by secular authorities over the life of the church and its administrative activities, for it deprives the church of its independence and initiative."[111] With the emperor's formal if reluctant approval, the Synod now laid plans for a church council to reconstruct the church and collected detailed "opinions" from diocesan prelates on the proper direction of reform.[112] Although some prelates found themselves deeply enmeshed in the reactionary Black Hundred movements, most remained apart and concentrated instead on seizing the opportunity for fundamental church reform, above all in the relationship between church and state.

Nor did the parish clergy prove more committed to defense of the old regime. Although hints of their unreliability were evident earlier, it was only the Revolution of 1905 that exposed the depth of disaffection and opposition among the parish clergy. Although

110. For high church politics in the early twentieth century, see Smolitsch, *Geschichte der russischen Kirche*, 306–330; Gerhard Simon, *Konstantin Petrovič Pobedonoscev und die Kirchenpolitik des Heiligen Sinod, 1880–1905* (Göttingen, 1969), pp. 249–264; N. F. Platonov, "Pravoslavnaia tserkov' v bor'be s revoliutsionnym dvizheniem v Rossii (1900–1907 gg.)," *Ezhegodnik muzeia istorii religii i ateizma*, 4 (1960): 103–209; John S. Curtiss, *Church and State in Russia: The Last Years of the Empire, 1900–1917* (New York, 1940); John M. Geekie, "The Church and Politics in the Reign of Nicholas II," Ph.D. dissertation, University of East Anglia, 1976; and James Cunningham, *A Vanquished Hope: The Movement for Church Renewal in Russia, 1905–1906* (Crestwood, N.Y., 1981). Cf. the traditional account in P. N. Zyrianov, "Pravoslavnaia tserkov' v bor'be s pervoi russkoi revoliutsiei," *Istoricheskie zapiski*, 95 (1975): 314–355.
111. A. R., *Istoricheskaia perepiska o sud'bakh pravoslavnoi tserkvi* (Moscow, 1912), pp. 26–31.
112. These diocesan replies have been the subject of repeated study. See, for example, John Meyendorff, "Russian Bishops and Church Reform in 1905," in *Russian Orthodoxy under the Old Regime*, ed. Stavrou and Nichols, pp. 170–182; and P. E. Immekus, *Die Russisch-Orthodoxe Landpfarrei zu Beginn des XX. Jahrhunderts nach den Gutachten der Diozesanbischöfe* (Würzburg, 1978).

some clergy did join the Black Hundred movement, more stood among the liberal opposition or, upon occasion, even with the radical left.[113] The parish clergy produced a number of prominent Christian socialists and radical publicists, who believed that "the only solution for the clergy is this: to support the interests of the peasants, to speak out in defense of their political and economic rights."[114] Even V. I. Lenin conceded "the presence of a liberal reformationist movement among a certain part of the young clergy," and a reactionary bishop complained bitterly that the parish clergy, "if not openly sympathetic to the revolution, were either passive or secretly supported it."[115] But, like the bishops, parish clergy were interested primarily in religious reform and tended to coalesce in a "renovationist movement."[116] The movement reaffirmed demands voiced earlier by Belliustin, including changes in the ritual itself that would make Orthodoxy more comprehensible to the folk: "The accessibility and comprehensibility of the language used in religious services is something absolutely necessary, given the very nature of the liturgy as a socioreligious act."[117]

Most important, the shortcomings of the old order survived almost without change to the very demise of the ancien régime. A declaration of clerical deputies to the State Duma in August 1915 demonstrated that even after decades of endless reforming

113. The most exhaustive recent account is Geekie, "Church and Politics." Apart from the contemporary ecclesiastical press, which clearly mirrors this attitude, see especially the informative memoirs of N. P. Rozanov in OR GBL, f. 250, k. 2, d. 1.

114. V. Myshtsyn, *Po tserkovno-obshchestvennym voprosam* (Sergiev-Posad, 1907), pt. 2, p. 36. See also the writings of G. S. Petrov, *Tserkov' i obshchestvo* (St. Petersburg, 1906), and Arkhimandrit Mikhail, *Khristos v veke mashin* (St. Petersburg, 1907) and *Pastyr', vybory, Duma* (St. Petersburg, 1906).

115. V. I. Lenin, *Polnoe sobranie sochinenii*, 55 vols., 5th ed. (Moscow, 1967–70), 9:211; the bishop is quoted in J. W. Bohon, "Reactionary Politics in Russia, 1905–1909," Ph.D. dissertation, University of North Carolina, 1967, p. 145.

116. The key manifesto of the movement is available in Gruppa Peterburgskikh sviashchennikov, *K tserkovnomu soboru* (St. Petersburg, 1906).

117. Quoted in N. S. Gordienko and P. K. Kurochkin, "Liberal'no-obnovlencheskoe dvizhenie v russkom pravoslavii nachala XX v.," *Voprosy nauchnogo ateizma*, 7 (1969): 325–332.

and counterreforming, the church was in no wise closer to the resolution of its long-standing problems. Thus the duma clergy complained that they were still dependent on the baneful emoluments, and warned that "so long as the present system of abnormal and humiliating form of support for the clergy exists, the clergy's authority in the eyes of the people will not be raised." Like Belliustin in an earlier day, they denounced their ecclesiastical superiors for careerism and indifference to the priest's needs: "The bishops hold themselves too high and far away from their co-workers in church affairs, the parish priests. The clergy do not see paternal leadership on the part of the prelates; instead, one finds a cold, often bureaucratic relationship based largely on paper." And like Belliustin they decried the bishop's unbounded authority over them, expressed in his power to "transfer without trial and investigation, to retire from active service by administrative order, to imprison without trial, and to place on trial without sufficient grounds." And like Belliustin they demanded that the parish clergy be accorded a larger role in church administration and such basic rights as the election of superintendents.[118]

By 1917 the commitment of bishop and priest to the old regime had reached a breaking point. Disappointed by the deflection of its reform plans in 1905, appalled by the enormous abuses of the Rasputin affair, the bishops gradually gave up hope on the autocracy. That attitude found its surest expression on the eve of the February Revolution, when the Synod declined to issue a proclamation in defense of the monarchy.[119] Far more radical still were the parish clergy, who often gave enthusiastic support to the radical social demands of the popular classes, not sporadically and as individuals (as in 1905), but on a broader organized basis. Thus the All-Russian Union of Democratic Clergy and Laymen endorsed a program of radical ecclesiastical and social change—democratization of the church and "Christianization of human relations," condemnation of capitalism, redistribution of land to

118. "Pechat' i dukhovenstvo," *Missionerskoe obozrenie*, 1915, no. 11, pp. 286–298.
119. A. V. Kartashev, "Revoliutsiia i sobor, 1917–1918 gg.," *Bogoslovskaia mysl'*, 4 (1942): 75–101.

the peasantry, and profit sharing for the working class. While such declarations reflected the mood chiefly among the more radical and especially urban priests, equally striking pronouncements came as well from the rural clergy. Thus a diocesan assembly in Voronezh adopted a formal resolution agreeing to "support peasant demands: (1) for the abolition of private ownership of land; (2) for equal land use; and (3) for labor norms."[120] This movement—a combination of social radicalism and demands for fundamental "reformation" in the church—flourished briefly in the 1920s as the Living Church (*Zhivaia tserkov*), which took to a logical conclusion the program espoused earlier by such activist priests as Belliustin—for a vernacular liturgy, effective religious instruction of the faithful, consecration of priests as bishops, and a closer nexus between church and people. It was that popular aspiration which ultimately impelled the Soviet regime to suppress the Living Church, preferring a more conventional patriarchate to popular reformation from below. Hence the 1920s marked both the climax and the conclusion to a movement begun decades earlier and first inspired by a dissident provincial priest and his *Description of the Clergy in Rural Russia.*

120. V. N. Dunaev, "Vystuplenie krest'ian Voronezhskoi gubernii protiv reaktsionnykh deistvii dukhovenstva," in *Sbornik rabot aspirantov Voronezhskogo gosudarstvennogo universiteta,* vol. 1 (Voronezh, 1965), p. 146.

I. S. BELLIUSTIN

DESCRIPTION OF
THE CLERGY
IN RURAL RUSSIA

There are a great number of questions of the highest importance which await a solution and which call for the meditation of all serious spirits. I do not hesitate to say that, of all these questions, not a single one can rival that of the clergy's education and character development. Give Russia a clergy worthy of its high mission, and Russia will easily take her place in the front ranks of Christian nations; suppose, on the contrary, a clergy without learning, without independence, without development, without zeal, without respect, without authority, and the same progress that makes Russia a completely material and superficial civilization becomes a source of new dangers. Thus the future of Russia depends upon what becomes of the clergy; the future of the clergy depends upon the education it receives, upon the care taken to initiate it into sacred learning and to form a sacerdotal spirit in it. Consequently, the future of Russia is intimately bound to this great question of ecclesiastical schools.

—Père Jean Gagarin, "De l'enseignement de
la théologie dans l'église russe"[1]

1. Gagarin's article appeared in a volume edited by Gagarin and Charles Daniel, *Etudes de théologie de philosophie et d'histoire* (Paris, 1856), pp. 1–61. It was solely on account of Gagarin's article (from which this epigraph is taken) that the Committee on Foreign Censorship prohibited the public sale and circulation of the volume in Russia. See TsGIA SSSR, f. 779, op. 4, g. 1858, d. 38, l. 1–1 ob. (resolution of January 8, 1858).

RURAL PRIESTS

> He that rebuketh a man afterwards shall find more
> favour than he that flattereth with his tongue.
> —Proverbs 28:23[2]

It is sad and painful to see how degraded and demoralized the
rural clergy has become. It is even sadder, even more painful to
see that the clergy itself is partly responsible for this state of affairs,
and does not even have the right to console itself by saying that
we suffer everything for Christ's sake. It does not behave in a
manner that would arouse in others the veneration that is always
vital for its service, so elevated and sacred; nor does it inspire in
parishioners a sincere, warm feeling—the kind of undying love
that would indissolubly bind priest and parish together in a common quest for the celestial calling.

What has caused this unsatisfactory condition of the clergy?
Wherein lies the evil?

To answer these questions, we shall follow the life of a rural
priest from the years of his childhood. That does not take us too
far back: the only thing that develops in life is what was sown
by oneself or others. And that which has so profoundly denigrated the rural clergyman is the inevitable result of his education.
Naturally, someone with such an education, if placed in quite
different circumstances, could become absolutely different. But
the condition of the rural clergy almost seems to have been purposely devised in a way to ensure that the old evil grows, matures,
and brings forth its bitter fruits.

---

2. The textual message here is cited in Greek, without translation.

Without the slightest hesitation, I shall tell the whole truth. And only the truth. May the Lord summon me to the Day of Judgment if I dare say even a single word that is false.

ELEMENTARY EDUCATION

Student Housing

We shall concentrate primarily on the sons of priests, not their lower ranking subordinates, the sacristans.[3] Whatever a priest may be like in service, not one wants to see his children physically and morally ruined; all, without exception, take good care of their children so long as they are in their personal charge. I say this without the slightest fear of being exposed for exaggeration.

Well, it is time for the boy to study, so the priest brings him to an ecclesiastical school, located in a district or provincial town. The first thing he needs is a place to live. But extremely few priests (no more than two or three in a hundred) have the wherewithal to place their sons in the apartment of someone respectable, such as a government official, merchant, or reliable urban priest. The great majority must seek housing that is as cheap as possible, particularly if the priest has two or three sons in school (a rather common phenomenon). So where is housing for them found? In the living quarters of a half-impoverished townsman, retired soldier, or widow (God only knows what she does to earn a living), or a local sacristan (who is almost always on the same level as a half-impoverished townsman). And it is to the supervision and care of this scum that an eight- or nine-year-old boy is entrusted!

What does one find in such housing? Loathsome poverty, invariably accompanied by filth, by rudeness that borders on bestiality, by the most abomindable vices that they do not even bother to

3. As the income of a deacon or sacristan was one-third to one-quarter that of a priest, it would be still less adequate for the education of sons.

conceal. And these are the boy's first impressions—the very first, which, as all experienced people realize, are permanent! It would not be so terrible if he only had to see this. But no, they force him to be an instrument of, even a participant in various abominations: they send him to the tavern for vodka, or to steal kindling and firewood when there is nothing to burn in the stove. Worse still, they put him in a position where he himself has to resort to crime. Thus, after they have consumed in two or three weeks all the provisions that the youth brought for several months, they feed him the kind of bread and soup that are nauseating just to look at. What is he to do when he is constantly hungry? If he is meek, then in a few months he turns into a virtual skeleton; if he is bold, he will thieve and indulge in similar activities. Only last winter, in the town of N., I saw the following: at 6 P.M., amidst the ferocious cold of a December day, a ten-year-old boy sat on the porch of a church, shivering terribly from the cold and crying.

"What's wrong?" I asked. "Why are you crying?"

"I'm afraid to go back to my boarding house."

"Why?"

"The landlady sent me to buy some vodka, but it was already time for class to begin, so I went to school instead. When I came home for lunch, she gave me a fierce thrashing, threw me out, and said it will be even worse for me tonight."

I went with the boy to see the landlady. The widow of a petty clerk, she was still rather young, but quite drunk. It was impossible to discuss the matter with someone in that condition (especially when it is a drunken wench), so I decided that it would be better to see the school's inspector. What happened? To all my explanations and pleas that he save the boy from this ruinous life, he only replied that "it's none of your business, and don't poke your nose in when you're not asked." According to information that I received subsequently, it turned out that this wench, who was drunk from morning to night, enjoyed the special protection of the inspector, and that boys are sent to her at his personal order (and in fact he sends only the boys of very

[67]

well-to-do fathers). Six unfortunate boys live with her! And such cases are the most ordinary thing in all provincial towns.[4]

When the boy comes home for vacation, his parents cannot recognize him, so changed is he, physically and morally. They transfer him to a different boarding room, but that merely drags him from one pit to another. If we add the fact that the boys almost always suffer from skin diseases (primarily phtiviasis, lichen, thermintus, farvus, scabies, which are widespread in all the schools),[5] and that they sometimes contract diseases that are disgraceful and terrible even to call by name, one gets, I think, a clear idea of the quarters in which pupils of elementary church schools live.

Even those who live in the best boarding rooms are not immune to those physical and moral sores, for they contract these infections from their fellow students. They have just one advantage: some measures are taken for their sake to deal with these problems, and the evil does not develop so quickly and uncontrollably.

It is in the midst of these destructive influences that a boy must spend six whole years, the best and most important years of his life! True, from time to time their parents bring them home, but what can even the most intelligent parents accomplish during a vacation that lasts just two to six weeks? At best they will manage to have some physical disease treated, but that is all—you cannot cure moral sores that have been developing for years in just a few days. Moreover, following the harmful example of their peers, the boys soon acquire the knack of concealing these moral deformities. Of course, here—as in everything else—there are exceptions, but they are rare: a boy requires an extraordinarily fortunate personality to resist the bad examples that are constantly before his eyes. Are there many such boys?

Someone may object that "school authorities are supposed to take care of these matters." Indeed they are. But there are hardly

4. Marginal comment by Chief Procurator A. P. Tolstoi: "This is why Father Nikolai has not enrolled his sons at the district school and is instead having them educated at home until they are ready to enter the class of rhetoric [level one] at the seminary" (OR GBL, f. 302, k. 2, d. 12, l. 3 ob.).
5. Belliustin names these various skin diseases in Latin.

any more remiss in performing their duty than those entrusted with authority in the church. Student housing, in fact, is a source of income for the school's superintendent and inspector. Once they have taken one thing or another from the landlords and landladies, they give these people complete freedom and power over the boys in their charge.[6]

District Schools[7]

All the filth and evil of private boarding rooms that corrupt the youth's soul would not have such catastrophic effects if the school itself acted as a counterweight. But no, to our great and irreparable misfortune, the boy sees nothing better at school. Here are the same filth, the same hostile people, only in another form; here are amazingly horrible disorders, only of a different form and character.

Just what are the school buildings like? Someone who saw them for the first time would find it difficult, in most cases, to guess what they are for. No, they are not barracks, stables, or cattle sheds, but something infinitely worse! Like the ruins of something built in immemorial times, most of the buildings are extremely dilapidated, propped up by innumerable supports; the wind sweeps through them freely, the slightest rain leaks in, even big snowdrifts can pile up inside in the winter. Even if the walls are sound and whole, and even if the rain does not come in (something that is quite uncommon), it is nevertheless quite terrible for the boys enrolled in such schools. It is considered the most unforgivable luxury to mop or sweep the floor; even on the occasion of a visit by the bishop they just sprinkle about some sand and juniper berries, and that's it. Nor do they believe that it is necessary

6. Tolstoi's marginal comment: "True!" (OR GBL, f. 302, k. 2, d. 12, l. 4 ob.).
7. The elementary ecclesiastical school, formally called the *dukhovnoe uchilishche*, existed in several district towns of each diocese—that is, in roughly a third of all the district capitals. Hence all the clergy who served in villages or other district towns had to arrange for their sons to live either in the school dormitory (if space permitted) or among local residents (the usual case).

to heat these schools (even though funds have undoubtedly been allocated for this purpose), even if the winter is cold—as it was last year, for example. The schoolrooms are so crowded that the pupils look as if they had been squeezed between the jaws of a vise. In the winter, the snow that has been tracked in or blown in by blizzards melts, filth covers the floor, and the whole classroom turns into a marsh. It is in such buildings as these that the youths study; it is from the midst of all this that priests and even bishops will later come![8] . . .

Thus pupils go from their filthy boarding rooms to classrooms that are even filthier. The boardinghouse is warm, at least; in school they must wrap themselves up in two or three layers of clothes in order to keep from freezing. But what happens then? Once they are all seated and the air warms up, it becomes intolerably stuffy. In the meantime, their legs are unavoidably planted in the marsh below, and they become so chilled that they eventually go numb; when class is over, the pupils hobble out as though they were on crutches. How do the boys endure all this? Those who are weak by nature simply perish; the healthier ones get off with fevers and other ailments.* Is that difficult to believe? Just look at the district schools in Moscow, Iaroslavl, Tver, and Vladimir provinces, and you'll be convinced. While I do not know about schools elsewhere, I do know these exceedingly well. If you like, here is evidence that should, one hopes, require no comment: "Let's look at the state schools," wrote a learned observer of north Russia about Bezhetsk,[9] but the venerable supervisor at

---

*In December last year the temperature dropped to 30 degrees below zero [centigrade, or $-22°F$], but in the town of X authorities did not heat the school (which, moreover, is a stone building) the entire year. Consequently, in December alone thirty pupils nearly froze to death: a third were saved because they were taken home in time, the rest bear the scars of frostbite. This winter the same thing happened again.

8. Tolstoi's marginal comment: "True" (OR GBL, f. 302, k. 2, d. 12, l. 5). The emperor himself had occasion in 1858 to discover the truth of Belliustin's account: "Upon visiting the seminary in Nizhnii Novgorod the emperor became very dissatisfied with the extreme lack of cleanliness, the dilapidated condition of seminary buildings, the unkempt beds, and the general disorder in the upkeep of the institution" (TsGIA SSSR, f. 797, op. 28, otd. 1, st. 2, d. 215, l. 12).

9. Bezhetsk, garbled in the printed text as a nonexistent "Bozheuk," was a small town with 7,000 inhabitants in Belliustin's home diocese of Tver; coincidentally, it was also the town where his father was still serving as priest.

the district church school did not want to show him his institution, because its buildings were extremely dilapidated."* The supervisor, for his part, showed good judgment, for it is impossible to show our schools to a layman: only our bishops can fail to be appalled by such schools. The visitor in Bezhetsk heard what he would have heard anywhere else—a refusal to show the school. Just have someone who is curious inspect these schools during the winter to see what they are like. Even the most tolerant person would not last more than a half hour; he would be deafened by the chorus of coughs and wheezing; he would feel dizzy from the stifling, foul air; his olfactory sense would not endure the suffocating nitrous atmosphere.

Is it possible that ecclesiastical authorities are taking no measures to ameliorate these conditions? Strictly speaking, one cannot say that: if a ceiling begins to collapse, they order that supports be erected; if a floor gives way, they order that a beam be laid across the gap; if a wall buckles, they put in three or four supports.

Oh, how sad, how painful—how terribly painful—it is when you think what the upper clergy in other lands do, and compare them with ours! Ours do not have even the slightest concern about the education given the very estate of which they are the head, which they themselves rule, with which they—even if unnaturally [as monks]—are connected. If the school collapses, that is not their affair; they not only refuse to sacrifice their own wealth (God alone knows where it goes), they do not even want to petition for necessary improvements. In other words, they feel no pity for someone else's children. If their own children studied in church schools, they most certainly would not permit conditions to deteriorate to their present level.

Administration and Teachers

My heart shudders as I turn now to describe the people to whom parents entrust—without conditions or limits—their sons,

Moskvitianin, 1848, no. 12, otd. 1, p. 112.

the best things in their lives. What I have to tell is unheard of and unimaginable, but absolutely true. May the Lord be my witness that this is the case.

Above all, our teachers are not chosen from among those students who are most talented in pedagogical classes, or those who perform best in the subjects to be taught. Instead, they appoint those who have money and are available; or those who rank at the head of their class. Of the former category nothing need be said. The latter rank at the top not necessarily because they know the subject they are to teach in district schools, but primarily because of their success in theology. Hence it is that they are often excellent students in theology but have difficulty, for example, even reading Greek. But what happens? None of this is taken into account when they appoint seminary graduates to teach in district schools. In the government's elementary schools, by contrast, if one wants to teach, he not only must complete a full course of study in the gymnasium but also must pass an examination, primarily in the language that he wants to teach (at present, that requirement even includes an examination at the university). There is nothing of the sort in church schools: a student petitions to become a teacher, often without even indicating the subject or the school. As soon as a vacancy occurs, they appoint him to the position, without so much as asking (if only out of curiosity) whether he knows the first thing about this subject. The result is predictable: most of the teachers in district schools are monumental ignoramuses. Even after teaching for several years, they have only a nodding familiarity with the rudiments of the subject they teach. Even that evil would abate if these teachers remained permanently at their posts; to some extent, necessity and years of practical experience would make them familiar with the subjects they teach. But in fact each eagerly looks forward to becoming a priest as soon as possible and does not deem it necessary to take his subject seriously, knowing that all this is absolutely useless to him once he obtains a clerical appointment. In fact, then, he will serve five or ten years, without the slightest benefit to his pupils, and then leave. His position will then be given to another student, with the very same knowledge

and the very same goals. Herein lies the entire history of instruction in our district schools.[10]

Most teachers display only one ability—that of collecting money.
This evil has sunk deep roots everywhere, but nowhere does it
appear so fearlessly, so brazenly, with such terrible demands, as
in the schools, district boards, and consistories of the holy church. When
a father brings his son to school, he must appear before the superintendent and five teachers. "Appear before" means "deliver
money to." On such occasions they demand that impoverished
sacristans give two silver rubles to the superintendent and at least
one ruble to each of the teachers. A priest must give four—or at
least three—times that amount. I said "must give" because the
amount is determined not by the cleric's desire or his wealth but
by the will of the person receiving the money. And here pleas,
even tears, are of no avail: anyone who insists he cannot pay is
summarily ejected from the premises (in a moment we shall see
what becomes of him). This same scene is repeated after Christ-
mas, Easter, and summer vacations, throughout the entire course
of a boy's studies.

"But why do they give?" you ask. Because of the grief that
befalls any boy whose father fails to pay the designated sum;
vengeance that is cruel, implacable, and bestial, tormenting the
boy from morning to night. The boy's torment knows no end or
limit. And what terrible torture it is! Let me just say this: on a
single day, two teachers subject the pupil to as many as two
hundred blows of the birch rod.[11] The blows are absolutely merciless, because the teacher stands there and screams, "Harder!
Harder!" The student who actually performs the birching on his
peer knows full well that if he appears at all lax, he is threatened
with the very same punishment; so he uses all his strength to
satisfy the teacher's demands. Yet that is not enough: just as the
boy rises from the floor, the teacher strikes him—with his hand,
a book, or whatever he happens to lay his hands on—across the

10. The high turnover in school teaching staffs is discussed in Freeze, *Parish Clergy*,
p. 116.
11. Tolstoi's marginal comment: "And sometimes more—up to 500 blows" (ibid.,
l. 8 ob.).

ears, the head, or the cheeks; or he tears out whole tufts of hair, etc., etc. This scene is repeated two or three times a week. But the pupils do not even dare to think of complaining to the supervisor, for such a complaint would inevitably be followed by punishment for the students who complained, not for the teacher. In the business of robbery the school superintendent and teachers act as a united force and support one another. And who is it that receives these punishments? A mere boy, eight to fourteen years old! Neither good marks nor excellent behavior are of any use; an inveterate scoundrel enjoys the affection and favor of all the teachers and the superintendent if his father gives them so much to drink that they can barely stand upright, if he brings them lots of everything, from money to eggs.[12] By contrast, a perfect boy but the son of a poor priest is flogged to death—literally flogged to death. No more than two years ago at N. school a twelve-year-old boy was thus punished, not because of some terrible prank but because his father failed to deliver a cow that a teacher had demanded. The boy was carried home and died the next day. Such things are no rarity. But why didn't the unfortunate father complain? And, in general, why don't they complain about the plunder and robbery committed by schoolteachers and superintendents? Later we shall see why.

There is no end to these extortions, and they all involve trivial matters. But there is one issue of vital concern: promotion from one class to the next, and especially from the district school to the seminary. Here is an example of how it works. In 1855, a month before the final examinations, authorities at school N. sent all the students home with strict orders to return with a certain sum (the inspector himself fixed the amount due), and warned them that anyone who brought less than the designated sum would remain in the same class, and anyone who brought nothing would be expelled. The largest sum (demanded from many priests) was fifty silver rubles, while the smallest sum was five silver rubles (which the poorest sacristans were to pay). What were the

---

12. Tolstoi's marginal comment: "They do give! They used to give Rector Nikodim as much as 150 and 200 rubles!" (OR GBL, f. 302, k. 2, d. 12, l. 9 ob.).

fathers to do? The threat of expulsion would doubtless be carried out. Their sons would either be expelled (what is one to do with boys at such an age?) or denied promotion to the next class (what are the effects when a boy must remain an extra two years in the same class, not to mention the problem of the teacher's inevitable vengeance?).[13] Some, primarily the fathers of scoundrels, hastily did as they were told. The majority, especially those who had absolutely no way of sending the designated sum, or who counted on the fact that their sons fully deserved promotion, appeared before the superintendent. Here the hard bargaining commenced, and some concessions were made. Those who dared pay nothing at all, and who even threatened to complain to superior authorities, were ejected from the inspector's office in disgrace. What was the outcome? If the father paid up, the boy was promoted; if he did not pay, the boy was either denied promotion or expelled.

Some of the fathers, in fact, did file a complaint with the executive board of the diocesan seminary.[14] What happened? They summoned the superintendent for an "explanation"—an "explanation," when they should have launched the most rigorous investigation possible! But that's the way it always turns out in the church: if some poor soul gets caught, he is crushed by investigations; if someone of means commits every imaginable abomination, they "summon" him to the provincial capital (you can guess why—for bribes—and that is the end of it). In this instance, no one knows what the superintendent said, but he returned home with consummate equanimity and continued his misdeeds with even more audacity than before.

A word about formal complaints is in order. Why indeed don't people complain? To understand why, let's take the example of the father whose boy was flogged to death. He in fact came to

13. Belliustin's complaint about "remaining an extra two years in the same class" refers to the biennial course system. Each class consisted of a two-year cycle of courses; any pupil denied promotion had to traverse the entire cycle and hence lost not one but two years.
14. The executive board (*seminarskoe pravlenie*), composed of the rector, inspector, and bookkeeper, formed the main administrative board of the seminary, with only nominal and sporadic supervision from the bishop, consistory, or a higher authority in the church's educational bureaucracy.

the town and prepared a complaint. But he still had two sons enrolled in the school; if he did file a complaint, then he would have to withdraw them immediately or their fate would be the same. Yet he could hardly provide for them in his home town: what would he do with them if they left school? He thought it over, wept, grieved—and left it to God's judgment. Another example that one might cite occurred about ten years ago in school X, where the brutality of the superintendent and inspector became so intolerable that the pupils began to flee from the school. Subsequently, a complaint was filed with the executive board of the seminary. Given the gravity of the matter, the rector of the seminary himself went to investigate. What did he do? He spent an entire week at the superintendent's residence without leaving the premises—God alone knows what he did. He then appeared at the school, meted out the most brutal birching to the pupils, and reported to the executive board that the pupils had rebelled and that he had suppressed the uprising. . . . Boys—just eight to fourteen years old—"revolted"; even their fathers, in the face of the cruelest tyranny, amidst a million injustices, would not even dare to think of such a thing! . . . It once happened that a seminary professor was dispatched to a certain school, where he conducted an honest investigation and exposed all the base deeds of the superintendent and teachers. What was the result? The superintendent made a hasty visit to the seminary rector and to the bishop's personal secretary. A new investigation was ordered. Predictably, it completely vindicated the guilty; the professor who made the original inspection was pushed out of the seminary with a negative recommendation. After all that, who would dare conduct a strict, just inquiry? So what is the use of formal complaints? After all this, can anyone still ask why people do not complain?

But let's assume that the complaint reaches the executive board of the ecclesiastical academy,[15] that the most honest and upright

---

15. Like the universities, each of the four ecclesiastical academies had an external board (*vneshnee pravlenie*), which was responsible for overseeing the seminaries and district schools in its region. Comprised of administrators and professors at the academy, the board was able to exercise only nominal supervision, for the press of academy business left little time for more than occasional and superficial inspection trips to the seminaries and district schools.

person has arrived to investigate, and that (and here is the most important condition) he can establish the truth without fear of harmful consequences to himself. What will he do? Interrogate the pupils? But will not the local authorities terrify the boys into mute silence beforehand? Will they really dare to say anything in an official interrogation, when they still do not know whether afterward they will still have the same superintendent and teachers? Will their fathers actually dare say anything at this investigation when they are fully convinced that to do so will cause difficulties for their sons (if not in the district school, then later in the seminary)? I myself have seen how a professor of rhetoric (now the archpriest of a cathedral) brutally persecuted a good pupil solely because his father exposed a superintendent for concealing and embezzling the stipends allotted for indigent pupils. In almost every class he would turn to the pupil and say: "Your father is a troublemaker and informer; you are the same kind of scoundrel, the same kind of base creature, the same kind of bandit," and other things too embarrassing to write. In the end he managed to have the boy expelled from the seminary altogether. Moreover, may not the authorities' vengeance against informers reach the fathers themselves? Even if we assume that everyone is bold and that the guilty party is punished, what is the difference? Someone else will come and start acting just as they do in all the other district schools. They will not change things in the least, figuring (and here they are probably right) that people will not complain every time, that such an honest investigation will not take place very often.

No, individual complaints will not change a single thing!

If only they would appoint special investigators—if not for all the schools, then at least for the majority of them. Such investigators, however, absolutely must be laymen, chosen primarily from those who have recently graduated from the university. Have them live for two or three weeks in the town, telling no one who they are, as they proceed to query pupils in their boarding rooms and on the street. After that, when they have dressed as poorly as possible (*conditio, sine qua non*),[16] have them examine

16. "A necessary condition."

the schools five times during the day, especially before and after classes. Have them examine everything closely—from the teachers' appearance to their treatment of pupils and method of teaching. Finally, have them go into the villages as simple travelers and ask the pupils' fathers what their sons' schooling is like, what conditions are like in the schools. . . . If only this could be done! . . .[17]

Oh, then everyone would see and know what our schools are like! Then everything I have said would be confirmed! More important, they would discover things that I have not dared to mention! . . .

Only then, after this evil has been thoroughly studied, can one rip it out by the very roots. Until that happens, whatever we do will be in vain; until that happens, the most well-intentioned decrees will have not the slightest effect.

Studies

First I shall describe *what* is taught, then *how* it is taught in the district schools.

The main subject, which receives the overwhelming share of attention, is Latin. Cornelius Nepos is the measure of intellectual ability and achievement for pupils: how much effort and torment goes into the task of pounding this eternal nightmare into the pupils' heads![18]

It is a strange, incomprehensible phenomenon, possible only in the education of Russian clergy: the heart of education for a future village priest is a dead language, which will be about as useful in real life as Sanskrit! To be a good pastor, now one must first be a good Latinist: without this training you cannot become a priest, for without a knowledge of Latin (which at present has

17. Tolstoi's marginal comment: "That is true" (OR GBL, f. 302, k. 2, d. 12, l. 12–12 ob.)
18. Cornelius Nepos (c. 100–c. 24B.C.) was a Roman historian, known mainly for his biographies; his prose—simple, clear Latin—was deemed highly suitable for classroom use.

become superficial and quite limited)[19] you cannot be promoted from the district school to the seminary! . . . For a whole six years the boy wastes his abilities on the study of a language that he will forget in his first two years of priesthood, for in all his life he will not encounter a single letter of that language! It would make sense if they taught him Slavonic with equal attention; that, at least, would provide excellent preparation for his future service. If he knew Slavonic well, he would not be stumped by questions from self-taught peasants. It would also be understandable if they obliged him to learn the *Cheti-minei*;[20] each lesson would provide material for talks with his future parishioners, not to mention the beneficial effect that this study would have on his young heart and soul. But no, they force us to cram into our heads some kind of Alcibiades and Cimon—and, what is more, in a foreign language![21] What can you expect from an education that is founded on Latin, something utterly useless for a rural priest? Indeed, can this even be called an education?

Some will interject: "But knowledge of Latin is necessary for those who later enter the ecclesiastical academy." True. But do many advance from the seminary to the academy? As a rule, just two to five out of a hundred; of the rest, some seventy to eighty go directly into diocesan service.[22] Now which figure should determine the curriculum? Obviously, the latter. In fact, however,

19. The decline in Latin progressed steadily in the prereform era. As Metropolitan Filaret (Drozdov) observed in 1838, "the decline of Latin is now more or less universal, varying only in degree" (A. Nadezhdin, *Istoriia S.-Peterburgskoi pravoslavnoi dukhovnoi seminarii* [St. Petersburg, 1885], p. 412n).
20. The *Cheti-minei* was a traditional compendium of spiritual literature intended for systematic reading each month and comprised of saints' lives, interpretations of the Scriptures, works of the Church Fathers, and the like.
21. Alcibiades (c. 450–404 B.C.) was an Athenian statesman and general, known for his leadership against Sparta in the Peloponnesian War and his later work in the service of Sparta; he has been alternately blamed for the decline of Athens and exalted as a competent, unappreciated leader. Cimon (fifth century B.C.) was an Athenian general and statesman.
22. In 1855, as Belliustin prepared this memoir, the church had only 340 students at the academies, while 13,835 were enrolled in the seminaries (*Izvlecheniia iz otcheta po vedomstvu dukhovnykh del pravoslavnogo ispovedaniia za 1855 god* [St. Petersburg, 1856], appendix, pp. 62–65).

it is just the opposite. As a result, the overwhelming majority completely waste six precious years and prepare nothing useful for the real life that lies ahead for them.[23]

Some will say: "The study of languages develops a youth's mental abilities." Let's assume that this is true. In that event, however, what is required is not the trivial, absurd, and lifeless study that one now finds in ecclesiastical schools. And why shouldn't pupils study modern languages, such as French, German, and English? The rural priest would find study of these languages twice as useful as Latin: those with inquisitive minds would have the means to pursue their education in the village, since each district has two or three landlords with a library in one or another modern language. Moreover, those priests who need supplementary income (and what priest does not?) could augment theirs honestly by giving language lessons in the homes of noble landlords. Quite apart from the personal material benefit for the priests, what infinite good their service could render! They could draw closer to the landlords and exert a continuous beneficial influence on the nobles' family life, which has become so profoundly corrupted of late. Hence they could rear a new generation of nobles in a strictly Orthodox spirit; that upbringing would be the opposite of what is provided by Western tutors, who always sow in their pupils a contempt for all that is Russian in general and Orthodox in particular.* "But," some will object, "they already study French and German at the seminary." My goodness, it would be better not to teach them at all than in the way they are now taught. . . . Moreover, German and French should be taught from the youngest possible age if anything is to be achieved by these efforts. But I shall have more to say about language instruction later.

A second subject that is deemed important (but not so important as Latin) is Greek. To begin with, it is taught poorly in *every* school. I can say categorically that in all Russia there is not a

---

23. Tolstoi's marginal comment: "That's not so" (OR GBL, f. 302, k. 2, d. 12, l. 18 ob.).

*Those who oppose the study of modern languages in the seminary do not see all this, but then, how could they? They are too removed from real life. They would think differently, though, if they themselves were rural priests.

single teacher of Greek who knows enough to understand and explain how the language in the writing of St. Macarius of Egypt differs from that in the work of St. John Chrisostom (we shall not even ask about Hesiod and other secular writers).[24] Even if he were taught Greek properly, so that he could really master it, of what use would it be to a future village priest? Some might respond: "He can study the scriptures in the original and read the works of the Greek Fathers of the Church." But where, in what village, can one find a single line of the Scriptures in Greek (I shall not even mention the Church Fathers, whose works are rarely published and are extraordinarily expensive)? Nowhere. In other words, he studies this language solely in order to forget it. In fact, he does not even wait for the end of the seminary course to forget Greek, but hastens to do so while still at the seminary. For proof, just examine a graduating class of students (from any seminary) and you will find that only five or ten in a hundred barely make an acceptable translation of some passage from the reader; another ten or twenty can distinguish one part of speech from another; the rest cannot even make out the ancient script used in such books.

Next in importance is catechism and biblical history. These subjects, which should be the fountainhead of education, rank third in importance. And where are they taught? In the elementary district schools! People may find this incredible; indeed, it *is* difficult to believe. But just ask how much time is devoted to these subjects and the content of examinations for pupils transferring from the district school to the seminary, and you will be convinced that even in the seminaries they regard catechism and biblical history as things of little consequence. That is also the way they are taught in district schools; teaching is limited to forcing the pupil to memorize and memorize. He commits it all to memory, invariably with almost no understanding of what he has memorized (this is particularly true with regard to texts). Hence his heart and soul are not touched by a single beneficial thought, a

---

24. St. Makarios of Egypt (Alexandria), baptized at the age of forty, died in A.D. 404. St. John Chrysostom (known as Zlatoust in Russia), A.D. 347–407, was perhaps the greatest of the Fathers of the Greek Church. Hesiod was a Greek poet of the eighth century B.C.

[81]

single sacred feeling, a single high-minded impulse. He learns by heart what one should or should not do, but does not understand why; at the age of thirteen or fourteen he cannot explain why one thing is right and another is wrong. What is the cause of all this? He has learned the catechism like everything else: they relied entirely on his memory and paid not the slightest attention to stirring his heart, to implanting sacred truths in his heart, to luring him onto the path of virtue.[25]

Next comes Russian grammar. We shall not delve into the monumental stupidity that could occur only in an ecclesiastical school—namely, that of making dead languages the chief subjects while relegating one's mother tongue to a status of minor importance. Instruction in Russian grammar is in a pitiable condition in our church schools. Here, too, the pupils simply memorize rules, without understanding either the spirit or the mechanics of the language. As a result, orthography remains a stumbling block for many pupils, not just in district schools, but also in the seminary. To see that this is no exaggeration, just give the pupils in any seminary an examination; just peruse the writing of any rural priest who has confined his education to what he received in the seminary.[26]

Instruction is still worse in other subjects, which are not deemed to be "primary" or even "secondary," but some kind of supplement.

Ecclesiastical music, that wild, dissonant singing which our ancestors enjoyed in hours of revelry, receives considerable attention.[27] Never mind that much of this subject, which is so tortuous for the pupils, is no longer observed in rural churches or even in monastery churches. Never mind that, in lieu of these primeval rules for church singing,[28] the state has published books on church

25. Tolstoi's marginal comment: "This is true!" (OR GBL, f. 302, k. 2, d. 12, l. 14 ob.).
26. Belliustin exaggerates here; as the clerical responses to a reform questionnaire in 1863 demonstrated, most could write very well indeed (see the massive files in TsGIA SSSR, f. 804, op. 1, r. 3).
27. Tolstoi's marginal comment: "Nonsense!" (OR GBL, f. 302, k. 2, d. 12, l. 17 ob.).
28. Tolstoi underscored the word "primeval" (*dopotopnyi*), used here of course in a pejorative sense (ibid.).

music (for the chapels of the imperial court) that is simple but adapted to the spirit of our service, and is equally impressive and good, whether performed by a whole choir or a single sacristan, the only requirement being that it be performed accurately and that the singer (or singers) have harmonious, well-controlled voices. Not the slightest attention, however, is paid to this singing used in court chapels; instead, the pupils kill time on traditional church music books [*obikhody* and *oktoikhi*].[29]

Let's now discuss *how* one is taught in district schools. I have already pointed out that pupils are forced to memorize, and in fact, it would be entirely fair to say that the entire course of study amounts to nothing more than rote memorization, a science of cramming.[30] They do not pay the slightest attention to a pupil's abilities. "Learn everything from point *A* to point *B*," says the teacher, without considering whether all the pupils are capable of doing so. Never is he the least concerned to ease the labor of those whom God did not bless with an exceptionally retentive memory. The time comes for the pupils to show what they have learned; a few are prepared, but the great majority are not. Some come unprepared because of laziness or mischief; others because of insufficient ability. But what happens? The teacher does not bother to examine the work of his pupils; it is easier and more convenient just to punish everyone who is unprepared, and he has them punished as he sees fit. What is the result? The pupil who is diligent but of limited ability is lashed along with the lazy and mischievous; as a result, he abandons his studies and becomes lazy too. What is the difference? he reasons: you get punished whether you work all night and fail to learn or do not study at all. Hence a boy whom patient, gentle, and concerned supervision could transform into a good pupil becomes incorrigibly lazy instead. For no reason at all, they destroy those few gifts that he received from the Lord; his interest in work is extinguished. It often happens that such youths are promoted to the seminary and even

29. *Obikhod* and *Oktoikh* are titles of books compiled for traditional church singing.
30. The persistence of rote memorization in church schools is discussed in Freeze, *Parish Clergy*, pp. 122 and 132–133.

[83]

manage to graduate from it; but it is someone else that does all the seminary assignments (with any remaining gaps being filled by "gifts" from their fathers). That is why it is not unusual to see a seminary pupil in a state of total inertness, physical and spiritual; he sits for hours on end, his eyes half closed, untroubled by concerns, anxieties, or ideas. Not even a glimmer of an idea flickers within him.

Actually, a pupil spends almost half of his time in school on the so-called constructions. It is in order, I think, to explain just what kind of operation this is. First the teachers dictate something in Russian; then above each word they designate the Latin or Greek word in its basic form. The pupils are supposed to change the grammatical form in order to create an idea that corresponds to the Russian text. The purpose of this whole exercise*—there must be *some* purpose behind even the most inane actions—is probably to train pupils to make translations from Russian to Latin and Greek. But of what use is all this for a future priest? Let us assume something that couldn't possibly happen:[31] namely, that he has fully mastered the subject and makes superb translations into any of these languages. But what is the value of that? Of what use is that ability? What will he translate? For whom? For what?

Here, with involuntary and unbearable sorrow, I must say that even though everything else is moving forward, the clergy alone

---

*Here is what the most learned pedagogues say about such exercises: "One hears that schools force pupils to seek out a certain Latin construction as they read the classical authors: here is yet another way to destroy talent, to dull a mind that is naturally bright" (Davydov, *Ob izuchenii latinskogo iazyka* [On the study of Latin], Moscow, 1842, pt. 6, p. 343). It is even worse in church schools: here such exercises are not performed during the reading, but for this purpose they simply pull a passage out of context, often without meaning. They pervert its sense with the most preposterous translations into Russian and force the pupils to distort it yet again by retranslating it back to the original. Here is how they destroy talent in the district schools, and how they stifle a boy almost daily in the schools and on holidays in his rooms! . . . Even if our omniscient pedagogues in the church cannot grasp this, the least they could do is to read how those who are knowledgeable in pedagogy regard such matters. But they do not want to do that either! . . .

31. Tolstoi's marginal note: "He is mistaken" (OR GBL, f. 302, k. 2, d. 12, l. 17 ob.).

stand still—on the very same spot where the Poles, our first teachers, first put us.[32] To this very day, the subjects that they deemed essential are still held in the same high regard; even the teaching methods remain unchanged. Likewise, the means used to compel pupils to study—fear and punishment, which are sure to spoil any chance of success—remain in ecclesiastical schools, notwithstanding the apparent reform.[33] "Reform" is a high-sounding word; but just what has been changed? They have introduced some subjects that our fathers and grandfathers did not study; they have relabeled classes, replacing *fara, infima,* and the like with "higher," "middle," and "lower" divisions. Is that really all? Without the slightest hesitation I can say: "Yes, that is all." They have made superficial, quite insignificant changes; internally, however, everything is just as it was in preceding centuries.[34] In fact, one could even argue that our present education is infinitely inferior to and less significant than that which our fathers and grandfathers received: they, at least, knew something really well, for they graduated from those schools as superb Latinists. But what does a pupil from a district school and seminary know thoroughly nowadays? Nothing, not even Latin!

The pupil has now completed the district school and, one way or another, has transferred to the seminary. When he leaves the district school for real life, what does he take with him? Nothing whatsoever! Almost everything on which he has spent six years is useless; he has learned everything just so that he can forget it, sooner or later. Has he not completely wasted the best years of

---

32. The original curriculum of the seminary did come from the West, for it was modeled after that of the Jesuit grammar schools; see Freeze, *Russian Levites,* pp. 90–91.

33. Here Belliustin is referring to the "transformation" of 1840; engineered by Chief Procurator N. A. Protasov, it added such courses as agriculture and medicine in order to make the seminary education more "useful." For details, see Freeze, *Parish Clergy,* pp. 125–133.

34. Belliustin's plural "centuries" is a curious error, implying that church schools dated back at least to the seventeenth century; apart from the Kiev and Moscow academies, however, it was only in the eighteenth century that the church constructed a real system of formal education for the clergy.

his life? For what purpose did he endure so many punishments, experience so many torments, shed so many tears? It would not be so bad if he had only wasted the years, squandered them pointlessly! No, it was during these years that the seed of evil was sown in his young, sensitive soul. What did he see constantly before his eyes in his rooming house? Filth and vice. What did he see in school? The same filth. What did he see in school authorities and teachers? Evil, cruel hirelings, whose sole aim was plunder—bold, unchecked, unpunished plunder. He saw that his teacher (who was often drunk) recognized neither law nor justice, had no conscience, and administered punishment or pardon to pupils in the most capricious way. The youth also saw that the only way to escape punishment was to pay bribes, as much money (or in kind) as possible. *This* is what he saw constantly for six whole years! . . .

It would be odd if an adult breathed that noxious atmosphere for six whole years and did not become infected. So what can one expect from a mere boy? Indeed, he becomes terribly infected. His moral sensitivity becomes dull and distorted; he feels no disgust as he looks upon the most vulgar debauchery. They are insanely cruel toward him; and he becomes cruel himself. They extort money from his father; he, too, extorts at every possible opportunity—if, for example, he is a teacher's aide or student supervisor.[35] In a word, he absorbs everything bad in his private quarters and at the school. So that is the foundation of his education, which is supposed to prepare him to be a future servitor of the Orthodox church! One does find exceptions; despite such a ruinous system, good pupils do emerge, apparently saved by the Lord Himself. Such exceptions, unfortunately, are rare.

And to all those who blindly condemn the clergy, I say this: You are so merciless in persecuting unfortunate priests with ridicule and contempt, but if only you had to run this gauntlet that

35. The teacher's aide (*avditor*) tested each student's preparation daily and filed an appropriate report for the instructor; the student supervisor or elder (*starshii*) was the inspector's aide and was responsible for overseeing the personal conduct of pupils (especially of those who boarded in private residences).

passes for education with us, God knows whether you would emerge purer, whether you would lead a life that is any better! . . .

Will not the seminary correct all that is wrong in the pupil? Will it not excoriate the evil? Let us see.

A SEMINARY EDUCATION

The purpose of every specialized education is to prepare people to be worthy of one or another form of service. The more elevated the service, the more rigorous must be the analysis of its educational program, which should contain only those things that lead directly to the prescribed goal and turn a boy into a man worthy of a given calling. This curriculum may be far from encyclopedic, but so what? Just make sure that this education is sound, that it is so ordered and directed that the student loves his future work with his whole heart and soul and devotes himself so completely to his work that nothing can distract him afterward. Familiarize the student with all dimensions of his work beforehand, and teach him the methods that most reliably lead to success. That is enough. If he is educated in this way, he will make a useful contribution in his service.

No one, I hope, will disagree that, as heaven is higher than this world, priestly service is superior to all forms of civil service. That means that the educational program of those who prepare for this service should be subjected to the most rigorous analysis. This education should admit only that which will prepare students to become true, zealous, and exacting servitors of Christ, prophets of his teachings of salvation, and tireless shepherds of his flock. Only subjects that help one to reach this overarching goal should be included.

If we look at the seminary curriculum, what do we find? Theology, philosophy, rhetoric, mathematics, physics, agronomy, medicine, etc., etc. What is all that supposed to prepare one to do? If a foreigner were to read this program of study, he would

[87]

find it utterly baffling, especially when he saw that it allotted two years for theology and the same amount of time for both philosophy and rhetoric. Evidently they want to make the seminarian simultaneously into something of a theologian, something of a philosopher, something of a rhetorician, agronomist, and medic. But what does common sense and experience say must result from such a curriculum? Absolutely nothing. In education everything that is *a little* is virtually equivalent to *nothing*; the more there are of these *a little*s (as in the case of the seminary, for example), the more surely the total sum of such an education will be close to *zero*. Hence the seminarian emerges as neither a theologian nor a philosopher nor an agronomist nor a medic! . . . All these subjects fly past him, for all are taught in only vague, general terms; not one of these subjects stirs real feeling in his soul or evokes enthusiasm and interest, because he has not become properly acquainted with any of them. It seems that blind fate, not rational will, controls his education: not one pupil in an entire seminary class can understand what he is preparing for. By the time he graduates he has no special enthusiasm for anything; he is equally ready to become a priest, teacher, petty clerk, or whatever you name.[36] Is that really an education?

If the seminary curriculum is absurd and senseless, the actual process of education in the seminary is still more so. One has to wonder: Is not everything purposely arranged to guarantee that seminarians will become complete ignoramuses with enormous pretensions? Let us begin first with the administrators and teachers.

The chief figure in the seminary, the person who exercises the greatest influence on the pupils, is the rector. He is always a monk, a choice that defies explanation: the principal overseer and director of the education of youth, the majority of whom are preparing to become village priests, is someone who has renounced the world forever, with all its concerns and demands—that is, someone who (at least ideally) is dead to all that is alive

36. Criticism of the disastrous proliferation of subjects was virtually unanimous; this curricular problem was one of the first objects of a synodal reform inquiry in 1858 (see "Iz zapisok arkhiepiskopa Leonida," *Russkii arkhiv*, 1906, no. 4, pp. 606–608).

in this vale of tears called earth. He invariably holds a master's degree; in other words, he is learned, even a most learned man. But is such abstruse learning of any use in real life? Are not the most renowned wise men invariably children in mundane matters? Where did he—this man with a master's degree or a doctorate in theology—learn about daily life, knowledge of which comes solely through experience and remains inaccessible to pure reason? Not behind the walls of a theological academy or in some monastery (of which he is the chief administrator): even if he wants to know the realities of life, he simply has no opportunity to do so. Real life has everything: the highest forms of both good and evil, in all their nakedness, both the angels of heaven and the demons of the netherworld. Is it really possible (that is, permissible and appropriate) for a monk to plunge into this whirlpool? If it is impossible, then what understanding of life can he have? It would be one thing if the majority of youths were preparing for an ascetic life; in that case it would make sense to appoint a monk as rector. But here the youths are preparing for battle with the flesh, with the entrancing power of the Prince of Darkness, and with the world alongside. What can the rector's lessons (very learned, but purely theoretical) teach them about true, reliable means to wage this battle successfully?

No, education of future priests should be left to the control of a priest, who is not so much learned as experienced in life, having himself encountered all that awaits the pupils later in their onerous sphere of service.[37] Rather than having him explain all the scholastic subtleties of theology, have him explain the behavior of human passions—diverse, infinitely variable, often strikingly apparent, still more often barely detectable and visible. Have him show the youths how to combat these passions! That kind of training will give the future priest an invaluable, irreplaceable resource; even the most elaborate courses in theology are no substitute for this! I shall not even deal with the fact that if the rector is a monk, he is in the years of man's most terrible passions, is

---

37. Tolstoi's marginal comment: "True, but the ideas are confused" (OR GBL, f. 302, k. 2, d. 12, l. 23 ob.).

free to dispose of his time and great means as he wishes, and through his example often destroys the little good that he manages to communicate in words. Nor shall I talk about those fatal excesses to which his human frailties sometimes lead. . . . If someone wishes or needs to travel the length of Russia, have him listen attentively to what people say about seminary rectors. What he hears will astound him—of course not everywhere, but in many, many places! . . .

Seminary teachers for the most part have master's degrees, but such degrees are rarely as useful for education as they should be. The reason lies in the system for appointing seminary professors, according to which not the slightest attention is paid to the candidate's pedagogical ability. If he graduated from the academy, that is enough to become a professor, even if he cannot intelligently combine two words when speaking. Moreover, most are appointed to teach not the subjects they know best but those for which vacancies first occur in a seminary. Such appointments are made even if the candidate has not the slightest knowledge of the subjects. In short, the appointment of professors does not involve special examinations or trial lectures, as is the case in secular schools. Instead, everything is left to fate. An expert in mathematics, for instance, is pushed into philosophy, about which he knows and understands as much as his future pupils—and yet he is made a professor of philosophy. Or someone who has done well in philosophy is cast by fate into a mathematics class, something absolutely alien to him: "Teach it," he is told. . . . There are also students who go through the entire academy and learn nothing. What happens? They dispatch such a type to teach one of the secondary subjects; he serves three to four years, and they see that as a teacher he is intolerably bad ("bad" in seminary jargon—in ordinary human speech, that means he is absolutely worthless). Then they transfer him to another subject, then a third, and on it goes until he becomes a priest or is old enough to qualify for a pension. . . .

Given such an ingenious system, what is the quality of instruction? Oh, if people with a real education could only hear what and how things are taught in the seminary! . . . I do not know

[90]

what feeling would be stronger in them: laughter at the pathetic, miserable caricature of education; pity for the unfortunate youths, who, God knows why, have been condemned to eternal ignorance; indignation that the time, energy,and work of pupils are pointlessly wasted; or disgust that monks, having seized control of everything, are guided by money and satisfaction of all their passions (from vanity to . . .), and give less thought to the well-being of those entrusted to their care than they would to a horse. . . . But we do know that no one can leave the seminary in a tranquil state of mind once he has discovered what instruction there is like. All the instruction there—from theology to Hebrew—is just "marvelous, superb, zealous, productive, inspiring. . . ."

Take, for example, theology—the queen of learning, the most important field of all human knowledge, the foundation of our education and life. With cold indifference the professor reads his lecture (some sort of abstract from his lecture notes at the academy, or a garbled translation from some German Lutheran theologian);[38] the students listen with the same cold indifference and can hardly wait till it is over. The professor orders them to learn it; everything now depends on how well they memorize it. Thus only the students' memory is put to work; the teachers give no thought to seeing that the great teachings of salvation move the student's soul, penetrate deeply into his heart, and become his very flesh and blood. What is the result? The pupils regard theology just as any other subject—that is, as an onerous burden, from which they would do anything to be free. They remember what they have memorized only while they are still at the seminary; after they have lived for a year or two in the parish, they have forgotten everything: they cannot satisfactorily explain a single dogma, and from the entire course of theology they have only a dim recollection that X gave lectures on something or other. Even moral theology is left to memory alone, without the least application to life: dryly, lifelessly, they say that your duties to God are such-and-such, to loved ones such-and-such; they talk

---

38. The impact of German Lutheran scholarship is discussed in G. V. Florovskii, *Puti russkogo bogosloviia* (Paris, 1937).

as though they were saying that once upon a time there lived Semiramis or Astyages, things that are of no concern to anyone.[39] As a result, the pupil who heard in a morning lecture that something is forbidden does it that very evening. If he is caught, they hasten to punish him, never troubling to make him conscious of the baseness of his conduct, never explaining to him all the ruinous consequences of such behavior. Hence the boy who is punished regrets not that he did something iniquitous, only that he did not know how to conceal it. He becomes used to every form of lying, cunning, and deception.

Some may interject: "This is an exaggeration: there are pupils with excellent morality."

Yes, such do exist, but they are only two or three in a hundred. Moreover, they owe this excellent morality not to their seminary education but either to the good fortune of being educated under their fathers' eyes or to a natural tendency toward virtue. Is this an exaggeration? No, that will not be the judgment of anyone who has studied at the seminary himself or who wishes to speak the truth before God and conscience. From the bishop to the lowliest seminary inspector, all have just one concern: to see that the pupil before them trembles. They never give the slightest thought to winning their pupil's trust, love, and childish obedience so that he may open his soul to them, with total sincerity, as though to his own parents. As a result, every prank, if the culprit is caught, entails punishment. It is unheard of for the seminary authorities to consider and weigh the import of the deed, to determine whether it was intentional or not, whether the cause is a corrupted heart or the excesses of inexperienced youth, and whether accordingly one should order physical punishment, be content with a strict reprimand in his peers' presence, or have a fatherly talk with the boy in his office. "Punish them all without mercy, so they will all be fearful"—*that* is the heart of seminary administration. But who does not know that fear of punishment is used only as a last recourse to stop someone from

39. Semiramis was a mythical Assyrian queen, known for her beauty and wisdom; Astyages was the king of Medes in the sixth century B.C.

doing evil? No, awaken in him a love of goodness, a desire for a virtuous life, and he will be good; amidst all the temptations and seductions of life, he will remain virtuous. "Train up a child in the way he should go: and when he is old, he will not depart from it."*[40] But that is not the way it is in the seminary! What good can one expect from such education? The youth is not attracted to virtue. Once he becomes a man, regardless of the rank he holds, he neither comprehends nor values goodness; he is easily and quickly lured into evil, suffers a terrible fall, and is powerless to lift himself up! Evil becomes habitual for him and becomes his second nature.

Consider the instruction in philosophy. When you see how and what is taught in the seminary under this pretentious rubric, you feel like either laughing or crying. They do not have the pupil seek truth through his own thinking; no, they force him to learn (sometimes even in Latin) some positively absurd compilation of quasi-philosophers from the seventeenth and eighteenth centuries, a compilation devoid of sense and meaning, drawn from ten different authors who are infinitely different from one another, thrown together by some self-made professor of philosophy. The unfortunate pupils break their skulls trying to master this senseless, worthless "wisdom"; once they have memorized it, they

---

*Proverbs 22:6. This text is omitted from the Slavonic Bible. Its basic idea is this: If a youth has been put on the right path, he will not deviate from it throughout his life (*Egchainismos*: restoration, reinforcement, *instauratio*).

40. Belliustin cites the textual passage in Greek (with some misspellings or typographical errors); hence his paraphrase in the footnote. The passage is omitted from the Greek (Alexandrian) text of the Old Testament, prepared in the third century B.C. and substantially different from the Hebrew texts that underlie modern translations of the Bible. For the Greek text, see *The Greek Septuagint Version of the Old Testament according to the Vatican Version* (London, 1851).

The selection of this passage suggests Belliustin's extraordinary degree of independence from church authority. In the 1840s a professor at the St. Petersburg Academy, G. Pavskii, had translated the old Hebrew texts and had the translations lithographed for his students' use, but his choice of texts and his translation of them into modern Russian soon created a furor. In 1856 the Synod, now free of the Nikolaevan influence, did elect to prepare a modern translation of the Bible, and in 1858 (not long after Belliustin wrote) commenced publication of individual books of the Bible. Unlike the Slavonic Bible, the modern Synodal translation includes this passage from Proverbs.

glibly answer questions at examinations. In reality, however, the student is unable to explain what he is doing and why. He has not thought deeply about anything, for they have forced him to learn, learn, learn; and to learn the letter, not the sense, even to the point that if a student substitutes an equivalent phrase, the professor (with notebook in hand) immediately stops him and orders him to answer just as it is written. All this learning will disappear without a trace; even while the student is still at the seminary, he regards all these studies as something dark, impenetrable, hidden from divine illumination.

Is it necessary to discuss the other subjects? Hardly. If that is the way they teach the things they regard as important, you can imagine what happens with the others. In the latter case, pupils either miss the class altogether (and kill time playing cards in their rooms) or lay in a store of novels and with the utmost serenity, paying not the slightest attention to the professor, corrupt their souls by reading the most ridiculous works of the French school. But I shall say a few words about agronomy and medicine, two courses recently added to the seminary curriculum.[41]

The goal behind the introduction of agronomy seems marvelous: the priest himself will practice agriculture according to modern science, not tradition, and will transmit his knowledge to the parishioners. Hence the economy will flourish, both for the priest and for all his flock. What could be better? All the schools have qualified teachers, graduates from special schools of agriculture. But then things go awry. Even if the teachers never do anything, even if their subject is despised by church authorities, even if not a single graduate can distinguish one soil from another, or marl from gypsum—none of this matters: the subject was nominally introduced, and that is the only thing that concerns the authorities.

But let's assume that fate makes the subject fare well: is the goal itself good? Is it attainable? Can the priest become a *trained* agronomist for his flock? I shall answer these questions by offering a few more. What are the majority of seminary pupils trained for?

41. Both courses were added in the Protasov reform of 1840; they were not part of the curriculum when Belliustin graduated from the seminary, in 1839.

Is it not to be priests in villages and towns? Of course it is. Do not authorities want these pupils subsequently to be priests not just in name but in reality—that is, to work zealously and indefatigably to save their own and their flock's souls? Of course. If that is the case, are they really unaware that the priest (who has one to two thousand male and female souls in his charge), after performing his main duties, has little time left for anything else, whatever that may be? Did I say that he has little spare time? If the priest understands (as he should) that he must give a strict accounting for each soul, he will find that even twenty-four hours a day do not suffice to protect some parishioners from temptation, to strengthen faith and virtue in others—in a word, to lead them all to the goal of the celestial calling. How can you find any free time here for agronomy? How can you think about that when you have to perform liturgies and to make the necessary preparations for them; compose a homily; visit the sick, bringing material and spiritual assistance; prepare the dying for that final terrible moment; reconcile the quarreling—in short, be all things to all men all the time, if you wish to be a worthy priest? It is possible and necessary for a resident squire to be an agronomist, for that is the chief goal of his life; but it is impossible for someone who is a priest in the true sense of the word.

If someone should object that "the priest now has a parish allotment at his disposal and cultivates it," I can only say that, to our great misfortune, this is true. In the appropriate place I shall discuss the consequences. At the most, we should allow the priest to keep a small garden, not as a business but just as relaxation from the things that disturb and exhaust his spirit. The point is that agronomy, even if taught perfectly, is useless to the priest's real life, for it is not part of his calling or proper activity.

Let's even assume the impossible: that a priest has the time and passion to be an agronomist. But where is he to obtain the capital to engage in modern agriculture? Even if by some miracle he found the means, his strips of land lie together with those of the sacristans: should he wish to introduce something new and better, they would not (and could not) do so. So what can he do? He sees and realizes all that is wrong with his economy, but he is in no position to do anything about it. So he does everything just as his fathers and grandfathers did—that is, he is "milling the wind." So why teach him agronomy?[42]

I anticipate still another objection: "Not all seminarians become priests: those who do not find clerical positions could become stewards on gentry estates." On those grounds one could introduce hundreds of other subjects as well if one considered all the nonclerical professions that students *might* enter! As it is, there are so many subjects that the pupil does not master a single one of them, even the main ones; if we added more, then the pupils would most certainly be driven completely mad. More important, this is not what we need. True, there is a surplus of pupils compared to clerical positions. But if one wants to provide for their future, establish a rigorous process of selection: leave some in the seminary and prepare them specifically to become priests; send the rest to agricultural schools, where they can be properly trained as stewards, something that cannot be done in the seminary. In brief, prepare each boy for his future work, not for everything under the sun.

Let us now consider medicine. Although this subject has been formally introduced into the seminary curriculum, it is there in name only, when in fact it should really be ranked alongside the main subjects. Our Saviour not only taught but also healed, an example that is extremely significant! What better model could one take for the education of the modern priest? But that is not the way we do things in the church: we have to be clever and smart; we have to introduce tens of subjects utterly useless to the rural priest and his parishioners, to disregard for no reason at all subjects that could be extremely useful. There are no doctors in the villages; as a consequence, quacks and sorcerers, who deserve every penalty and punishment, have complete freedom to destroy the souls and bodies of the unfortunate peasants. The result is that sometimes hundreds die from the kind of disease that could be completely eliminated by timely, intelligent measures. There

---

42. Antipathy to agriculture was virtually universal among the parish clergy; the clerical questionnaires in TsGIA SSSR, f. 804, op. 1, r. 3, offer eloquent testimony.

are, to be sure, district doctors; but what is one doctor for several hundred thousand peasants living in each district? Suppose he is as zealous and active as you can imagine; nevertheless, it is physically impossible for him to attend to all the sick in every corner of a district, which often stretches over a distance of three hundred to five hundred versts. But such a [zealous] doctor is a phenomenon unknown in our district towns; all these gentlemen prefer tranquillity, comfort, and—frequently—the bottle to their work. They reside permanently in the district town, and visit the countryside only for murder inquests or to treat ailing nobles. It is unheard of for a doctor to go to a peasant's home, even if it lies just five versts from town. At examinations in his own residence, too, he is always careless and incredibly rude, and he demands fees that are far beyond the means of peasants. If you add to that a prescription costing two, three, or more rubles (inexpensive prescriptions do not exist), with highly dubious prospects for success, you can understand why peasants fear the doctor as much as any disease, and would rather endure the most intolerable suffering than seek help from a doctor.[43]

How can one correct this evil? There is but one means: make the priest a doctor—a real doctor, not in name only. Do this and the effect on peasants will be wonderful, miraculous! Constantly in his parishioners' midst, he can take timely measures: who does not know that timely action quite often will save someone who is ill, even if the means are extremely modest? Having fortified him during the ailment, the priest can look after his daily development and recovery. All that will help parishioners, and it will also give the priest many wonderful, reliable means to achieve the principal goals of his service! For the doctor of the body, the soul of the sick person is always accessible; when the organism is weak, the soul is more receptive to all impressions, advice, and suggestions. Thus, even as he treated the body, the priest could penetrate deeply into his parishioner's soul, once and for all establishing permanent access, and thereafter could easily direct it to

43. Tolstoi's marginal comment: "That is fair" (OR GBL, f. 302, k. 2, d. 12, ll. 33 ob.–34).

the path of salvation and steadfastly lead it along this path. Here, while raising the ill person from the sickbed, the priest could sometimes reach a person's inner being; true spiritual ties simply cannot be attained in the machine-like, cold, hurried, and lifeless confession that now exists. Heavenly Father! As doctor of the soul *and* body, how much good—so pure and lofty—could this person sow around him. . . . Gratitude, trust, and finally love would bind the pastor to his flock; these things would form the basis of all relations between them—not those obligations that make the peasants so indignant, such as weddings, burials, and other rites entailing emoluments. There is no point in trying to describe the full benefits that would ensue if rural priests had a knowledge of medicine; they exceed anything I could say. I am not exaggerating in the least. From experience I know what a priest-doctor, an empirical doctor, means—not just in his own parish, but in the whole neighboring area. . . . He is a general adviser, a friend, to whom the people turn for assistance, even in the most terrible spiritual illnesses. What would it be like if every priest were a true doctor?

But is it possible to achieve this goal? Oh, quite possible, if one only wanted to. Seminary studies last six years; just abolish the subjects of little or no use to the rural priest (rhetoric, philosophy, mathematics, agronomy, Greek, and Hebrew); reduce church history and general history by half (one knows nothing anyway, whether he takes the full or abbreviated course). The time thus saved will be quite sufficient to permit a full course of medicine, including the auxiliary sciences. But there is one necessary pre-condition: professors must be appointed by authorities at the Medical Academy according to the strictest selection, and both the professors and the instruction itself should be under the direct, strictest supervision of the universities and Academy. If these rules are not adopted, the whole effort will be spoiled and things will be no better than they are now. Moreover, pupils who complete the course should be examined at the universities, not the seminary; this procedure will provide a reliable check on the professors' knowledge and zeal. Some may object: "Not everyone has the means to journey to the capitals and live there for a certain time." But for what purpose are funds being accumulated by the Committees for Assistance to the Poor of the Clerical Estate?[44] Would it not be better to use these sums for so useful a purpose? Finally, to encourage everyone, give the best positions in the diocese to those who hold a degree in practical medicine.

It may also be objected that "this plan would require new professors and an anatomical museum: how is one to pay for them?" They should—and easily could—implement this proposal immediately, if only they wanted to. After the elimination of superfluous subjects and professorships (which now are allotted salaries to no purpose), professors of medicine can assume these positions.[45] As for the apparatus that is required, it is only necessary to establish strict control over the seminary's money and supervise its bookkeeper closely: in three or four years it will be possible to purchase everything you need. If that does not suffice, then levy an assessment on the churches and monasteries. What is 1,000 rubles for some monasteries, or 300 to 500 rubles for some churches? It is just a tenth of their annual revenues. If that is still not enough, then one can find a million instances showing that our government is exceedingly generous with funds when it receives a direct benefit; it would most certainly render assistance in this instance. Is not an increase in the largest possible number of village doctors directly useful to the state? A healthy population increases the strength of the state. But now, given the complete absence of doctors, it is distressing and painful to look at some villages. Wherever the peasants are employed in industry (especially in the capitals), in such areas entire villages are infected with that horrible disease [syphilis] which destroys the present population and is transmitted to the next as well. Medical education could be established in the seminary to take care of this need—if, I repeat, they really wanted to do it.

As for seminary instruction in French and German, there is little to be said. They are taught by professors who do not know

44. The Committees for Aid to the Poor of the Clerical Estate were established in 1823, with a capital endowment of 150,000 rubles (*PSZ[1]*, vol. 38, no. 29583).
45. Tolstoi's marginal comment: "That's not easy to do" (OR GBL, f. 302, k. 2, d. 12, l. 35 ob.).

how to read them (there are no exceptions here), and as a result the pupils simply do not learn them. In other words, the time designated for their instruction is completely wasted. The same must be said about Hebrew. Nor do the pupils learn Latin and (especially) Greek; here, too, time is wasted.[46]

Time is wasted first on one thing, then on another: just how much time is *usefully* spent in the seminary? People will be surprised if I say no more than two hours a day. They will be still more amazed when I add that professors, who know that pupils do not study their subjects, devote just fifteen (at most thirty) minutes a day to their class, and often use that brief time for some banal conversation, anecdotes, etc. Even professors in the main subjects are only a little more zealous in their work; an hour (at most an hour and a quarter) is regarded as completely adequate for the class. What do the pupils do during such prolonged intermissions? They indulge in the most vapid talk; or read every vile thing they can lay their hands on. . . . Given all this, judge the sum of information that pupils acquire in the seminary!

We have seen what the seminary does for a future priest, that is, the degree to which it prepares him for the great tasks of the pastorate. Now I shall examine his living quarters. The majority of pupils at the seminary—as at the district school—live with the poorest townsman, soldier, widow, or clerk—that is, with people of exceedingly dubious morality. Even if they almost always occupy two, three, or more separate rooms, encounters with the landlords are constant and their influence on the students is inescapable. What must be the influence of such people? What must be the effect of such influence on pupils, whose moral sense was already dulled in the district school, whose soul has been contaminated, whose entire being is predisposed to accept evil? The results are terrible, awful!

In comparison with the district school, the respective roles of the landlords and students have now changed: previously the pupils served the landlords, now the landlords do the pupils'

---

46. Tolstoi's marginal comment: "True" (ibid., l. 36 ob.).

bidding. . . . To see a pupil with a pipe, cards, and vodka is quite routine; sometimes it is worse, indeed so bad that it is impossible to speak of it. "But do the seminary authorities not look after them?" Yes, there is an inspector, his aides [*pomoshchniki*] and student elders [*starshie*]. But as for the elders, little need be said: they are pupils themselves, and always the first guests at every drunken feast. As for the inspector and one or two aides, what control can they exercise when there are several hundred students? So what if they visit the pupils one, two, or three times a week (usually in the evening)? The rest of the time, and particularly at night, the pupils are completely on their own.

No, it is not enough just to check on the pupils once or twice a week: indeed, one should never take his eyes off them, day or night. Is that possible when the pupils are scattered all across the districts, streets, and alleys of a town? Obviously not. Consequently, the seminarians should not live in private boarding rooms; it is not in these cesspools, infectious and fatal, that the future priest should pass his time; he needs, above all, purity of body to qualify for his lofty, celestial rank. So he should live in a general dormitory, under the constant and indefatigable supervision of authorities.[47] A youth, even one with good inclinations, is so easily led astray onto the treacherous path of vice; he needs very close supervision, to be warned, to be stopped in time, to be restrained from falling. What can one say about a youth who has been surrounded from childhood by an infectious atmosphere of vice? What about those who have themselves traversed this path, who must know the evil emanating from private rooms, and who later became bishops: why should they not make an effort to build dormitories to house all the pupils? Every father would gladly pay for his son's maintenance in the dormitory, if only he could be sure that the supervision would be vigilant and that there

---

47. The need for sufficient dormitory space (essential if proper moral training was to be provided in these ecclesiastical boarding schools) also greatly concerned the Synod's reform committee on seminaries in 1860–62. See the main memorandum by its chairman, Dmitrii (Muretov), in OR GBL, f. 316, k. 66, d. 31, and the committee's formal proposals to the Synod, in TsGIA SSSR, f. 796, op. 141, g. 1860, d. 367, ll. 255–437.

would be no abuses. Private boarding rooms are a permanent nightmare for parents, permitting them no peace of mind, night or day. Their fear is both natural and understandable.

But here, as with everything that would be good and useful for the clergy, there is an excuse: "There are no funds for the construction of dormitories." How can that be? When the state does not begrudge millions of rubles for the improvement of the clergy's material condition, you say: "There are no funds for dormitories." But have you tried to explain to the state all the evil, all the harm caused by private rooms, the absolute necessity of educating the youths under one general supervision? No? Then how, in seeking to justify your inexpiable indifference, can you refer to a lack of funds? The government, constantly concerned about the welfare of all its subjects, has deigned to provide [some] rural clergy with a salary. Did you bring the question [of dormitories] to the government's attention? Did you petition about the dormitories, which are something the rural clergy especially needs, even more than salaries? You did nothing of the sort. Indeed—though who could believe it!—there are prelates who rejected the Tsar's gift, who dared to contest the intention of God's Annointed (an intention inspired by God Himself) to extricate the pathetic, unfortunate clergy from the depths of calamity, from all that so degrades and depresses them.

"The rural clergy do not need salaries," declared some bishops, in all their infinite wisdom, in all their benign unconcern for their subordinates.[48] "They do not need a salary"—in other words, the rural clergy are to remain forever in the same terrible, downtrodden, hopeless condition in which they have been up to the present. Is this how you want to preserve forever your illegal, godless, terrible authority over the white clergy? Do you wish to know, as you secure your tyranny, what "Judge of the Earth" means? For the sake of your own wealth, you have condemned them forever to resort to those illegal, shameful, criminal, contemptible

---

48. As the church archives make clear, most prelates in fact supported the demand for clerical salaries; only a small minority resisted such proposals, primarily on the grounds of canon law and Scripture (which affirmed the *voluntary* nature of clerical support). See Freeze, *Parish Clergy*, chap. 2, for details and references.

levies on parishioners that are popularly referred to as "revenues" [emoluments for performance of rites and sacraments], because they have no other means. "A salary is not needed." So say you: alone, after voluntarily condemning yourself to deprivation and monastic poverty, after taking a strict vow renouncing all concern for worldly possessions, you assiduously amass tens and hundreds of thousands of rubles in income each year. But even that is not enough: you regard each monastery as your private estate, even as you continue to draw your salary. What do you need all this money for? For food, silk, velvet, cassocks of sable, support for "nieces" and their offspring? . . .[49]

Oh, how perverted things in the Orthodox church have become! Saint Sergius, for example, wore sackcloth and linen; now a certain monk X drapes himself in a 10,000-ruble cassock (if not more expensive)! . . . But you say that there is "no need" to give a salary to the rural priest—who lives in his own house; who has a legal, God-given family of ten or more dependents (not those "nieces" who spring from nowhere); who educates two or three sons at the seminary; who must arrange marriages for two, three, or more daughters! . . . He must be content with some hundred rubles per year; even that he collects by violating every conceivable propriety, not to mention law and justice! No, this is not mere Machiavellianism, but something so evil, so hostile to the white clergy, so ruinous for the entire church, that I do not know what to call it. . . .

No, if you should say that before granting salaries we need to reeducate the clergy, then it would be clear that you do wish your subordinates well, that you are concerned about the church's welfare. Yes, indeed, improvement of the clergy should begin not with salaries but with a radical transformation of its entire way of life and especially of its education. Without such reforms, a salary will achieve nothing. Moreover, under the distorted ruinous education that clerical youths now receive, a salary would

49. Belliustin is alluding here to a sensational affair at a local monastery, where the abbot was found to have masked illicit relations under the guise of visits by his "nieces." See the report of the Third Section in TsGAOR, f. 109, op. 223 (85), g. 1850, d. 15, ll. 55 ob.–56.

even cause them harm: in the hands of those who do not know how to make proper use of it, a salary would be like fire or a knife in the hands of a child. Before granting salaries, have dormitories built, so that all the pupils—from childhood to the end of their studies—can be reared at state expense and under the continual supervision of teachers and administrators who have good intentions and who are experienced in the purity of life. I said at *state* expense, because that is the only way to establish equality in the clergy's condition, without which envy (and its consequences) are unavoidable. And unless the cost of education is borne completely by the state, childless clergy will always be rich, those with large families will always be indigent and suffering. To repeat, one should begin to improve the clergy with educational reform, and then complete the process by [granting] salaries.

Finally, I shall say a few words about an important abuse, one that could be permitted only in the education of youths preparing for the priesthood—whether in the village, city, or capitals makes no difference. It is this: Seminary pupils are obliged to attend mass only on Sundays and major holidays. From that fact alone you can see that the program for educating clerical youths was not composed by one of God's parish priests!

Now the course of study is completed. Twelve, fourteen—and sometimes more—years: these are onerous years, made all the worse because the student did not study even the main subjects with desire, zeal, or interest, but solely because of extreme necessity (and whether or not he was living in good or bad conditions). Now new questions arise: What is he now? What does he have to offer? What path should he take?

Do not ask him *what he is*. Otherwise, you will be unpleasantly surprised by his answer: "I'm a graduate of the seminary." By the sound of his voice, his manner, and his physiognomy he'll let you know that this is not just anybody, not just an ordinary person—this is *someone who has graduated from the seminary*. Yes, one must give the seminary its due: if it sows and nurtures little that is good and worthwhile, it shows an extraordinary capacity

[104]

to develop whatever is bad in a person. An unpretentious seminarian is a phenomenon rarely seen. Pride—petty, trivial, inane, yet displayed obtrusively and clumsily—all this is stuffed into a seminarian and especially the graduate, from head to toe. How the seminary manages to develop such a deadly vice in such terrible quantity is one of its mysteries (something that I have little desire or need to unravel). I shall only say that the seminarian's self-esteem, if he goes on [to the academy], turns into satanic pride, into the most insufferable pedantry, into egotism without limit or measure. If he becomes a priest, especially in the countryside, he is transformed into some kind of pathetic, ridiculous creature, demanding that everyone pay him honor and respect (although he has no right to either), permitting no one to forget himself in his presence (while he is most often the first to do so). In a word, he is an exceedingly irritable, obstinate, and unsociable creature. There are exceptions: some seminarians become the most wonderful, most noble souls, the epitome of honor and achievement. Similarly, some village priests have abjured the foul spirit of the seminary. But these exceptions are rare, unnoticeable in the general mass, and there is no need to speak of them. In general, one can discern a seminarian immediately, whether he is wearing a cassock or an official uniform, whether he is draped with crosses or stars: it is a virtually indelible characteristic! . . .[50]

And it is easy to discern what is inside him. Just strike up a serious conversation and force him to express himself, and you will see that he is totally vacuous, lacking any positive, fully mastered body of knowledge. Sometimes an articulate seminarian showers words on your head; but in vain would you seek a lively, conscious, perceptive idea in this torrent of words. You'll find

50. The supposed indelibility of clerical origin and seminary education provided grist for contemporary humor. One story popular in the mid–nineteenth century told of several bureaucrats of clerical origin who sought relief from the summer heat by bathing in a nearby river. As they emerged naked from the water, a peasant who had lost his way stopped to ask for directions. "Not knowing who they were, he was at first perplexed as to how to address them, but then discerned what breed they were and cried out: 'Hey, sacristans, listen!' " (OR GPB, f. 550, F. IV, d. 861, l. 385 ob. [Zapiski M. P. Veselovskogo]).

nothing of the sort. It could not be otherwise after the kind of education he received in the seminary: it developed only his memory, and suppressed the ability to think on his own. (The actual purpose: the less they think, the less they will reflect; the less they reflect, the more easily and readily they can be moved about like pawns, etc. In other words, stop up their eyes and ears, and they won't think either.) While he still has a fresh recollection of what he memorized at the seminary, he talks ceaselessly, but does not know how to explain why it is this way and not some other. As a result, a vacuous, insignificant sophism immediately throws him into confusion. For the same reason, during entrance examinations for the university he refuses to describe, for example, the Kremlin, and asks that he be given an easier theme— such as "the immortality of the soul." And for him that really is easier: he recently memorized a lecture on the immortality of the soul; he needs only to transfer what he memorized onto paper and the essay is ready. But to describe the Kremlin, one must think a little independently, and that is not something he learned to do in the seminary. Then, too, he would need to know history; however, he memorized history during rhetoric [the first two years of the seminary], so that by the end of his studies he has completely forgotten it. So what on earth could he write about the Kremlin? Indeed, even if they ordered him to describe the village where he was born, he would be at a loss and would ask for an easier theme, such as the unity of peoples in Christ.

Where does he intend to go? He himself has no idea—which shows how wisely and usefully his education has been designed and managed! Naturally, it is simplest for him to become a priest: even if he does not feel the slightest heartfelt attraction to this rank, his father, forefathers, and kin are all servitors of the church at a higher or lower rank. So he too seeks a priest's position in some village. If he succeeds, he becomes a priest; if he fails, he still seeks to attain this goal in some roundabout way (what this means I shall describe later). If all this comes to nothing, he requests a teacher's position. If this too fails, he petitions—just as cold bloodedly, without any sincere interest—to become a petty clerk. . . . In a word, there is no rank that the seminarian will

[106]

not seek, so long as he can expect to earn his livelihood in it. Consequently—what a terrible, bitter "consequently"—he becomes a priest, for the sake not of Christ, but of a loaf of bread. . . .

Some will say: "From the ranks of seminarians have come very learned people, even professors in the university and state officials, and model priests in the capitals." But just ask such people: Was it the seminary that developed their abilities and made them important people? Was it in the seminary that they realized their calling and role? If they wish to answer truthfully, then—without the slightest doubt—they will reply: "No! No! No! . . ." Here is how one great figure came from the seminary: Fate drove him into the university and there, for some reason, he attracted a professor's attention; or he chanced to give tutorials in the home of rich, educated people, who wiped off the dirt and expunged the foul spirit of the seminary; and his career was made. If, however, he had relied on the means, spirit, and direction that he received in the seminary, he would have been lost. Or, in another case, fate thrust such a person into the theological academy, associated him with noble people (noble in spirit and life, not in formal rank), people who think and act nobly; they took the trouble to educate that hideous creature from the seminary and transformed him into a model priest. If that does not happen, he can graduate from the academy, perhaps even acquire a smattering of knowledge, and take over the best clerical position in the capital; yet such a person brings no joy, honor, or beauty to his rank, remaining either a great acquisitor of money or a querulous troublemaker. Or perhaps fate cast him, after completing the academy, into the chancellery of some magnate; he caught somebody's eye, and that person took him under his firm control, put him under his own roof (to teach his children, to handle his private affairs); and later he became a state official, like Count Speranskii.[51] Had that not happened, he would have become mired in his own foul seminarian mentality. Perhaps, after incredible labor, he attains

---

51. M. M. Speranskii (1772–1839), son of a village priest in Vladimir diocese, became one of the most prominent figures in Russian state service in the first decades of the nineteenth century.

the highest ranks in the civil service, but such a high official is especially onerous and terrible for his subordinates. . . .

But just let fate cast these people into the rural priesthood, and they will be no better than the others. After all, even now, of the number who become rural priests, there are [many] with great spiritual powers that are undeveloped, even untapped; all their powers perish in the whirlpool of life. The only exceptions are those who go to a village where there is a landlord with a true education; here the priest is saved. The landlord takes care of him, knocks that seminary foolishness out of him, kindles his ability to think, puts the family library at his disposal (such landlords always have splendid libraries), and provides support (not luxurious, but reliable) that spares the priest the coarse duty of cultivating his land or making shameful assessments on parishioners. The result: a model priest is formed. But are there many such landlords in an entire province? No. Hence there cannot be many such priests, and as the exception is quite rare, there is little to be said.

What, then, should one say more generally about the education that the pupils receive in ecclesiastical schools and seminaries? We have seen how pointless, ridiculous, insignificant it all is; we have seen how little benefit pupils derive from the district school and seminary, how much evil they take away from these schools. Consequently, we have every right to declare: Everything in the district schools and seminaries—from their very foundations—must be changed and transformed if authorities want the education of clerical youth to be more than mere learning. I would state my own profound convictions, based on prolonged observations and much reflection, on what proper education should be. But what would be the point? Who will listen to the words of someone traversing a path so insignificant, frustrating, and thorny? Everyone realizes the necessity of a fundamental transformation; yet new schemes are composed in the office of a famous, prominent person, who is surrounded by every comfort and can no more fathom a rural priest's life and needs than he can see the water in rain clouds. Authorities will introduce new subjects, change the textbooks, but the spirit will remain the same; everything will stay just as it was. But some talk about combining the seminary and secular gymnasium; that will just confuse the unfortunate clergy once and for all!! . . . But that is the way things are always done here. Thus it is necessary to reform the village; projects are drafted in the most luxurious offices; they are discussed in the most elegant rooms; yet no one asks the village itself what is needed. But why ask? they will say. The "dark people" do not understand themselves what they need. . . . They do not understand?! Well, when they try to implement those plans written in luxurious offices, we'll see what becomes of them!

THE VILLAGE PRIEST

Appointment

The best student—that is, best according to seminary records—need not dream of receiving a good position in the diocese. Such positions are usually given out to the bishop's relatives; if he has none, then the swine who surround the bishop will get them. "Swine" is strong language; but what else can you call the bishop's lackeys, servants, secretaries, and choirboys? What kind of people are they? The lackey is always someone driven from the district school or seminary because of dissolute conduct; it is the same pupil who was a watchman somewhere for several years, then a novice, and came to the bishop's residence; somehow or other, he then wormed himself into the position of lackey there. If he shows special ability in service, he rises to the rank of personal servant, enjoying the broadest trust. The secretary is the most brazen, unscrupulous, merciless clerk; compared to him, the clerks who work in secular courts are mere lambs. . . . And the choirboys are nothing but a nest of drunkenness, debauchery, violent uproar; incredibly unscrupulous, they are forever plundering churches, monasteries, and the entire clergy, and nothing ever satisfies them. They accompany the bishop on visitations to villages in the diocese, where they rage at the priests and church elders, brazenly demand vodka and money, and curse (if sober) or permit themselves still worse (if drunk). And they do all this without the slightest fear of punishment, because they are protected by the prelate's mantle. . . . They are always joined by archdeacons and subdeacons, who are distinguished from the choirboys only in their dress; in all other respects they are identical to each other. Can this contemptible gang be called anything but swine? And it is this riffraff that obtains the best positions! Nor is that all: if a good position appears, one of them claims it and then transfers it to a brother, sister, or niece, or simply sells it. He then repeats this trick three or four times until, to the disgrace and dishonor of the clergy, he becomes a priest himself.

The student can receive a mediocre position, but under one condition: that he pay for it. Twenty years ago this evil was not so widespread, but of late it has become incredibly common. The reason is that the number of seminary graduates has sharply increased, and as a result, up to ten people (sometimes more) apply for the same position. However, the position is not given to the person with the best seminary record, but to the one who pays the most. It is sold either by the bishop's personal secretary, who always has great influence, or by his servant, or sometimes by the two together. The better the position, the higher the price; it sometimes rises to as much as 200 rubles. But it is not all over when you pay these gentlemen, for you must also pay off the consistory: it must review the documents and compile an "opinion," and such things are not done gratis. Unless everyone is satisfied (the members of the consistory board, the secretary, and all the clerks), the opinion will go against you. . . . What are the thoughts of the future priest? He has no time now to reflect upon what he is entering into, or to prepare his mind and heart for a miraculous paradise: all his thoughts, concerns, and contemplation are focused on one thing—money! money! Where can he obtain some money! To avoid returning to this topic, I'll note here the other fees extorted for installation into the priesthood. Namely, one must pay the archpriest, archdeacon, subdeacon, and choir-boys immediately after the rites of ordination—that is, immediately after receiving the sacraments, on the very spot of ordination. One has to fight off a whole horde of the most rapacious, insatiable beasts with money and pleas, often with foul language! For the decree to the consistory and for the ordination certificate, one must pay the secretary a certain sum (beyond the regular tax); otherwise, they will detain you for months. Altogether, one must spend from 60 to 100 silver rubles.[52]

Now where is a seminary pupil or graduate, who is invariably poor, to obtain so much money? Having no particular place in mind, he usually seeks a fiancée for himself—not just any fiancée, but one who has a bagful of money. Hence he is not concerned to choose a friend for life, but to find as much money as possible. After he has bargained for a few potential fiancées, he decides in favor of the one that can pay the most, although she may have every kind of failing, moral and even physical. The bargain struck, he receives both money and a position.

The mediocre student has one other possibility: he tries to "join a home." That means he is seeking a priest who, because he is old or because he is under investigation for some offense, must surrender his position. In this case one does not pay the slightest attention to either the fiancée's merits or her parents' family life (and ask whether one can live peacefully and undisturbed with them). The only thing that counts is the position itself; the girl can be twice the fiancé's age, stupid, ugly, and so forth.

If for some reason he cannot arrange his affairs in this manner—that is, he does not want to take a girl for money (which is extremely rare, however) or thinks that they are still not giving him enough (which is extremely common)—then even if he is twice as good a student as everyone else, even if he applies for every position, he will nonetheless remain without a position five or ten years.

---

52. In 1839 Nicholas' government introduced the silver ruble, its value fixed at 3.5 times that of the assignats (Walter Pintner, *Russian Economic Policy under Nicholas I* [Ithaca, 1967], p. 210).

This is why inferior students, with lower class ranks, who value themselves more cheaply, find positions more quickly than the best students (this applies still more to those ranked at the bottom of the class, who, because of their inferior value, price themselves still more cheaply). In other words, the diocese first receives the worst students of the seminary; the other students, after many futile attempts, give up and become teachers or government clerks.

Here it would be appropriate to note how much money they receive for taking fiancées. In the provinces best known to me (Moscow, Iaroslavl, Tver, and Vladimir), a seminarian qualified to become a priest receives 500 to 1,000 silver rubles, in addition to the dowry itself. As a result, only the daughters of rich priests or deacons (or even sacristans, if they received an inheritance from some monk, etc.) become the wives of rural priests. How their fathers acquired this wealth does not matter, whether it was through honest and honorable toil, unscrupulous extortions, criminal exactions from parishioners, or even unforgivable fraud (for example, when the superintendents rob the church treasuries, etc.). The daughters of honest but poor priests with large families either remain old maids or marry sacristans, petty government clerks, or other undesirable types. Even if they are beautiful, God-fearing (because of the need and deprivation of their childhood), gentle, patient, thrifty, and of wonderful morality, it doesn't matter in the least.[53]

Family Life

So now the former seminarian is a rural priest. He has joined a home or assumed a vacant position. Let's look at the family life in both situations. I should note that I am describing the majority, but certainly not all. One can find better, more lofty cases than

53. For similar critiques of clerical *mariages de convenance*, see the diocesan reports of 1863, summarized in Freeze, "Caste and Emancipation: The Changing Status of Clerical Families in the Great Reforms," in *The Family in Imperial Russia*, ed. David L. Ransel (Urbana, Ill., 1978), pp. 124–150.

the ones I shall describe; because they occur so rarely, however, I shall not discuss them in this or the following sections.

The seminarian enters a household. Dire necessity, not free will, dictated this decision on both sides—the original household and the seminarian who enters it. On the one hand, the girl's advanced age or the priest's loss of his position for misdeeds prevent the priest from being too discriminating in the choice of a fiancée, from seeking the one who is intellectually and morally best, and oblige him to take the cheapest he can find. On the other hand, the need for food and shelter forces the seminarian to agree to the most onerous terms on joining a family with many members (and sometimes with open disorders), and moreover to take as his wife some sort of monster, in a moral if not physical sense. The consequences of such fatal deals become apparent all too soon. The cheapest candidate hardly manages to become a priest when he proves the truth of the proverb: "If it's cheap, it's no good." And from the very first he does not know how to conceal his moral decadence. The conflict always starts with the terms of the contract: the former cleric demands literal compliance, while the new priest at first cannot, then does not want to comply. His noncompliance gives rise to quarrels, which are morally harmful for parishioners when they see two priests (indeed, closely related ones) quarreling; these quarrels turn into irreconcilable hostility, then into lawsuits and a division of property.

The one person who could reconcile the two sides—the young priest's wife—for the most part just fans the flames. It was not by mutual attraction of the heart that they married; hence she has not the slightest influence over her spouse and is in no position either to reason with him or to calm him, even if she wishes. But often she does not even want to, especially if she has become hardened and thick-skinned. Her husband, whether intelligent or stupid, has entered this house with his own needs, his own inclinations, his own stubborn seminarian spirit, and he wants to establish his own order in the house. And the more stupid he is, the sooner he sets about the task. His wife, accustomed to the old order, is in no position to understand and believes that the only way she can have an influence on her husband is this: to

[113]

agree verbally with all he says, then to go against him in every-thing. This is the beginning of a conflict between man and wife that ends in hatred. To vex and irritate her husband gives his silly wife satisfaction; the husband naturally repays her in kind. There-after, in disputes between her husband and her parents, she always sides with the latter and, whether he is right or wrong, showers insults on him, torments him with reproaches, casts aspersions on his parents and all his kin, etc., etc.

What is the result? The young priest begins to despise every-thing, even the very walls of the house he lives in. To be home is sheer torment for him, and he seeks every opportunity to be away—out in the parish, with the sacristans, in the church watch-man's house, anywhere but at home. Partly because he lacks his own internal moral fiber for support, partly because of an evil predisposition acquired at the seminary, he takes to the bottle—at first to stifle the sorrow, but then because the bottle has become a necessity, a passion. Wherever there is a bottle to be found, he will be there too, invited or not; and often he is neither invited nor wanted. He has to perform the priest's duties: to conduct a marriage, to bury the dead, to say prayers for a woman who has just given birth, and so forth. But before everything comes the bottle. At last he parts with his father-in-law and remains alone with his wife; having come to despise her and having acquired the habit of drinking, however, he does not improve. Thus he drags out his life, tainted and scandalous. It often happens that he gives himself up to the most vulgar vices; when one is drunk and despises his wife, what will he not think if?

You can imagine what kind of children come from such an unhappy family. Worst of all is the fact that from early childhood they grow accustomed to despising their parents and nourish none of a child's usual feelings toward his parents. Somehow having grown up and become independent, they would never dream of supporting and caring for their parents at the end of their days. A son who denies his own father and mother a crust of bread; who does not think of visiting them even to say a few kind words during the most serious illness (not to say render assistance); who casts vulgar curses on his parents and on a holiday drives them from his house in ignominy, etc., etc.—such phenomena are not uncommon. Should one expect from those reared in such a family brotherly love, that pure and holy love which compels you to regard your brother as yourself? That sacred love is missing here. From time to time brothers see each other, but only on holidays; they do so not to console each other or share their joy, but to bicker among themselves amidst a furious orgy. . . . Is this not the foundation of that great fragmentation of the clergy, which causes each priest to regard his fellow clergyman, if not as an enemy, then at least as an ill-wisher, someone who is envious, etc.? Indeed, a bad brother will never be a good neighbor, a good colleague, or a trustworthy fellow servitor. If the heart is not warmed by love toward close ones, the result is always evil, and only evil, toward others.

In general, the practice of bringing the new priest into his predecessor's home while the girl's father and mother are still alive is an evil that should have been brought to the government's attention long ago. We may assume something that is exceedingly rare (perhaps true in just 5 percent of the cases)—that the fiancé and fiancée like each other; that, having become man and wife, they fall in love with each other; and that even the contractual terms are bearable. Yet the very fact that the household has two masters leads to mutual dissatisfaction: one is accustomed to living in the old way (that is, in filth and simplicity), the other to live more cleanly; one performed all the work himself, the other does not want or even know how to do so; the one loves raucous holidays, the other cannot stand them, etc. Conflict between the old priest and the new one, however well intentioned their aims may have been, is inescapable. In a word, feuds are inevitable.

Whose side does the wife take? She cannot remain neutral: the parents, annoyed that things are not done the way they like, vent their irritation on the daughter. Should she defend her husband? That means turning her parents against her and hearing their rebukes and curses from morning to night. To be reviled together with her husband? It is painful and terrible for her to lose his love

[115]

and attachment. What is left for her to do? To endure, weep, and suffer. Two or three years of this troubled and long-suffering life completely saps her strength; those with poor health soon perish, even those with a strong constitution rarely are able to ward off consumption. That is why widowhood among rural priests is so common (four to five in ten). But even before this terrible catastrophe, the husband, who loves his wife yet sees her forever in tears and perpetually despondent, and who lacks the means to set things straight, seeks consolation in the bottle. While his wife is still alive he is careful—love for her restrains him from going too far; but her death is the harbinger of his complete fall.[54] Then he seeks in the bottle not consolation but total oblivion; with the help of that ruinous poison, he seeks to suppress the anguish of loneliness, dissatisfaction with his family, all the sorrow of his life. If the seminary had fortified his spirit to withstand the tempests and adversities of life, if it had taught him to understand and love scholarship, if it had developed and strengthened his faith in Providence, he could hold out. But what can sustain him when he has left the seminary with nothing of the sort?

A priest should be allowed to enter a household in only one case: when the old priest is dying and leaves a large family. Here awaiting the new priest is nothing but want and poverty with two families to support, his own and that of his predecessor. But here, at least, there will be no conflicts, because the orphans' status makes them pliant and undemanding, and material want is easier to endure than family squabbles. Here too, however, the contractual terms between the two sides must be strictly weighed, examined, discussed, and confirmed in writing by diocesan authorities to avoid future disputes (over the betrothal of girls, for example, or support for the boys at a district school).

At this point someone may ask: "But what should a priest do if he can no longer serve because of ill health or age? If he renounces his position and does not accept a son-in-law, he will be left penniless."

---

54. Tolstoi's marginal comment: "This is excessive" (OR GBL, f. 302, k. 2, d. 12, l. 54). For Metropolitan Filaret's critique of such estimates, see his memorandum of 1860 in TsGIA SSSR, f. 796, op. 141, g, 1860, d. 1019, ll. 1–12 ob.

Exactly: penniless—in the most literal sense of the word. The condition of a priest who has no position is incomparably worse than that of an invalid: the latter at least can collect charity; the priest is forbidden to do so. Here, thanks to our bishops, is the clergy's condition: a petty official who has served thirty-five years (his entire duties amounted to nothing more than sewing or gluing together court files) is released with a pension and has reliable support; a priest, after serving thirty to forty years (or even longer), has nothing in his old age and infirmity! It happens that in the most terrible poverty he goes to the bishop for assistance. After long delays they occasionally grant him something. But how much? Ten to fifteen rubles a year![55] Whether you want to or not, you have to accept a son-in-law, even though you know beforehand that this will be anything but paradise; but at least you will not die of starvation.

That is how our wise, well-meaning bishops tolerate every form of evil, fully aware that it is evil (lawsuits between fathers-in-law and sons-in-law come to them for resolution), so that the old order will not be changed in the least, so that improvements in the clergy will not be permitted. . . . "Let them live as best they can—that will best serve our interests." This canon, so wise and modern, finds expression in all their behavior and decrees. But to understand how the clergy live once they have resigned their position, I shall relate one of the many cases known to me. A soldier who has reenlisted for a second term and served forty years is completely provided for in his old age; the teacher of any parish or village school receives full support after twenty-five years; but an archpriest, earlier the best pupil in the seminary, then the best of priests, his entire life passed in such intense toil that disease developed as a direct consequence of this heavy mental toil, is accorded one right: to die of starvation!! . . .

Consequently, the evil that ensues from having seminarians

---

55. Reports from diocesan authorities confirm this view; see, for example, the annual report for 1850 in TsGIA SSSR, f. 796, op. 132, g. 1851, d. 2357 (all dioceses). Contrary to Belliustin's assertions, however, these reports demonstrate that the bishops did not regard existing support as adequate, but they had neither the power nor the resources to alleviate the situation.

enter another family can be eliminated only when priests are given a pension for their old age. But will this reform ever be made? There is no reason to hope that it will. Consequently, this evil—with all its terrible consequences—will exist forever.

What happens if a pupil assumes an unoccupied position? Here, it would seem, are all the conditions for a happy family life: a life of two together, without any outside meddling, should draw the young husband and wife together, even if they hardly knew each other before the marriage. In fact, however, such is not the case. I explained earlier how things are done in the clergy: one does not seek a friend in life, but money; when he takes the money, he also has to take whatever fate sends along with it. It is rare, however, that fate does not mete out punishment for such a perverted order, rare that you obtain a good wife along with the money. It could hardly be otherwise. The daughters of rich priests are a spoiled lot, willful, accustomed to sloth and extravagance; if, to make things worse, her father is also a superintendent, then she is also immensely pretentious (it is inevitable: because of her father's status, the priests in his district bowed to her, the sacristans threw themselves at her feet). Education, which would eliminate (or at least moderate) such deficiencies, is simply unavailable for the clergy; hence all the shortcomings are prominent, striking, obtrusive. Just imagine two of the most immense pretensions—that of the seminary, that of the superintendancy—coming into conflict: what kind of battle must ensue? How must it appear? Naturally, there is nothing good here. From the very first quarrels begin over the most trivial matters; both sides are irritable and unyielding; the quarrels give rise to that intolerable situation in which the husband and wife seize every chance to humiliate, to wound, to sting each other; here the wife complains to any and all about her bitter fate; do-gooders appear to meddle in their affairs, offering inappropriate advice and reproofs that only aggravate the vexation. It always ends with the husband, if he drank vodka at the seminary, in two or three years becoming an incurable alcoholic; if he did not drink, he begins to do so, and, though less quickly, still develops a passion for the bottle.

It sometimes happens that the husband and wife get on together and there is neither strong affection nor animosity between them. But here the troubles are different. Of the money received for taking his wife, only a trifle remains; yet he has to build a house and set up his household. Where is he to obtain the means? In this case the wife takes command: "My father built up a fortune like this: he demanded a certain sum for weddings; if the parishioner did not want to pay, he applied various forms of pressure; they cursed him, but all the same they had to pay. He demanded a certain sum for prayer services; otherwise, he refused to conduct the service, etc. Do you understand?" The new priest in whose soul the seminary failed to instill honor, honesty, or even simple worldly wisdom (make yourself worthy and they will give you everything you need) is easily convinced by such counsel, and before the first year is up he extorts a terrible fee for every rite. Previously, parishioners paid too little for prayer services, marriage, and other sacraments; now they have to give a larger sum. . . . Rare is the priest (no more than five in a hundred) who does not begin his work in this way. The consequence is predictable: parishioners are outraged, regard the young priest as a petty official, that is, as some kind of inescapable evil; they pay, but with the most profound indignation, with secret (sometimes overt) curses. It sometimes happens that the whole parish is up in arms; because peasants have no fondness for quarrels, they take matters into their own hands and set a price for everything, less than the old one. The priest struggles and resists, but *volens-nolens* must given in. In either case the priest has sundered any possible ties between him and the parishioners from the start, and the rest of his life he shall not be able to mend the harm he wrought in the first three or four years.

Such, with few exceptions, is the family life of rural priests! Rare is the happy marriage, in which the husband sees in his wife a friend, aide, adviser; in which the wife, by force of will and mind, guided and directed by true love, transforms her husband from a seminarian into a human being!

How can one eradicate this evil? How can the family life of rural priests be improved?

[119]

Above all, it is necessary to educate the priests' daughters.[56] Education by the family, given the clergy's present condition, is impossible; public education is needed. God bless our Tsar's family, which has already laid the foundations for such education, having constructed two schools for girls of the clerical estate. But two schools for all of Russia: is that not just a drop in the sea?[57] Then, too, however small the sum required for educating the girls, most rural priests find it simply beyond their means—60 to 70 rubles a year, when the annual income of the rural priest is 100 to 150 rubles (or, very rarely, 200 rubles), on which he must maintain his house and support two or three sons at the church school or seminary? Even half that sum would be intolerably onerous. Moreover, at present the priest's wife must manage the entire household, that is, look after the livestock, reap and thresh the crops, and so forth; girls reared in these schools, however, are simply unable to perform such work, and that is why future rural priests are afraid to marry girls with this marvelous education. Only if we reform the living conditions of rural priests and educate wives for them (that is, in each provincial town establish schools to educate priests' daughters at state expense) will the family life of rural priests improve. Such an improvement would have so many wonderful benefits for future generations!

But in any case, whether this reform is adopted or not, we must use the strictest measures to eliminate immediately the deeply rooted custom of taking money for brides. Of course, this measure must be preceded by a complete abolition of the shameful, despicable sale of positions (which deserves the severest punishment possible) and all the disgusting bribes that are exacted for

56. Belliustin's concern about female education was hardly unique; as the chief procurator noted in his annual report for 1852, "the need to educate daughters is being deeply felt everywhere in the clerical estate" (*Izvlecheniia iz otcheta po vedomstvu dukhovnyhkh del pravoslavnogo ispovedaniia za 1852 god* [St. Petersburg, 1853], p. 56).

57. The imperial family established the first such school for clerical daughters in 1843 (in Tsarskoe Selo) and had opened three more by 1855 (in Iaroslavl, Kazan, and Irkutsk). Three more such schools were established by diocesan authorities (in Riazan, Khar'kov, and Tula), but relied on the local clergy for financial support. See *Ob uchilishchakh devits dukhovnogo zvaniia* (St. Petersburg, 1866).

ordination into priesthood. Let the divine grace of priesthood be given freely, without payment to the miscreants who surround the bishop or work at the consistory. Then a student could seek a wife and take only the one who won his heart, even if she were the daughter of the poorest priest. There is no need to say what it means for a person to have a wife he loves: what an immense, beneficial influence she can have, even if she is uneducated, but raised in an honest, strictly Christian family.

Someone will interject: "A young priest needs money to build himself a home." That is true. But why not build and maintain a parsonage in each parish? "But that it impossible: it would cost too much money." What! In our *overwhelmingly Orthodox land this is impossible, but it is possible for Lutherans?* They provide for the pastor in every respect, from parsonage to fuel; with them he need not acquire the necessities of life, kopeck by kopeck, through every conceivable ruse; with them he is not soiled by dirty labor, not coarsened by physical toil. With Lutherans everything is possible, but here it is not? Oh, Orthodox Rus'!! Notwithstanding all this, you wise men are not abashed to hurl reproofs and evil mockery at our clergy, and to ask: Why are they not like the Lutheran clergy? "From the midst of Lutheran pastors come both scholars and preachers; their family life is wonderfully developed," etc., etc., say the critics of our clergy.

All that is true. But, in noting this phenomenon, why do you not want to discern its causes? Put our clergy in the same condition as the Lutheran clergy, and then compare. Educate the youth properly; educate a wife for him; release the priest from the filthy, murderous life in which he now vegetates; give him reliable, if modest, support—do all this, and I dare to vow by all that is holy that you will not recognize our clergy and will be proud to point it out to people of other faiths. Clergymen possess great strength, but they are demoralized. Everyone oppresses them: from the bishop to the consistory guard, from the gentry parishioner to the lowliest stable boy. You need scholars, preachers; such men would emerge from among our rural priests if only they were spared this terrible tyranny and permitted to breathe freely. . . . You want the clergyman to be good, yet you ignore the fact that

[121]

he is pompous, he drinks, and so forth; you refuse to tolerate just one thing—that he be intelligent and think; if such heresy is discovered, he is persecuted with the most brutal malice. . . . Ask your own conscience: could you, would you, dare to be better if you were in such an oppressed condition?

Means of Support

It is difficult to imagine who has less support, who is more vulnerable to mere chance in his material support than the rural clergyman. How are these uncertain means of support acquired? What is their relation to the priest's service? Oh, how much evil lies in these means of support!! They consist of *agriculture* and *emoluments*.

Emoluments

If you gave a prize for inventing a way to inflict the maximum humiliation and disgrace, to convert a lofty and miraculous calling into a trade, then surely one could not find a better means to do so than those unfortunate exactions from parishioners known among the clergy as "revenues." The priest administers a short prayer service, and thrusts out his hand for a reward; he accompanies a deceased person to his eternal resting place, and again he holds out his hand; a wedding ceremony has to be performed, and he even bargains over his fee; and on holidays he goes about the parish with the sole purpose of collecting money. In a word, no matter what he does, he has a single aim: to obtain money. Oh, here is the height of dishonor and shame: even when he has reconciled a confessing sinner with God, he takes money; even when he has administered the sacrament of communion, he does not recoil in horror from money. . . . Is he not simply a hireling? And how must the parishioners look upon him? Walk across Russia from end to end and listen to how they revile the clergy because of these accursed emoluments. . . . After all this, what benefit is to be gained from the priest's service? What moral

[122]

influence can he exert on the parishioners when they understand perfectly the primary goal of all his actions? And, lacking in authority, what kind of pastor can he be? Given this order of things, what is the point of a pastorate anyway? . . .

Oh, may the memory of Nicholas I be blessed forever! May the Saviour bestow all the blessings of Heaven on him for wanting to uplift the bitter, sad condition of rural clergy! He could not know how downtrodden it is, yet he wished to bestow imperial money on Christ's poor servants.

And may eternal damnation come to those egotists, those Machiavellis, scribes, Pharisees of the Christian church,[58] who— by calculations that are truly satanic—rose in opposition to salaries for the rural clergy.

Speaking of emoluments, I said nothing about abuses that are so common, such as the exaction of five to ten rubles (or more) for conducting a marriage. Nor did I speak of other things of a similar nature. To talk about these things is too onerous and sad; even without abuses, it is painful to look at the prevailing order of things in the Orthodox church.

But one cannot cast stones at the priest for making these dishonorable exactions. He can do nothing else, because he simply has no other means at his disposal. However much these abuses may outrage the soul, to some degree you have to forgive him if you examine his material condition. The priest lives with a family that rarely has fewer than ten members and sometimes includes as many as twelve to fifteen persons. How much does he need each year to support his family? Let us suggest a minimum, that is, the amount required by a peasant (who needs no cassock or similar things) with a family of ten: 120 to 180 rubles. In addition, the priest has one, two, and sometimes three sons at the district school or seminary: for two boys he needs at least 120 rubles a year for clothing, room and board, and travel to and fro (not to mention the bribes demanded by the teachers). In addition, the

---

58. Matt. 23:27: "Woe unto you, scribes and Pharisees, hypocrites! for ye are like unto whited sepulchres, which indeed appear beautiful outward, but are within full of dead men's bones, and of all uncleanness."

[123]

priest has unmarried daughters, so he has to set something aside for them, too; would you vouchsafe to calculate how much? What, too, will the needed repairs on his house cost? And the annual payments to the district board and superintendent? Unless the priest applies pressure to his parishioners, however, the very best parish will yield just 150 to 200 rubles, and the typical parish produces only 60 to 100 rubles. What would you have him do in such circumstances? You will say: "Pray and rely upon divine providence." But he was not taught to do this before he became a priest; on the contrary, they took from him and robbed him; from childhood to ordination he has been used to regarding exactions as something ordinary, even inevitable. So calmly, without troubling his conscience, he does the same thing that everyone else does, especially if he has the kind of wife described above. Then, inhibited by nothing, stopped by no one, he applies every conceivable kind of pressure. True, bishops are quick to punish clergy for this evil once complaints arise; since they do not indicate more honorable means of acquiring the necessities of life, however, the persecution serves no useful purpose. Thus their persecution only causes the priest to resort to the ruses used by bureaucrats (that is, to take illegally, but in such a way that one cannot be exposed). Moreover, the strictest persecution, if not accompanied by the bishop's own good example, only arouses contempt for even the most just measures.

Abolish dishonest exactions from parishioners, let there be no monetary deals between them and the priest, and you will restore peace between them. Then the parishioners will look with trust and love upon their pastor, and will listen to his every word with reverence. I will offer an example of what it means to give a priest proper support, and I hope that our all-wise bishops who oppose clerical salaries will not object. I shall quote the words of an intelligent person who has conducted research on the Chuvash people:[59]

59. The Chuvash, who lived in Kazan province (east-central European Russia), were descendants of the Bulgars, spoke a Turkish tongue, and represented a mixture of Finnish and Mongolian people. Absorbed into the Russian state in 1552, they had long since been Christianized and made adherents of the Orthodox church.

Earlier, when the priests took emoluments from them, the Chuvash were more pagan than Christian, and despised the priests with all their hearts. Recently, however, their relations with priests changed completely and in the most favorable fashion. What caused this miracle? It was this: the priest was given a salary from the state treasury and also was assured punctual delivery of support in kind [*ruga*], and thereby became fully independent of his flock. Hence the priest no longer had to indulge the weaknesses of his spiritual children and to overlook their misdeeds; and the flock has no cause to be indignant about levies or to complain of avarice. The consequences of these mutual relations between them is now beginning to manifest itself in respect from the flock, in their obedience, in their readiness to perform those demands by the priest that are grounded in religion.*

The very same thing that earlier existed among the Chuvash is found in villages all across Russia: people detest the priest precisely because of his levies. Despising the priest, they are ill disposed toward his very service and look with hostility upon religion itself. Here is the origin of that profound ignorance among our Orthodox people about everything that concerns their faith. Our *Orthodox* folk, and I say this without the slightest exaggeration, do not have *the remotest conception of anything spiritual.*

Do authorities wish to correct this deplorable state of affairs? There is but one means: provide the clergy with proper material support. The consequence will be just as beneficial as it was in the Chuvash case. But it is necessary to provide this support immediately. Moral degeneration is rapidly and uncontrollably spreading through the lower strata of society; measures are urgently needed to contain and heal this ulcer, which is more fatal than the plague and cholera; within a few years it will have infected everyone and no countermeasure will work: it will be too late to correct the evil. But our bishops—who bear primary responsibility for taking care of Christ's flock—do not want to recognize these facts. I did not say "cannot" but "do not want." That is precisely the situation: they do not *want* to know.

*V. A. Sboev, *Issledovaniia ob inorodtsev Kazanskoi gubernii* [Investigations of the native peoples in Kazan province] (1856), p. 8.

Agriculture

Where the land is good and the priest tills it with his own two hands, he enjoys good support. The priest and his family are not only sated but, when God blesses him with a good harvest, he also is able to sell some of it. But look closely at such a priest: is there even the slightest hint that he is a priest? Look, here he is hauling manure: can you go up and ask for a blessing from someone steeped in nitrogen and filthy from head to toe? Or there he is, drying out the barn for grain storage: can you possibly suspect that this monster, covered with soot and draped in rags, is a servitor of the Heavenly Lord? Here he is plowing, in an old dark caftan reaching to his knees: if that is not a boorish peasant [*muzhik*], then what would you call it? But if one turns from external appearances to his internal condition, my God, what coarseness of feelings, what a lack of understanding! Wholly preoccupied with taking care of his livestock and land, he regards his primary [spiritual] role as something ancillary, which just interferes with what he considers his main occupation in life. If he is needed in the parish (especially if it is during working hours), he is distracted from his field work unwillingly, peevishly, often with curses; so he hastens to perform his religious duties in just any old way in order to get back to his own affairs. When a holiday comes, he has to perform a liturgy. Oh, what an onerous, insufferable labor this is for him; he would rather thresh the harvest in two barns than serve one liturgy. . . . He serves (he has to), but how? Inattentively, absent-mindedly. He himself is in a rush, above all seeking to get away from the church as soon as possible; the sacristans too are rushing, and read and sing as if they had laid bets on who could finish first. . . .

In a word, the farmer-priest is just a peasant, distinguished only by his literacy; otherwise he has a cast of thought, desires, aspirations, and even a way of life that are strictly peasant. After about ten years of such a life, he has so thoroughly assimilated this course and dirty way of living that it is sheer torture for him to spend two or three hours in good society. Indeed, he even finds it onerous to dress decently. For him the epitome of pleasure

[126]

is to fraternize with the peasants in noisy, wild drinking bouts; with joy he sets off to the tavern, drinking house, wherever— just so he is invited; if they do not invite him, he will unabashedly go and get senselessly drunk with a friend from his parish. . . . Here is how he spends a typical winter evening. The priest has cleaned up his livestock and is now free; true, he might engage in reflection or at least read something. But no: he did not learn how to think in the seminary. Read? That means he would have to work with his head, but it has been a long time since anything went on there. Solely occupied with physical labor, he under- stands nothing else; he finds intellectual activity simply impos- sible. And so off he goes to join the street corner gang, and passes the evening engaged in utterly vacuous and absurd gab.

Some will say: "He has voluntarily brought himself to this con- dition. He could be a farmer and still perserve the dignity of his rank." Can he? Of course, it is possible. But I would ask anyone you please to experience this life for themselves—for example, to try to think about lofty and beautiful subjects as they dig around in manure; to write something intelligent and useful in the eve- ning after a day that began at three in the morning and was passed entirely under the burning, scorching rays of the sun, so that there was not even time for lunch; to live in expectation of many more days, even weeks, of the same; to read in the barn, which is on the verge of collapsing, where sparks from the burning brand [used to provide light] threaten at any moment to set the barn on fire. Just let them try; once they have had this experience, they can tell us themselves what is possible under these conditions.

No, a farmer-priest cannot be a true priest or even vaguely resemble one. Whether from necessity or free will (it does not matter which), it is impossible to preserve one's moral purity once he becomes accustomed to unending physical filth. The priest, for the most part, lives by his spirit, that is, it is of great importance that he develop his own spiritual life. But how can he do that? When he is wholly immersed in concern about his family (that it be well fed and dressed), about his household (that it not suffer ruin from such things as lack of hay, straw, or manure); when he, like a simple day laborer, tirelessly and without rest, with all

[127]

his strength kills himself at hard labor all summer long? A life so overwhelmingly physical invariably destroys the spiritual life; that is why the farmer-priest has no thoughts or ideas of anything beyond his daily life, not even the desire to liberate himself from this dirty rut in which he is so completely mired.

There are priests who are in no condition to work themselves—from a lack of health sometimes, but usually because they do not know how to do it. That's what the seminary course in agronomy is worth! They do not even learn how to hold a plow and scythe in their hands! Consequently, they resort to other means to till the land, namely, they perform most of the work by means of so-called parish assistance, *pomoch'*.

The essence of *pomoch'* is to gather the largest possible number of parishioners for one or another kind of task. But the device is laden with so many troubles and difficulties and yields so little profit that the priest turns to it only as a last resort. Our peasant likes to be stubborn when his help is needed; as a result, the priest must plead and beseech, bow down humbly to each one, and recite both his past and future services; otherwise the peasant will not come and help. When he does come, he does so not to work but primarily to drink: *pomoch'* is inconceivable without vodka. The work begins with vodka; it continues with vodka; it ends with vodka. In this case the misfortune is twofold: if you do not give the peasant plenty to drink, he will work poorly out of annoyance; if you do, he will work poorly because he is so inebriated that he cannot work well. Hence cultivation of the soil with *pomoch'* is always wretched. But what it costs to give drink to twenty to forty people, especially peasants, who are not easily overcome by alcohol! As a result, cultivation in this manner is very expensive. Then, too, sheer chance can further increase the cost of such labor and its inconvenience. The peasants have been given food and drink; it begins to rain and the work is over for the day—and so the peasants go home. It would be only half as bad if it were just the wasted expenditures; but time has been lost in vain, and one must wait until next Sunday to get the work going again. But what does a week mean for work in the summer? One week usually spells the difference between a good harvest and failure. Thus cultivation of the land through *pomoch'* provides the priest with the worst possible support. Grain that he obtained from the soil costs him as much as it would if he bought it. Thus all his pains, toil, anxieties go virtually unrewarded. That is why most priests would have abandoned the soil long ago if only it were possible.[60]

Moreover, this method is not free from pernicious moral consequences: (1) This work always takes place on Sundays or major holidays, because the peasants would never abandon their own work on weekdays for any purpose. What example is the priest setting here? How can he demand that the peasants devote the Sabbath to God when he himself is the first to violate this commandment?[61] (2) Drunkenness is strongly developed among our lower classes; it is the principal cause of their poverty and of most crime. How can the priest protest against this ruinous contagion when he himself—with his own hands—serves liquor to his parishioners until they are drunk? (3) The peasants' vices are many and of the coarsest variety; the priest should use all his strength and means to excoriate them. But the clergy know that if they attack these vices, they will arouse the guilty against them. How can the priest take action when every unmasking and correction is sure to annoy the sinner, who will never come again to work for him? Involuntarily, at first he is tolerant and silent, but then he becomes accustomed to it, and his parishioners' coarsest vices come to seem ordinary and inescapable, something he need not speak and act against.[62] And finally, (4) one deeply rooted custom has survived among our common people to this day: namely, that the guest should not drink without his host. The priest brings the peasants something to drink, but they will not raise their cups until their host does so. If he does not drink, the guest is insulted,

60. Tolstoi's marginal comment: "Not true" (OR GBL, f. 302, k. 2, d. 12,l. 66).
61. Tolstoi: "True" (ibid., 66 ob.).
62. Such ideas were baldly affirmed in the clerical questionnaire of 1863. A priest in Vladimir diocese wrote: "The thought of parish assistance [*pomoch'*], which is in the priest's mind all summer, makes him dependent upon the people and greatly inhibits his freedom vis-à-vis the parish, for fear that an angry peasant will not help or will keep others from coming to perform this voluntary labor" (TsGIA SSSR, f. 804, op. 1, r. 3, d. 21, l. 25–25 ob.).

an offense he will not soon forget. The same thing happens during *pomoch'*: if the priest will not drink with the peasants, the whole effort is wasted; it takes but one refusal to drink and thereafter no prayers on earth will suffice to persuade the parishioners to return and work. I know well some priests who, at the time of their appointment, not only felt no inclination to drink vodka but positively detested it. What happened? Work begins; at first the parishioners looked upon the sober priest with amazement, but then they all ceased to come and help with his field labor. What was he to do? Somehow he entices two or three of them and "pays his respects," that is, gulps down a few drops; at first it seems disgusting, but the longer he does it, the more tolerable it becomes; so that gradually he is drawn into drunkenness. He begins to drink and everything is just as it should be: the peasants no longer refuse to help. What would you have him do in view of all this? If the priest were provided the main necessities of life, if he had no need of the help of peasants (who, in accordance with an age-old, ineradicable custom, are rewarded with vodka), he would not sink so low. At least he would not fall in the very first years of his service as priest. But, having withstood the first few years (the most difficult ones), especially if he did not develop a fondness for vodka at the seminary, all his life he would remain abstemious and sober. Even if he had acquired this fondness he would not develop it into a passion; he would have fewer occasions, few motives to drink. But now, a Sunday or holiday means *pomoch'*, and that means vodka. How can he abstain? On Sunday he drinks because of his dear guests; on Monday because of a headache; and with each passing year he adds still another day for some reason (in honor of one thing or another).

And so in the end the day he fails to drink is terribly onerous, and he feels called upon to satisfy this passion on every occasion. He has to hire a worker, carpenter, stovemaker, or the like to do some repairs at his home; the priest begins to bargain, but it ends in vodka. If this work has to be done at the church, the same thing happens. How well do the woodworkers, gilders, and their ilk know how to exploit this situation! Where they foresee work, they first pay two or three visits to the priest to make his acquaintance, and bring an abundance of food and drink. Then they begin negotiations with the priest, now hopelessly inebriated. You can imagine what happens; again, it ends in a two- or three-day drunken binge. Now the work is started; sobered up, the priest realizes that things are going badly, but how can one rise up against a contractor so generous with food and drink? It sometimes happens that the priest does protest; the contractor, however, has the means ready—he calms the priest down with some more alcohol. The work is at last finished and at the time of the final payment the scene that took place at the initial contracting is repeated. The result: an unforgivable amount of money has been spent; the job was done inexcusably poorly (it needs to be redone almost immediately). But what can the priest do now that he has settled his accounts with the contractor and given him a signed certificate that the work was done well and that he is fully satisfied with it? That is the end of it. Nor did such an episode even serve as a lesson for the future; the next time this kind of work is required, the very same thing is repeated. That is the terrible result of this passion, which sometimes begins with the need to satisfy the wish of parishioners coming for *pomoch'*.

Yes, land can more or less provide the priest with his means of subsistence, but at the same time it serves as a source of profound and irremediable evil. To improve the clergy's material condition, one must either completely eliminate the landholding or provide the means to cultivate it with freely hired labor. It would be best for the clergy to be completely free of it: distracted by nothing so irrelevant and disturbing as agriculture, he could focus on his real work, pastoral service; let him see that—not toil in the fields—as his main goal and primary assignment in life. If he has land and relies on free labor, he nonetheless will remain a farmer, not a priest, for he will have to be with his laborers in the field from morning to night; otherwise, things will go poorly and their wages will not yield a proper return. Even he who has not completely forgotten his mission will still be just half farmer and half priest; that is, he will not do anything truly substantial

[131]

or long-lasting either for himself in the fields or for his parish-ioners in the church. Land was absolutely necessary for the priest in earlier centuries, when there were neither district church schools nor seminaries. Then the priest had, say, two or three sons— healthy, strapping fellows; what else should they do when they live at home if not plow together with their father, who had also grown up from childhood working in the fields? So they plowed, sowed, threshed, etc.; all this was both profitable and convenient for priests then, because they did everything with their own hands. Now, however, different demands are made upon their children; you would think that they could not possibly fail to change the clergy's living condition! But no! On the one hand, they have condemned him to vegetate, as his grandfathers and forefathers (back to St. Vladimir's time) vegetated.* On the other hand, they want him to satisfy modern demands, to be a priest not merely in name but also in reality. It is a perverse logic, possible only in Orthodox Rus'!

THE PRIEST, SOCIETY, AND THE CHURCH

Parishioners

The foregoing already gives some idea of the rural priest's rela-tionship with his parishioners. As a pastor he should have some influence over his parishioners; indeed, that influence should be total, unlimited, and uninhibited. In fact, however, it is just the other way around: wholly dependent on his parishioners for sustenance, the priest is subjected to *their* influence. Hence it is not the parishioner who absorbs something good from the priest, but the priest who absorbs the bad habits and evil tendencies of his parishioners. In general, the priest, in his relationship with

---

*Indeed, the clergy were rather more intelligently organized under Prince Vladimir [980–1015] than now. At least part, if not all, of them were supported by a tithe [*desiatina*]. But now there is nothing reliable or secure. It would be nice to know what miscreant laid the foundations for the present order in the clergy!

parishioners, finds himself in the most bitter, most pathetic, most absurd condition. His position is still more intolerable if there is a noble landowner in the parish, and it is the height of misfortune if there are several landowners.

Those unfamiliar with the way of life of gentry squires who permanently reside on their estates could not possibly believe it if you described accurately their material condition and manner of existence. Indeed, it is difficult to believe, so remote is it from the name they bear, "noble." We shall not speak of squires who are single or live apart from their wives, of whom there are a number in each district; their entire life can be summarized in a few words—the most profound depravity, which is shameless and concealed from no one, which reaches *ne plus ultra* development, even to the point where there is not a single girl on the entire estate who has not been defiled, not a single young woman who has not been shamed, not a single family where the landlord has not introduced his fatal contagion [syphilis].

But even landlords with families represent something so incomprehensible that it is hard to decide what class one should assign them to. In name they are "noble"; on that basis they regard themselves as a privileged class, given the right to live and act as they see fit, not inhibited by anyone or anything; every squire, even if he has just twenty to thirty male serfs, regards himself as an aristocrat, to whom all must subordinate themselves, whom all must revere. In short, to see the more horrendous vanity, expressed in the most petty trifles and shrouded in the most absurd form, you have to see a noble landlord living on his estate. To judge by external appearances, they are educated folk; in every home you will hear a French phrase, see a piano, find artists dancing, etc.

But look more deeply, study the internal life of these landlords: you'll be astounded, amazed, horrified by the vapidity and banality of their entire life. The men have cards, wine, dogs; the women have cards, gossip, intrigues—it is on these things that they spend their entire lives. Only in one out of ten homes will you find any kind of library. But do not ask for anything intelligent and serious here: these libraries are composed of the abominations

[133]

of the French school, and are the property and pleasure of young noble girls, who cannot yet participate in the pleasures of their father and mother.

Spend a few consecutive evenings with such a family. Perhaps the first time you will be intrigued by such banter (oh, how they all excel at that!) about the nobleman's dogs, about the misdeeds of the constable or marshal of the nobility, about political affairs (what else? each regards himself as a most profound statesman, counts all the government's mistakes on his fingers, and even lets it be known that everything would be just marvelous if they would only turn to him for advice). The next evening they will invite you to play cards; if you refuse, then it will be the same talk as yesterday; on the third more of the same; and so on, ad infinitum. It would do you no good to try to steer the conversation to ideas that are provocative, important, and engaging; they simply cannot comprehend such things and turn them aside with some banal witticism. Such are the great majority of our rural squires. There are exceptions, but as a proportion of the great majority, these exceptions are no more than one in a hundred. Besides the squire's vacuity, see how he regards his serfs and how he treats them—like workhorses, to whom he is absolutely indifferent. He regards his borzoi as incomparably higher and more important to him than any peasant; he takes care to see that the borzois are fed, but as for the peasants, he has only one concern—to squeeze out of them sweat, blood, and all their strength. . . . If you add the fact that it is a rare landlord who, in addition to his real wife and family, does not have a wife and family somewhere in the servants' quarters or in the washhouse (or some such place), then you have a good idea of what these people are like.

What must be the position of a priest who has such a treasure in his parish? What is he to do, as a priest, as a pastor of souls? Act according to the Apostles: forbid, beseech, demand at suitable and unsuitable times? Lord save us and have mercy on our souls! Just let a priest even dare hint to a landlord about disorders in his life, which is a poor example for his servants, his serfs, and that will be the end for the priest. The landlord himself will no longer receive him, and will forbid his peasants to do so. This happens often, for even lesser cause—if a priest refuses to administer marriage rites because of close kinship or against the will of the groom and bride, or to bury without a judicial inquest someone whom the master had whipped to death, etc. In such cases the priest is even left without subsistence.

Moreover, the landlord will complain to the bishop, describing the priest as he pleases. In our bishops' view, the landlord is always in the right, the priest always in the wrong; no formal investigation is even needed. How else could they decide such cases? During visitations in the diocese the bishop finds a sumptuous lunch, bountiful dinner, music and everything else at the squire's house; what can you get out of a poor priest, who lives in a stuffy, smoky hut and who is almost always content with meatless cabbage soup, horseradish, and other equally antimonastic substances? Why indeed sit at a priest's table and hear the deafening music of children? The noble's girls will provide the bishop with pillows and rugs, made by themselves (the girls always work), jam, and everything else necessary for the life of an ascetic. But what can a priest's wife give? At most, a piece of unbleached linen! Which offers the greatest advantage?

As a result, here is the way things work. The squire goes to the bishop to complain; apprised of this, the priest goes to present his side of the case. The squire, even if he is the worst of his kind, goes directly to the bishop's drawing room; the priest, even if he is the model of exemplary living, is kept in the unheated vestibule, even if it is 30 degrees below zero. The squire is there two or three hours; with unimaginable obsequiousness the bishop hears him out, promises to satisfy his demands, and gives his word— before he has even heard the priest's side—to transfer him to some remote place, to the worst possible village.

The priest is at last admitted to see the bishop, and by now he is chilled to the bone and worn out from the long wait (indeed, more dead than alive from exhaustion). Then this successor to the Apostles shows the priest no glimmer of kindness, but at the first moment strikes him down with rude, severe, threatening words: "What have you done out there, you fool?" After such a

[135]

welcome, the priest's entire organism begins to tremble; his vision grows dark; his ideas become tangled; his tongue goes numb. So, instead of giving a real explanation, he mumbles something. "And you even took it into your head to come here and defend yourself!" the bishop screams at him and, without having heard clearly what the priest said, shouts: "Get out of here!" So, without trial and investigation, solely on the basis of a verbal denunciation, solely because of the bishop's vast and unlimited power over the clergy, the priest is driven from his village in disgrace, where he was settled and established; he is now dispatched to some destitute parish to languish in poverty until the end of his days. The bishop who acted in this manner demonstrates that he is a person who fully understands the rules of contemporary life: "Pay no heed to what is just; do whatever is asked by those who can pay; despise and oppress those who cannot reward you with anything (never mind whether they are in the right or not). . . ." The noble landlords are in raptures over such a bishop, give him sumptuous dinners, and practically carry him about in their arms. What could be better than that? Moreover, landlords scream loudly and their voices can easily carry all the way to St. Petersburg. . . . But the priest's? If one shows him mercy, even justice, who besides God will hear his blessing? Just let him, the downtrodden, groan, cry profusely, perish prematurely, leaving his family in utter want— what is so terrible about that? He is a person too insignificant to worry about!! . . . .

As a result, the priest, fearing ruin (not so much for himself as for his family), remains silent before the most insolent, most dishonorable, most disgraceful escapades of the squires. In his presence, people in gentry homes utter insults against everything sacred (the most ordinary topic of conversation at the dinner table of landlords, especially when a priest happens to be present), malevolently ridicule the entire clerical estate (monks catch it even worse than priests), and insolently curse ecclesiastical institutions. At first he is outraged to the depths of his soul, shudders with a violent convulsion, but does not dare make the bold, outspoken protest that a priest should. The longer he hears such attacks, the more coolly he reacts; in the end he has become so

[136]

inured to this sort of thing that he himself contributes an anecdote. . . .

An unmarried servant girl has given birth. The priest would like to chastise her for debauchery, and indeed the squire's wife asks him to do so, saying that life has become impossible—all the girls have become so corrupted. But how can the priest chastise her? What if she is under the master's special protection? So he holds his tongue. Or, who knows, he may even have a drink of vodka and offer congratulations on the successful birth. . . . Now the master orders his best peasant to marry a girl who has already given birth to two or three illegitimate children. It is impossible for the peasant to refuse the slut (who almost always became that way involuntarily) before the master: you would be flogged so hard that you would remember it for a month to come, and still have to take the girl anyway. So the peasant beseeches the priest not to perform the marriage. What a hopeless supplication that is! The priest knows perfectly well all the tragic consequences of such a marriage, but how can he violate the squire's will? . . . And so he performs the marriage.

That is the way it always is. In the end he is no priest, but a mere lackey, just wearing a different costume. . . . On the other hand, the squire treats him well, receives him affectionately, and makes him a participant in his orgies. Never mind if the priest gets drunk and goes strolling about in the nude. That is nothing at all! They will all laugh about it and the next day help him feel better.

There is only one thing that they will not forgive: if he dares to be a true priest. But, given his relationship with the landlord, can he be a true pastor for his peasant parishioners? No. Right there, before your eyes, is the greatest evil, the most terrible evil, against which the priest does not dare to rebel: to persecute evil and vice in the peasant would mean that the priest must contradict himself too flagrantly. As a result, all his labor goes for nought. Then, too, the peasant has his own logic for everything; to all the priest's arguments they give the same answer: "It is true we are doing wrong, and we shall be punished for it in this life and endure Hell in the next. But the master does still worse, and what is the result? Here he is living in paradise and you promised him paradise in the next life too. . . . But if Hell is really the reward for such things, well, why do you not tell the master to desist from his misdeeds, why do you not threaten him with Hell like the rest of us sinners? The master can do this, but we cannot. Well, we have had enough. You just make fools of us and implant fear in us—most likely in compliance with the master's orders. . . ." How can a priest reply to that? He has no choice but to remain silent and weep over his terrible plight. If he is still conscious of his duties, his plight is truly terrifying: what will he hear at the Final Judgment after such a pastorship? Or he can go to the squire and smother the last spark of conscience in orgies.

If the parish has two, three, or more squires (sometimes there are up to ten landlords, who are of course petty serf owners, but whose pretensions are not a whit smaller than those of the magnates), then his life—even if he is totally obsequious—is intolerable torment. It is practically unheard of for neighboring landowners to live amicably among themselves. They are all acquainted and often visit each other; that, however, does not prevent them from slandering and blackening one another's reputation (to be sure, behind their neighbor's back). Petty, absurdly banal pride forces them to watch carefully that no one show greater respect to a neighbor than themselves. Should that happen, woe to the guilty party! "What! He did such-and-such for N., but not for us? Are we really worse that N.? But here is what N. has done." (Here follows a list of everything bad in N.) "Well, anyone who shows undue respect to N. is no better than himself—'like attracts like,' and so on. We'll show him what it means to scorn us! We won't receive him, we won't admit him to our house! No, we'll admit him, but then give it to him good, and then refuse to receive him again," etc., etc.

What is the priest to do in a parish like that? If he hits it off well with one nobleman and plays up to another, he arouses the animosity of all the rest. It is impossible to pander to them all, given the very nature of his service. One squire, for instance, demands that the liturgy begin at eight o'clock, another at ten. Or when the holidays come, the priest must go around to all the houses and sing a prayer service: if he goes first to N., all the others are mortally offended. "Why didn't you come to us first?" they ask, and refuse to receive the priest. Even if they do receive him, they give him a tongue-lashing that he will not soon forget. Sometimes they even complain to the bishop. . . . So here is the kind of amusement found in the very same parish: one squire cannot find words enough to praise the priest, while the others denounce him. The bishop, naturally, decides in favor not of the one who is in the right but of the one who is wealthy. Thus the priest is saved if the more affluent are on his side; he is done for if the affluent are against him, even if ten petty squires and all the peasants support the priest.

A priest has greater freedom to act in a parish where the parishioners are all state peasants and there are no squires. Yet here, too, as I noted earlier, the priest is inevitably subject to the influence of parishioners and cannot be a true pastor. In addition, there is a further circumstance that at present has a ruinous effect on the priest. Namely, to this day our common people still observe that ideal of hospitality which in ancient times distinguished our forefathers. In itself ideal, this custom is nevertheless manifested among our peasants too coarsely, until it becomes intolerable importunity. Say it is a holiday like Easter, and the priest conducts an icon procession. Each house offers hospitality, that is, vodka and something to eat. The prayer sung, they ask the priest to "pay his respects" to the master of the house: that is, to drink vodka and have something to eat. If the priest refuses, everyone in the family falls to his knees and will not rise until the priest has had a drink. This, too, does not work: the priest implores his hosts to rise and leaves without drinking. The host is terribly offended, of course; fuming with indignation, he gives the priest something for the prayer but does not accompany him to the next house.* Afterward, if the priest should dare approach the peasant about some need, it would just evoke a rude refusal—"You didn't

*But this is an expression of the greatest dissatisfaction. Ordinarily, the family escorts the priest from their house to the gates of the next house, where another family is waiting. So it goes through the whole village. When everything is over, the most elderly and respected of the crowd escort the priest to the outskirts of the village. Lord, even when the clergy is in such a state, the people display such zeal toward it! What would things be like if every pastor were a true pastor!

[139]

pay respects to me, and, well, I'm not your servant." That is the way it was in one house, then a second, then a third, and so on.[63] If the priest accepts the vodka, by the time he has gone through the whole village even the most cautious, sturdiest soul hardly has the strength to perform his duty. A priest who is less cautious or whose constitution is weaker simply passes out. And what scandals do not occur when the priest is in such a condition!

Obviously, all this is simply abominable, terrible. But I would ask anyone you please to put himself in the priest's shoes and tell us how *he* would act. Would he endure everything, the requests and anger, and not begin to drink in one of those houses? If he held out, then the entire parish would be furious with him. The time comes for field work, and not a single peasant will come to help. What can he do now? With his own two hands he himself can do but little. He could hire some laborers, but with what? It was just Easter; the peasant, if he is satisfied with the priest, will undoubtedly give him the customary gifts; if he is dissatisfied, however, he will toss him some petty sum and will turn deaf ears to entreaties or requests for more. Thus the sum collected at Easter was a mere trifle, and that has already gone to pay for household expenses, to send the son to the seminary, and the like. I ask you: what is the priest to do? And what would the deacon and sacristans say after receiving these niggardly contributions (how they speak and act in such cases I shall describe later)? If the priest had other, more reliable means, if he were not bound to engage in agriculture, it would be quite another thing. The parishioners' indignation would not be so terrible for him, for it would not lead to such losses, from which he suffers such terrible destitution. Was he given nothing or too little for the prayer service? What is so terrible about that? He is provided for and poverty does not loom over him like a threatening specter. Ten years of patience, and the peasants would become accustomed to see the priest as someone sober and abstemious, and would cease to torment him with insistent requests that he drink too. And in the clergy's present condition, truly bitter and ruinous, some bishops dare to proclaim that salaries are not needed! It is clear that they are well

63. Tolstoi's marginal comment: "Not so!" (OR GBL, f. 302, k. 2, d. 12, l. 76).

acquainted with the life of rural priests, that they have inquired closely into their needs and way of life! Honor and glory to such bishops, such "benefactors" of the clergy!

I would also like to add a few general comments here about parish processions. If they ever really decide to transform the clergy, then one of the most essential measures must be a complete ban on these processions. What are they for? If it is necessary to give a prayer service, then do it in the church. By contrast, see what happens in the village: drunken clergy give services; drunken clergy pray. What kind of prayer is that? Indeed, these processions are not something religious, but just a custom, established over the centuries, with the sole purpose of collecting money. Abolish this custom and you will in fact eliminate half the drunkenness and disorders in the clergy. The only thing that can be permitted is an icon procession once a year, but it must strictly observe the following conditions: each hamlet is to hold a separate procession, after first preparing themselves by fasting; on the day of the procession the priest is to sing a liturgy in the presence of the whole village, to depart immediately from the church with the icons, and to go throughout the entire village without removing his vestments; afterward (without stopping for one minute in the village) he is to return again to the church with the icons. Now that would be wonderful, a truly religious affair; it would therefore be sacred and help save souls. Otherwise, the girls and women will continue to drag the icons from one village to the next at Easter; they shout and squabble; afterward they pull the priest and his staff along in a cart. Is all this not a disgrace for the church? In the end, is this not the best possible means to kill any interest in religion?

Deacons and Sacristans

It is an amazing, incomprehensible, utterly inexplicable phenomenon in our church: the priest's aides—the rest of the parish staff—belong to the clerical estate! Deacons and unordained sacristans [*diachki, ponomari*] are part of the clergy! Actually deemed to form part of the clergy!

[141]

What kind of people are they? I shall first explain, if only briefly, their genealogy.

A pupil at the seminary or elementary district school has completely gone to seed: he is a drunkard, troublemaker, thief—in a word, so bad that he is considered intolerable even in our ecclesiastical schools, and so they expel him. Once expelled, for two or three years he loafs about aimlessly, completely free to perfect his various abilities. Then a sacristan's position somewhere falls vacant; he petitions for the post and obtains it. Thus, rather than expel him entirely from the clerical estate, rather than free the estate of this contagion, rather than dispatch him to the army as a military conscript (as the strictest justice requires), they make him a member of the clergy, a servitor of the church, admittedly a lesser servitor, but all the same a servitor of the church! . . . There are no exceptions here, because our educational institutions expel only incorrigible rogues; those who are untalented, even lazy, but who behave well are dragged from class to class until they complete the course of studies. So what kind of servitor of the church must he invariably be?

He was a perfect scoundrel at the district school, despite the thick rod applied by teachers fond of merciless punishment. If such punishment could not reform him, then what good can one expect from him in a position where he enjoys complete liberty and has a certain amount of means? It is impossible to expect anything good here, and as a rule you will not in fact find much. The lower servitors in the village (and urban ones as well), without the slightest exaggeration, can only be called a shame and a disgrace not only to their office but to all mankind. Incidentally, I am including the deacon as part of the lower servitors, since by background (he often comes from the ranks of expelled pupils), spirit, proclivities, and aspirations he is largely in league with the sacristans. These lesser servitors are as repugnant and base as anything that can appear in man. Any peasant is superior: he may be boorish, cruel, stubborn; yet he is hard-working, respectful toward his superiors, in his own way honest, and has some notion of shame and conscience; he gives himself up to vulgar vices, but he understands that he is acting badly and rarely falls to the point where he has lost all trace of humanity and sinks to the level of animals. The priest's aides, the deacon and sacristans, do not have even the slightest trace of all this! They are unimaginably lazy, unscrupulous, insolent, and lack the slighest awareness of their evil! In a word, these are animals, greedy, gluttonous, rapacious—slyly plotting more evil and ruinous frauds, rejoicing over the ruin of others, especially their superiors. . . .[64] And this creature belongs to the clerical estate!! He is also given the right to join the priest in all his activities, both in the parish and in the church, so that together with the priest he is to certify all parish records and church documents; he is supposed to oversee the income and expenditure of parish funds, etc., etc. Could one think of a more absurd order for the parish clergy?

It is with such people that the priest must live and work! With their help he must perform sacred liturgies and satisfy all the parish's needs! What must the priest's position be? I shall offer some examples to show the state of affairs.

It sometimes happens that the priest, at the outset of his service, would like to improve one thing or another, to perform liturgies more reverently, to conduct prayer services in the parish in a more seemly fashion. The sacristans and especially the deacon, however, always rise to oppose changes, and do so openly and impudently. Neither rational argument nor fear of punishment has any effect on them. Nor are complaints to ecclesiastical authorities of any help; a denunciation sent to the bishop, if it does not totally ruin the priest, will at least expose him to the torment of investigations (later I shall discuss how and why). The priest struggles and struggles, and then abandons the whole attempt.

To cite another example, the priest is sometimes not yet mired in the quicksand of life and for a time withstands all the peasants' efforts to have him drink vodka, as I described earlier. And for this he is deprived of just compensation for performing prayer services. Perhaps some priests would somehow endure this

---

64. The low professional and moral standards of sacristans, as well as their educational level, were indeed a source of continuing concern to the bishops. For details and references, see Freeze, *Parish Clergy*, pp. 158–160.

[143]

adversity, but they encounter a terrible revolt by the deacon and sacristans. At the very first houses in the village these people always manage to get insanely drunk; and in that condition what do such people not permit themselves? Consequently, they shower the priest with every loathsome curse, every disgraceful vulgarity imaginable. It often reaches the point where the priest has to save himself by fleeing from his enraged fellow servitors. Once they have slept it off, do they admit their guilt? Nothing of the sort. In fact, they do not sleep off the intoxication and sober up in the course of the entire holidays: at midnight, at noon, they are in the same condition, because every house has vodka in honor of the holiday. Thus to return with them to the parish would mean that the priest must risk his own health; however drunk they may be, they have not forgotten yesterday's scandalous episode and will try to start it again today. So the priest puts off the icon procession until the very end of the holiday. Now, at last, their insanity has somewhat abated, and the priest orders them to set off for the parish.

"We'll go," they reply, "if the priest receives full payment for the prayer service. Otherwise, we'll stay right here."

And they will not go, no matter what the priest does. It is impossible for him to go alone, so he too stays home. Thus passes one holiday, then another. The parishioners are beside themselves with rage; the other members of the clerical staff egg them on and get the loudmouths drunk; and soon a terrible storm breaks over the priest's head! It does him no good to try to explain what this is all about; they do not listen to him and drown out all his attempts to explain with shouts: "You yourself are terribly arrogant. Our deacon and sacristans are good people: they drink in our homes and treat us to the same in theirs. But you respect nothing. So we shall go to the bishop and complain," etc., etc. Who could enjoy listening to all this? There is but one means to calm the storm: the priest must satisfy his staff's and the parishioners' demand that he too drink. So the unfortunate priest gives in. Sitting solemnly at one table alongside his vile staff members, he takes turns at the bottle with them. . . . The deacon and sacristans exult in triumph, content that they have humiliated the

[144]

priest; sitting on the very same bench, partaking of the same food and drink, they already consider themselves his equal. Now he had better not dare to make any critical remarks, to demand what is expected of them: to one word of truth they will reply with a hundred of abuse. The abstemious, sober priest was a threat to them; now there is nothing to fear. Curse, carry on like a madman, play every conceivable prank, and he will not dare complain to the bishop: he was there himself. . . .

My God, my God! If one-millionth of all the holiday scandals were brought to light, what an eternally indelible stain would cover the church!!! Say the priest is performing a prayer service; behind him the deacon is playing on the harmonica, the sacristans are dancing, and the entire family of the peasant is roaring with laughter. Or the priest is blessing the water; and right there, outside the door, the deacon is in his surplice and pestering some woman, who fights him off with a curse and a shout. Or the priest is entering a home, but has to inquire where the deacon and sacristan have gone to. After a long wait they bring him the deacon, who has been pulled from some ditch, covered with filth, his hands tied with his own orarion [the shoulder ribbon of his surplice], because he tried to fight when they came for him. As for the sacristans, they say that it is impossible to bring them in because they behaved even worse and are tied up to some post. These and similar phenomena are not even the most striking and outrageous; it is sometimes worse—oh, how terrible it can be!

Here is another example of what happens in every parish, without exception, when the priest has to officiate at a wedding. First of all, the parishioner must announce his intention to the priest and staff three weeks in advance; in other words, he must bring vodka and host them all until they are full of food and drink. Then, throughout the entire period before the wedding, the deacon and sacristans seize every opportunity to visit this peasant, often with their wives, and each time the peasant must satisfy their wants—that is, ply them with drink until they drop unconscious. On the eve of the wedding the peasant must appear before all the clergy with bread and salt, with money for the wedding, and with the inevitable vodka. Though given drink, the clergy

[145]

nevertheless do not go easy on the peasant and always fix a pretty sum for the wedding. The peasant bargains, stalks out, returns, adds a half-ruble, a ruble, two rubles. No, they still will not give in; he gives them something more to drink, gets drunk himself, and somehow they settle the question. The peasants and wedding train arrive; the priest is in the church, but the deacon and sacristan are nowhere in sight. The peasants go after them, taking vodka, beer, meat pies; if the food and drink before the wedding were sufficient—that is, if the peasant was sufficiently tolerant and wealthy so that he gave them all they wanted to drink—then, after putting up some last resistance, they come to the church. If all that seemed too little, then it is no easy task to get them to come to the church. The wedding party stands around for an hour or two, sometimes from eleven in the morning until late at night; but all that is of no concern to the deacon and sacristans. One might ask what the priest does in such circumstances: as things stand now, there is nothing he can do. He gives them orders, but they do not obey; he himself often goes around to their houses, but to no effect. Finally the peasants ask them what it is they want. "Look here," they reply, "you didn't want to host us properly, so now for that you must give us ten (or at least five) pints of vodka. Otherwise, we won't go, and you can stand around here all week if you like." There is nothing to be done: the peasants send for the vodka or give them money. Satisfied, half dead [from drink], they finally appear at the church. What often happens next can be related to you by every peasant in Moscow, Iaroslavl, Tver, and Vladimir provinces.

How can this evil be eliminated? There is but one way: to make a radical transformation in the structure of the lesser church servitors, so that the church and parish have only one person who is officially appointed and confirmed—the priest. He should bear complete and sole responsibility for the administration of all affairs in the church and parish, without the slightest meddling by other people. Only if he acts independently, uninhibited by anyone or anything, can he bring improvements and order to church services, which at present are so perverted and denigrated. Without

[146]

this reform, all the reforms and improvements in the living conditions and work of the rural priest are pointless. Even if the priest is intelligent, honest, and God-fearing—that is, even if he is a true pastor—so long as the existing structure of the parish clergy exists he is not in a position to do anything serious. Every necessary innovation he makes will encounter arguments and altercations with the staff, followed by the inevitable feuds, animosity, and litigation. Patience is of no help here; these people, corrupted to the *n*th degree, are so insolent and obstinate that it is difficult to imagine what they are like. The struggle between honesty and the most brazen dishonesty, between knowledge and the most abysmal ignorance, between piety and the most vulgar impiety—that struggle is too unequal. For the sacristans have thousands of tricks, thousands of ruses to exculpate themselves before human judgment and to ruin the priest; the latter can act in only one way, which is sure to win him a place in heaven but is of dubious value in obtaining justice from the bishop.

Moreover, such struggles fill the soul with indignation: how can the priest offer a sacrifice at the altar when his soul is filled with indignation, his soul knows no peace? Oh, how often, between matins and mass, the deacon and sacristans deliberately try to sting, to wound, to annoy the priest; though he maintains his apparent equanimity, the priest performs the liturgy with a tormented soul, standing before the altar with the very same deacon who only this very minute was tormenting him! How often the sacristan, when handing the censers to the priest, right there says something rude to him. How often he is drunk, committing one or another outrage, laughing, or fuming in anger in the choir and even at the altar—all during the liturgy itself!

"To eliminate all this," some will say, "stern measures are needed."

No, no kind of severity, even of the harshest sort, will help. Let us suppose that they punish two, three, or ten people; thousands of others will still remain, and in fact those punished will be replaced by the very same kind of miscreants. After all, they mete out punishment—though quite rarely—even now; however,

[147]

that does not make the slightest impression. Furthermore, the more hardened and evil the person and the more inventive his dastardly deeds, the more cunning he is in concealing them. Hence such a person, if confronted by extreme strictness, will just be more cautious. That is, he will not torment the priest within ear-shot of outsiders, but will seek opportunities to do it when they are alone. And they do not have to seek far—such opportunities abound. To cite one example, the deacon and sacristan had cruelly insulted the priest at the altar; the priest could not endure the insult and dispatched a denunciation to the bishop. An investigation is launched: who heard or saw anything? No one. The rest of the staff swears by all that is holy (what does it mean for such people to take such an oath?) that nothing of the sort happened; the culprit himself complains to the bishop that the priest has slandered him. What is the outcome? They believe the three lower-ranking clerics more than the single priest, who is then put on trial before an ecclesiastical court for making a false denunciation.

Of the countless cases one could recount, the following gives a particularly good understanding of the priest's relationship with the sacristans. About fifteen years ago, one of the poorest churches of N. diocese had a priest who led an impeccable life. Demanding of himself, he was also strict toward the deacon and sacristans; that is, he insisted that they behave as they were supposed to. For that reason the priest seemed intolerable, and they tried every possible means to ruin him. But directly and openly they could do nothing, for his behavior was beyond reproach. So they sent the local ecclesiastical superintendent a denunciation filled with the most preposterous slander. The superintendent was typical of men in his position—that is, he was interested only in money. Because of the poverty of the parish and the priest's large family (he had nine children), he could not quench the superintendent's thirst for more and more money. The superintendent, consequently, became terribly angry with him. But the sacristans' slander was not by itself sufficient grounds to challenge the priest. True, he transmitted it all, with his own embellishments, to the bishop, and succeeded in arousing the prelate's ire against the priest. Still, all this was just words, not something substantive.

[148]

Finally, the superintendent told the sacristans and deacon that if they could just find an opportunity to ensnare the priest for something real, he would do the rest.

And here is the trick they came up with. They chose Good Friday to do it: what a satanic idea—the more lofty the day, the less circumspect the priest will be, since he is absorbed in his work, and will be less likely to suspect that they would dare to conspire for his ruin on such a holy day!! The priest comes to read the canonical hours;[65] the deacon and sacristans are standing at the altar. The priest begins the hours, but the sacristan [who is supposed to read] neither speaks nor moves. The priest orders him to read, but the sacristan just curses. The priest asks him to leave; the sacristan only curses still more strongly and fills the church with his shouts. The priest goes and reads himself, but the sacristan's voice drowns him out with curses. What choice did the priest have? Harassed and upset to the highest degree, he cast down his vestments and left the church. All day the priest wept bitterly; however, he did not want to initiate a suit during these holy days, and so did nothing. But the sacristan immediately set off for the superintendent with a denunciation that the priest had reviled him, even struck him at the altar, and in the midst of the service had cast off his chasuble and gone home. The same day the superintendent appeared before the bishop with this denunciation.

However ill disposed the bishop might be toward the priest, he did urge the superintendent to reconcile the priest and his staff, but that came to nothing and the bishop ordered a formal investigation. The priest, whose soul and conscience are pure, tells everything just as it happened. But no one was there to corroborate his words; the sole witnesses—the deacon and second sacristan—were co-conspirators in the whole scheme and under oath corroborate the first sacristan's denunciation. The result was

---

65. The various "hours" [*chasy*] recalled episodes during Christ's last day on earth: his judgment by Pilate and his sentence to death (the first hour), the descent of the Holy Spirit to the Apostles (third hour), the crucifixion (the sixth hour), Christ's death (the ninth hour). See P. Alekseev, *Tserkovnyi slovar'*, 5 vols. (St. Petersburg, 1818), 5:125.

[149]

this resolution by the bishop: "The priest himself has admitted that he left the church before finishing the service. As punishment for that, and in accordance with such-and-such an article in the law, he is deprived of his position and demoted to serve in the rank of sacristan for a term of six months." The chief culprit in all this, the sacristan, did not receive the slightest punishment. Some counseled the priest to petition the Holy Synod; but how can he complain, when the Lord was the sole witness? Indeed, if the priest were rich, he would have been exonerated without the Synod's help anyway; but a poor priest not only has no money to pay for the stamped paper [required for such appeals], but was not even able to prepare the barest essentials for Easter. Heavenly Father, what did he and all his family not have to endure during the six-month demotion and the year that passed before he found another position! . . . That they all did not die of starvation was due to one of his former parishioners, who remembered some service the priest had rendered and each week brought him a pood [36 pounds] of rye flour. That was how these poor people ate for a year and a half; even then, with just rye bread and water to live on, their bellies were hardly full. . . .

Such things are quite routine and will go on forever if the deacon and sacristans retain their present relationship to the priest. Salaries will not improve things; these people are simply incorrigible. If salaries are granted, there will still be the same envy (why, they will ask, does the priest receive more money and veneration?) and the same drunkenness (indeed, drunkenness will increase because their means will be greater). In short, everything will be a thousand times worse, the priest's life will be still more unbearable, disgraceful incidents will be still more numerous, and the entire clerical estate will sink still lower.

No, that is not the way to reorder the parish clergy if one wants the church to flourish and priestly service fully to achieve its goal. Deacons must be completely eliminated in the villages (and also in all the provincial towns, except in the cathedrals); sacristans should not belong to the clerical estate and should be excluded from it completely.

[150]

Description of the Clergy in Rural Russia

Let's begin with the deacons. What are they for? Of what use are they? What do Orthodoxy and Orthodox believers need them for? There is not the slightest need for deacons! Everything in the church and parish can be handled perfectly well without them. Morever, the evil and harm they do are endless. Of their misdeeds only the first thousand ever come to the bishop's attention; for various reasons they always emerge unscathed from all the other things they perpetrate. Journey across Russia from one end to the other, ask any priest in this entire expanse, and each—before God and conscience—will confirm that this is absolutely true. The deacon is forever slandering the sacristans before the priest, the priest before the sacristans; he is constantly encouraging sacristans and even parishioners to feel indignant and to rebel against the priest; he is forever sowing discord and provoking disputes. Yet the priest must nevertheless perform divine services together with him! The situation is quite different for episcopal services, monasteries, and cathedrals, and also for the cities and larger parishes; there, for the sake of a more solemn service, the deacons can be retained. There, under the jurisdiction of the bishop or archimandrite, who holds unbounded authority over them, they are not dangerous. But in the villages they must be eliminated as a most evil pestilence, infecting and destroying everything.

Sacristans should not be appointed to the church as they now are, but should be freely hired—as, for example, the church watchman is now. A pupil who is expelled from the school or seminary as worthless has absolutely no claim to be a regular part of the church. Let him be attached to the peasantry or townspeople and, if capable, be employed as a sacristan. If he is bad, corrupt, or a drunkard, the priest can dismiss him and hire someone else. In fact, however, he will be afraid to be bad, knowing that he will be deprived of his means of subsistence if he loses his position. He will be punctilious in performing his duties, courteous, respectful toward the priest, attentive to service, and not dare to quaff the parishioners' vodka so brazenly. In a word, only then will he be a sacristan, the kind that he should be, the kind that is described in the sacristan's installation charter. And how

[151]

great will be still other wonderful consequences of such a reform! District boards and consistories are now inundated with disputes and lawsuits among all the members of the parish staff; after this reform, there will be no trace of these things. Hence half the clerks can be eliminated, and those who remain will have nothing to do. The bishops themselves will not have to waste their time investigating and resolving these cases—sordid, shameful, outrageous cases that bishops, as monks, should not even have any knowledge of.

Thus, regardless of any other improvements that may be made in the clergy, this measure is necessary and must be implemented immediately—that is, deacons in village parishes should be eliminated and sacristans should become hired employees. I guarantee by all that is sacred that only this reform will once and for all eliminate the majority of abuses in rural parishes and that some abuses can be eliminated by this measure alone.

I foresee many objections to this measure: it could not be otherwise. Every innovation generates critics and criticism; the more beneficial the innovation is, the more ruthless is the opposition from those accustomed to the old order and the more determined they are to keep things as they are for their personal advantage. This reform, for example, will be opposed by all superintendents, all district boards, all consistories: their avarice could hope for nothing better than the present order. Thus the present conflicts bring the consistory secretaries tens of thousands in annual income; after the reform they would have to be satisfied with just their salaries—how could they not oppose the reform with all their strength? Hence their objections carry no weight: such people cannot objectively judge the matter because of their quite understandable prejudice and their sympathy toward such dishonorable people as the sacristans and deacons. But I can say categorically that all their remonstrances will be repeated by people who are completely ignorant of the life and conditions of the rural clergy. Here, however, nothing need be said: objections by someone ignorant of the matter at hand are simply meaningless. I am convinced that anyone who has experienced life with the deacons and sacristans, who has studied all aspects of their behavior, who

[152]

sincerely wishes the church well, who wants pastoral service to attain its goal, will agree with me and recommend precisely the reform proposed here as the only solution.

Some people will interject: "It is impossible to do this all of a sudden: what are we to do with all the present sacristans?"

What are we to do with them? There is no problem here: they would remain just where they are, in the present numbers, and whoever wants a sacristan's position can have it. But if some incorrigible miscreant cannot find any position, that is no great tragedy and nothing to be sorry about. On the contrary, we should rejoice that we have rid ourselves of one more ulcerous sore. The whole point is that such a measure will cause each sacristan to have second thoughts about his conduct and, against his will and wish, to correct himself and change from an animal into a human being. What is so bad about that? That alone would be sufficient cause to adopt this reform. Just let it be adopted, even if against the sacristans' will and wishes; if they are good, however, that will be accepted everywhere and with jubilation. Fear of losing one's position will be the best curb against all that is bad, and it is now the sole means to save them from their own fatal inclinations and tendencies. But in order to see that their correction is complete, and not just affected to obtain a position, and in order to strengthen them on the path of righteousness, one should also give them the right to enjoy their present privileges so long as they serve the church. If, however, they lose their position and fail to find a new one within a year's time, they forfeit all these rights. To avoid disorders in hiring and settling accounts with them, authorities should set them a specific salary once and for all, with the strict requirement that it be given out in full and without interruption. The sacristan's salary should be fixed in accordance with the number of parishioners, between 50 and 75 rubles. Because they have much free time, and so that it not be wasted and idleness lead to sloth, grant them the land that sacristans currently use. It will be a legal and honorable supplement to what is lacking in their salary.

Such should be the organization of the parish clergy for the sake of the church.

[153]

Superintendents

The immediate supervision over the clergy is entrusted to superintendents. This office is necessary in cities, where the clergy generally behave decently, and it is needed still more in the villages. Nevertheless, does it achieve at the present time the goal for which it was established? How well does it achieve its goal?

Above all, this position is exceedingly important (if it is understood and executed the way it should be), but it is very rarely entrusted to a priest of superior intelligence, education, and deportment. Such priests are never ingratiating and absolutely do not want to sacrifice hard-earned money to acquire and preserve an official position. But it is always necessary to purchase the post of superintendent, sometimes at very great expense. It is therefore given to a priest who is a pathetic mediocrity but an artist at making money. Naturally, having bought his position, he wants to recover his expenses and to turn a profit besides. As a result, the purpose for which superintendents are established is perverted at its very foundations.

Moreover, every civil servant, every district police officer, every petty clerk, not excepting even the messenger at a civil court, receives a salary for his work: it is only the superintendent who receives nothing. At the same time he has many expenses that are absolutely unavoidable; he must, for example, pay for his paperwork, hire messengers, etc. All this just provides further motivation for the superintendent to plunder the parish clergy placed in his charge.

Moreover, even if the superintendent is incredibly stupid and immoral, he will firmly hang onto his position if he is generous in his payments to the district boards and consistory. Indeed, he will be praised, rewarded, and held up as a model for others to emulate. He may be incapable of linking one idea to another or of writing two lines of intelligible, sensible prose; never mind, the board and consistory will write it for him, do everything that is required, and put things in order. But woe unto the superintendent who is intelligent and behaves in an exemplary fashion. He manages affairs himself, accurately and honestly; he behaves

[154]

in such a way that he does not require indulgence; hence he gives only some trifling sum to diocesan officials. What does he get in return? The most indefatigable, petty, base persecution. They cavil at everything, heap upon him censure and reprimands, and force him to redo some trivial report twenty times without indicating the problem. In brief, they employ every bureaucratic trick to force such a superintendent to resign his position. It always ends the same way: he loses his patience and resigns, and his post is given to someone more to the liking of the district board and consistory.

Finally, all work deserves compensation. The superintendent, if he performs all the work himself and is conscientious, holds an extraordinarily difficult position. There is no salary, so he seeks and demands compensation from those subordinate to him.

Given all this, what does a superintendent represent to our clergy? A tax collector, in the strictest, fullest, and most literal sense of the term. The goal of all his actions, his sole aim, is to collect as much from the churches and clergy as his strength and ability permit. Yes, the churches!! . . . Just discreetly ask any church elder, whether in a city or a village, and he will tell you what the superintendent costs him each year. . . .[66]

But for a superintendent to permit himself such things, his conscience must be completely vitiated. With few exceptions, the rural superintendents have exactly that kind of conscience, and I say this without the slightest exaggeration. If it were customary to call things by their proper name, then in all justice he would be called "evildoer," not "superintendent for good order and morality," because there is no greater evil than that which emanates from him.[67] Their thirst for money is insatiable; there is nothing they would not do to quench their thirst! Every conceivable oppression, injustice, and insult to those who live honorably;

66. The imputed peculation concerned the parish church's treasury, which derived its funds mainly from the sale of candles; responsibility for the treasury rested primarily with the church·elder (*tserkovnyi starosta*), a layman elected for a three-year term.

67. Belliustin's term *zlochinnye* (evildoers) is a pun on the superintendent's title, *blagochinnye*.

every conceivable leniency for those who live dishonorably—such is their usual code of conduct. Why? What is the superintendent's purpose? An honest priest, or perhaps one who does not behave exceptionally well but at least is cautious enough to avoid cause for complaint, always gives the superintendent a modest sum, does not permit him to touch the church's treasury, and himself tells the church elder how much to give the superintendent. By contrast, the priest who lives badly is silent and defenseless as he pays tribute to the superintendent; he often weeps, but hands over whatever the superintendent cares to demand; if the priest is incorrigibly bad, the superintendent himself—with his own hands—counts out money from the church treasury, takes as much as he pleases, and sometimes grabs everything he can hold in his hands, without even counting.[68]

Nor is that all: the superintendent is usually on the side of the deacons and sacristans, defends and supports them with all his strength. Why? So that, relying completely on their impunity, they will more often revolt against the priest, more often start feuds with him, and themselves appear and drag the priest into litigation before the superintendent. All this, however, is well known: wherever there is injustice, bribes flourish; the more sordid and disgraceful the case, the larger the bribes. That is why the church whose clerics live peacefully among themselves (or, if they quarrel, settle things among themselves) enjoys no favor with many a superintendent. That is why scandals and disorders in the rural clergy have reached such a horrifying degree: each knows, each is convinced that if he behaves badly or does God know what but slips two or three rubles to the superintendent, all his misdeeds will be covered up, and the superintendent's annual reports on behavior will rank him among the very best. But woe to poor priests: a trifling, insignificant incident, or an unintentional mistake, or blatant, preposterous slander—and all this is immediately reported to authorities with embellishments and addenda. Why? Because such a superintendent is an irreconcilable enemy of the poor and the honest. So the poor fellow

68. The superintendents' abuse of church funds was evidently a source of great concern to Belliustin, who registered similar indignant protests in his diary ("Iz zametok," GAKO, f. 103, op. 1, d. 1307, ll. 9 ob.–11).

perishes, without cause or purpose; but a wealthy cleric who deserves punishment twentyfold calmly continues his disgraceful way of life or, still worse, authorities set him above everyone else and bestow distinctions upon him. . . .

"But why don't the clergy complain against such foul superintendents?"

Complain? To whom? The district board? The consistory? Hardly. That kind of superintendent is a golden goose as far as they are concerned: the more corrupt he is, the more zealously they support him. They are all bosom friends to such a superintendent, from the chief secretary and members of the consistory to the very last watchman at a district board. On their very own shoulders they rescue him from every trouble: so how can you complain here? Complain to the bishop? The bishop's clerks and personal aides also will stand behind the superintendent like a mountain; together with the consistory, they will use every opportunity to laud him before the bishop, to offer him as a paragon of virtue. What chance is there that a complaint will succeed here? It would be sent for review to the very same consistory, which, prejudiced in the superintendent's favor, completely confirms the decision it made earlier. And the one who complained will be found guilty of making a false denunciation and punished accordingly. Indeed, he will be punished with unusual severity as a warning to others, so that they will not dare to think of similar deeds of insolence. A complaint to the Holy Synod in St. Petersburg? Oh, ugh! . . .

I have presented only the most ordinary and commonplace of the superintendents' misdeeds. I cannot bring myself to speak of their behavior during inspection trips: some are intoxicated, behave scandalously in priests' homes and even in the churches, heap abuse on those with whom they are dissatisfied, and—even in the presence of women and children—use the kind of language heard only among stable boys, etc., etc. It is all too shameful, depressing, and bitter to discuss.

How can this evil be extirpated? There is but one means: we must abolish the existing order whereby the consistories appoint the superintendent. For the benefit of the entire clergy, superintendents should be chosen by the clergy themselves, and for a fixed term of office. That is the sole, indeed the most reliable, means to replace evildoers with true superintendents.

It is strange, incomprehensibly strange, how this order has come into existence: when everyone else, in some fashion or other, moves forward, only the clergy stands motionless, just like the Chinese monarchy. How is it that in the second half of the nineteenth century it has the same charters, the same orders, the same administration that existed in the seventeenth, sixteenth, and even more remote times? The names change but the essence remains the same: the old term "steward" is changed into "superintendent," but the incumbents have not moved a single step beyond their predecessors![69]

All social estates have now been given the right to choose freely from among themselves people to serve in judicial and administrative positions. Even the petty townspeople and peasants have their own officials—whomever they want, whomever they deem the best. Only the Orthodox clergy are deprived of this right! Why have the clergy been so deprived? Are they really more insignificant in state affairs than even the peasants? Or are they so stupid—more stupid than any townsman—that they do not know how to select an effective superintendent, an intelligent judicial deputy for the civil courts, an honest and just member of the diocesan consistory?

No, it is due to the bishop's intemperate thirst for power: power that does not tolerate the slightest limitation, the slightest concession—power so despotic that it will never permit the free election of anyone or anything. If it were only possible, they would not permit us to breathe and think freely. *Pereat ecclesia—fiat nostra voluntas!*[70]—that is the motto of all their activity, the object of their most zealous concern. Here is the cause of everything terrible and ruinous for the church; here is the cause of stagnation in the

---

69. Curiously, Belliustin was ignorant of the real background of the superintendents: until the eighteenth century they had in fact been elected representatives of the parish clergy and were called "priestly elders" (*popovskie starosty*). It was only in the last quarter of the eighteenth century that bishops began to appoint superintendents (Freeze, *Russian Levites*, pp. 50–51, 54–55).

70. "Let the ecclesiastical assemblies perish: our will shall prevail."

Russian clergy. Whatever the cost, even if it means the destruction of the church, they try to preserve that power and significance which prelates possessed in the fifteenth to the seventeenth centuries. Other estates have virtually repudiated this control of the bishops; the clergy, however, remain in their grasp, and the bishops seek to preserve their terrible power as long as possible, at least over this group!! . . .

That is why they cruelly persecute every new idea, every new demand, the slightest attempt to break free of this intolerable condition. That is also why they oppose a salary for the rural clergy. Their intimate thoughts, expressed in every action, are the following: "So long as the white clergy are oppressed by material want, wholly immersed in filth, reduced to such a hopeless condition that they cannot think of anything better, we can humiliate, persecute, and oppress them as much as we please. So long as each priest before us is like a Negro in the American colonies (the relationship between priest and bishop is exactly like that between Negro and plantation owner), we can punish or pardon him as we see fit. But if his position is improved, if he sheds his disgusting black skin, he may begin to speak of his rights, as a member of the very same church. Who knows, he may demand still more—that he be treated like a human being, like a servitor of the Heavenly Father, and that we—even we [bishops]!!!—treat him with respect. It would be better to let the white clergy perish, if need be, to preserve our absolute power intact and unchanged!"

But if only the medieval system for choosing and appointing superintendents were changed, what wonderful consequences would ensue! Give the clergy the right to choose the superintendents from their own midst and to elect them for a three-year term (not more), and this disreputable tribe of evildoers will vanish. At least some of those elected will not be artists at thievery and ready to conceal any abomination, but rather will be the most conscientious, honest, and intelligent. The impact of such people, when they exercise a greater or lesser degree of influence, is quite inevitable. To give timely counsel, to admonish at the right moment, to explain the meaning of one or another act and its consequence—all this means that others will be led onto the path of virtue. To prosecute evil indefatigably, dispassionately, and energetically means that they will reduce the number of evils. That is what a superintendent should do and what, without doubt, an intelligent, conscientious, and honest one will do. A three-year term of office will provide the surest curb to any tendency to deviate and will guarantee that the superintendent himself is not attracted to something outside the law and conscience. The idea that in three years he has to hear words of either gratitude or indignation from those who chose him (indeed, in the presence of the entire clergy), with the honor of reelection to a new three-year term or removal from his post in disgrace, without hope of ever receiving this honor again—that idea alone will always keep him within the limits of the strictest truth, complete disinterestedness, and vigilant fervor toward his work. In addition, *volens-nolens,* every disorderly priest will think better of it and alter his behavior. Who does not want distinction among his peers? And to be accorded such distinctions by the peers themselves means that it was done on a just and worthy basis. Who would not want to become a superintendent? The electoral order would make it entirely possible: if worthy, you can become a candidate and perhaps they will choose you. If it did not happen this time, then perhaps it will in three years. Oh, what priest would, in that case, not use all his strength to break free of the marsh in which he is now mired?

In order that the superintendent have no cause to take money from those in his domain, it is necessary to provide him a certain sum to cover his chancellery expenses, to hire a copyist and messengers, etc., and to provide at least a modest salary for his labors. Some will interject: "How much will all this cost, when there are so many superintendents?" Well, what good is it to have as many as there are now? All they do now is increase the revenues for those on district boards and consistories. One superintendent with two assistants is quite sufficient for a district. To encourage the superintendent to discharge his duties zealously, honestly, and incorruptibly, to be for others a model of honest, temperate, and irreproachable life, it is necessary to establish special awards that would belong only to superintendents (for three years' service, for example, a cross on the ribbon of the Order of St. Vladimir, or something similar). If they would only do this as an experiment, then they would see that the measure I propose here is no daydream, that it was not the fruit of idle imagination, but is the only way to eliminate the present kind of rural superintendent, that sore and disgrace for the clergy. My suggestion is the product of long and tireless observations, deep thought, and innumerable consultations with priests who are exceptionally intelligent, serious, and well intentioned.

I shall say a few words about one further benefit that would result from the measure proposed here. At the present time the government is seeking to reduce official paperwork and to simplify clerical procedures.[71] But you should see what chaos reigns in district boards and consistories! Here, for example, a consistory receives a decree; the diocese has ten or more boards, so ten copies of the decree are prepared; each district has at least ten superintendents, so that means ten more copies. To cite another example, the superintendents must make reports to the boards and each of them writes as he pleases; it costs the board indescribable labor to compile something intelligible from all this cacophony; the boards report to the consistory, and here it is the same old story all over again. But if there were just one superintendent per district, if there were not all these intermediate instances (if, that is, decrees went directly from the consistory, and the superintendents' reports went directly to the consistory), then that alone would mean ten times less paperwork. In fact, why would district boards even be needed then? They would no longer have their chief task—to copy from morning to night this formula: "Having heard the decree from the consistory, which directed that it be distributed throughout the ecclesiastical domain, we hereby send

71. Late in Nicholas' reign the government formed a special committee to reduce red tape; its efforts are described in S. F. Starr, *Decentralization and Self-Government in Russia, 1830–1870* (Princeton, 1972), pp. 111–122.

it to you, the superintendent." Now is that not a truly meaningful and useful activity! Who, someone may ask, will conduct investigations if the district board is abolished? This task can be performed by the superintendent and his assistants. What about verification of various church reports or parish documents? The consistory has already assumed responsibility for the majority of such matters (aiming to enjoy for itself the exactions that previously went to the district boards); why should the consistory not handle everything else as well? As far as the clergy themselves are concerned, this reform will bring a significant reduction in their written work alone. At the present time every report (for example, those concerning births, deaths, and marriages) is compiled in three copies: one for the parish church, a second for the district board, and a third for the consistory. Does the board need a copy when it is in the consistory as well? References and certificates are never issued by the district boards and have no legal validity; so why present a copy to the board? Solely to feed the rats and moths, to expose the clergy to plunder when they present these reports? When district boards cease to exist, there will be no superfluous toils, so useless and unnecessary. Plunder itself will have diminished, and the city where the board is located will no longer seem to the clergy to be a den of thieves, the most merciless, unscrupulous, and brazen of their breed.[72]

The Consistory

Of late one hears complaints everywhere about terrible abuses in the lower echelons of civil administration. But what would happen if those who complain saw what goes on in our ecclesiastical boards and consistories? Truly, they would find that civil

72. Abolition of the district boards had in fact already been undertaken, and approximately one-third of them were eliminated in the period from 1841 to 1855 (*Izvlecheniia iz otcheta po vedomstvu dukhovnykh del pravoslavnogo ispovedaniia za 1841 god* [St. Petersburg, 1842], p. 9; *Izvlecheniia iz otcheta . . . za 1855 god* [St. Petersburg, 1856], pp. 6–7). The resultant savings, however, were used to augment the salaries of clerks in the diocesan consistory, not to provide salaries for superintendents.

courts, by comparison, are as different from ecclesiastical organs as a mild case of cholera from a fatal attack of that dread disease. Having seen ecclesiastical administration, they would drop their complaints about civil administration and fall silent.

The district board and consistory are judicial offices where, in the name of law, every truth is trampled so fearlessly and brazenly that it is difficult to comprehend it all. Every respectable person avoids these judicial offices and holds them in the most profound contempt; their very name has become synonymous with disgrace. What is so particularly bad about them?

Enthroned there is the most profound ignorance of canons and laws. Here I shall speak only of the consistory, not of the district boards: in the latter's case there is no need to expatiate—things are simply worse than in the consistory, more shameful than anything you can imagine. It goes without saying that members of the consistory board are priests—that is, archpriests who hold a master's degree from an ecclesiastical academy.* Perhaps some of them are capable of writing sermons, but not one has any knowledge and comprehension of juridical matters; this I can say categorically and without fear that I shall be exposed for lying. How can I fear anything here? Just have any member of the consistory board (such as the one in Tver diocese) examine any serious case, assemble the appropriate laws, and compose a decision: then you shall see whether I am telling the truth. The members of the consistory board are like the chief officials in townships: they sit and sign whatever is given them. No, that is not quite true: consistory members are higher than township officials—they

---

*At least they could teach the canons—*ius*—in the academies. As it is, the outsider would find it both ridiculous and pathetic to see how the lowliest clerk leads the gray-haired "men with master's degrees" around by the nose. That is how intelligently they have understood a clerical education, that is how well suited it is for its tasks! Learn everything that is utterly useless in life; do not have the slightest idea of things vitally needed to get along in life. If members of the consistory board were not such ignoramuses, it seems there would be few outrageous abominations [in the church]. A different, younger person with a master's degree and not entirely subjugated by the clerks would be happy to oppose any clear outrages, but, not knowing how, he is involuntarily silent, concurs, and signs the documents [like the rest of the consistory].

correct grammatical mistakes in the document. But all the same they still copy out the resolution prepared beforehand. It is a well-known fact, however, that nothing is more arrogant than ignorance. Consequently, consistory members seek to conceal their ignorance with external quasi-pomp. It is also well known that nothing is so jealous of true merit as ignorance; that nothing is so capable of every baseness and vileness as ignorance. That is why the consistory member always represents the kind of personality that one can hardly bear to discuss. He is accessible for 50 kopecks, a ruble, a bottle of rum, a pound of tea; but he is inaccessible for the best priest in the diocese if the latter has the impertinence to appear empty-handed. He is the friend and patron of a superintendent who is the most incorrigible plunderer, indefatigable persecutor of an honest priest who found it [demeaning] to knock about the consistory reception room without business or need. In brief, a single goal stands behind all his actions: bribes, come what may.

As for the clerks employed at the consistory, little need be said. If the members of the consistory board permit themselves such things, what will the clerk—a former seminarian, expelled from school for drunkenness and rowdiness—not permit himself?

The lay secretary is the very soul of the consistory, and—everywhere, always, without exception—he is the most brutal scourge of the white clergy. Rather than expatiate upon this figure, I shall say only that consistory secretaries count their annual income in tens of thousands of rubles. Where does all this money come from? How is it possible? It is perfectly obvious and understandable that he could not possibly acquire so much in an honest, upright fashion; he has to resort to all the clerk's ruses, to the most unconscionable tricks, to the cruelest oppression in order to squeeze such immense sums out of the clergy.

What is the condition of the clergy under such administration, especially that of the rural clergy, defenseless and downtrodden? It is surely no accident that the village priest (or those living in towns, for that matter) shudders more from news that he is summoned to the consistory for some reason than from news that cholera has broken out in his parish. In the case of cholera there is still the chance that the Lord will save you; there is no hope of salvation, however, once the consistory has fastened onto you. It does not matter whether one is guilty: he must bring the kopecks he has scraped and saved over many years; if he has no savings, he must sell the last of his livestock or the grain he has stored. Otherwise they will find the means, if not to ruin him completely, at least to blacken his service record with this disgraceful entry: "Was convicted and fined." Anyone who has had to deal with clerks, not to say consistories, will not doubt that they can do all this.

It is easy to understand how business is conducted where everyone, from the member of the consistory to its lowliest watchman, has a single goal: to plunder and rob. Here is one of the thousands of incidents that could be cited. In a certain village, five years ago, both the priest and the deacon became intoxicated and got into a fight; the deacon then filed a complaint at the consistory. The consistory launched an investigation and in the interim forbade the priest to perform services in the church. The priest journeyed to the consistory, which then lifted the priest's suspension and suspended the deacon instead. Next the deacon went to the consistory; now he was reinstated and the priest suspended instead. All this continued for more than two years, as each was in turn suspended and restored to service four times; in the end the local superintendent was at an utter loss to say who was suspended and who was not. Does all this seem incredible: It really is hard to believe that such a farce could be permitted in a matter so important as the administration of holy sacraments. I have told the absolute truth, however, and if anyone would care to check it, I can identify the village and persons involved. Here is how the affair finally ended: once they had squeezed everything possible from both of these clerics (the priest sold his livestock and by September had even sold his winter crop in advance), they transferred the deacon to another village but left the priest free from any punishment. That is the way business is always conducted. Even if the priest merely needs a birth certificate for

[165]

his son or daughter, he must pay 10 to 15 rubles for it. Otherwise, they will procrastinate for months.

In self-justification the copyists say that "we receive too small a salary," and the signers [the members of the consistory board] say that "we receive no salary at all—so how can we not take money?" But why not request a salary from the government? Is that impossible? If so, then levy a direct tax on the entire clergy, and be honest in all your actions, if you can. Each priest would willingly and gladly give 5 to 15 rubles a year if he were convinced that those employed in diocesan administration would no longer oppress him in any way, that they would not seek ways to blow up some trivial matter, that they would treat him as a priest and not the way proud vassals regard their tributaries, and that they would render justice in the event of need and not drag out cases for months and years.[73]

But will our consistories ever improve? It is hard to think or believe so! Perhaps only the fire that engulfs the earth on the Day of Judgment can efface the dishonor, shame, and disgrace that these offices have brought upon the entire clergy and their administration.

---

73. Both to conceal Belliustin's identity (by avoiding excessive references to Tver diocese) and to temper the political danger of the work, Pogodin deleted a passage accusing his former prelate, Grigorii (Postnikov)—now metropolitan of St. Petersburg—of heartless rule over good priests. The manuscript next contrasts Grigorii with his successor in Tver, Gavriil, whom Belliustin lauds in the most favorable terms:

> How joyous and bright it is for the soul when one speaks of a pastor who was fully worthy of his rank, of such a rare bishop. Unfortunately, such bishops are exceedingly uncommon. His accessibility is explained by the fact that [Gavriil] himself was a [former] priest [who had taken monastic vows after his wife died]. Consequently, he could judge from experience the bitter conditions of all priests and tried to ameliorate them through all the means and powers at his disposal.

But even such a well-intentioned bishop as Gavriil could not prevail, for his ill health permitted tyranny and abuse to flourish at the consistory: "Merciful God, what did the consistory not permit itself!! It openly trafficked in [the sale of] positions, official appointments, awards, and justice" (OR GBL, f. 231/III, k. 1, d. 66, ll. 2–3).

The Bishop

The chief goal of a bishop's service is to shepherd the flock entrusted to his care. To achieve this goal completely, he must know all of his flock's spiritual needs, which are infinitely diverse, because his flock consists of an entire *province*— that is, hundreds of thousands of people. Here one inevitably encounters both higher education and abysmal ignorance; both belief in all its purity and simplicity, and desperate disbelief, the most insolent freethinking, the most brazen impiety. But can the bishop possibly learn *all* the needs when he is a permanent resident of the provincial capital, and only rarely, in passing, inspects part of his domain, just that part which lies along the main postal roads?

It *is* possible. He has fellow servitors—priests, who by their very appointment are bound to assist their bishop in the great work of his service. Just let him draw close to them, appear before the priest not as some great ataman but as a true successor to the Apostles, to whom each priest could turn trustfully, sincerely, and lovingly, as if to his father. If the bishop did this, in two or three years he would become better acquainted with the spiritual and moral life of his flock than he otherwise could do in twenty years—if ever. Having learned the true substantive needs, not just imagined ones, as now happens (in such-and-such a class such-and-such a vice must be common), he can find the means to prevent and, insofar as possible, eliminate such vices.

Here, too, the priest can be a true and reliable adviser to the bishop. If a particular disease, such as cholera, appears in an infinite variety of forms, according to differences in organisms, so that a universal panacea is impossible, this is still more the case in the matter of moral ailments. Therefore it is not enough for the bishop to know where a certain vice has taken root; it is necessary to investigate to see how far it has developed, how it spreads, how it manifests itself in persons of different social estates, and how one should treat it. Who could know this more intimately, reliably, and precisely than the local priest, who is face

[167]

to face with this vice from morning to night? And who can better show the surest means to combat this vice than that same priest, who not only knows the degree to which the ailment has developed but also the people involved—that is, the spiritual organism of the ailing? Having consulted with local priests, the bishop would not begin to speak of *humility** to the *squire's serfs*, downtrodden and crushed, reduced to the condition of beasts of burden. Nor would he talk of *divine mercy to serf-owning nobles*, who need to be threatened with words of incorruptible truth. . . . *Nor would the bishop flatter and indulge a merchant for building an iconostasis, or invite him to attend the consecration: that merchant declared bankruptcy three times, plundered and dispossessed dozens of penniless families and cast them into the streets, and drove the heads of such families prematurely to their graves while forcing younger members of the family to earn their living through debauchery.* . . .

No, having learned the true state of affairs, he would expose vice. With the words of the Gospel he would pronounce judgment on impiety; he would level the strictest judgment on this insolent hypocrite (who intended with his iconostasis to make amends to God, conscience, the faith, his close ones, for his past acts of plunder); he would console, strengthen, and encourage the earthly sufferers with hopes for heavenly recompense, etc. And this

---

*I shall not indicate who said these words or when; I shall only say that they have been published. These (and similar) words, however, clearly reflect not a lack of common sense but other goals—[a desire] to please the powerful of this world, to rise with their help (which in fact they did). There is also an unpublished homily on the consecration of an iconostasis, where a thieving miscreant is canonized in his own lifetime and is counted among the greatest supporters of the faith, the church, and Orthodoxy. (And this praise was enunciated from the pulpit! It is a wonder that a bolt of lightning from heaven did not strike the person preaching such insolent blasphemy! God, how patient You are!) True, the censors found that it is impossible for a single bishop to canonize someone, even for building an iconostasis and for paying the bishop thousands of rubles. . . . A pity, truly a pity! It would have been so useful to publish this homily, with a small commentary, to translate it into other languages, and to disseminate it all over Europe, not just in Russia. Let people in other countries read, find edification, and be astonished at the progress achieved here in the task of preaching the Gospel.

sermon would not have a dull metallic clang, as now, but would be the Living Word, penetrating to the marrow of the bones, to the depths of a listener's mind. It would not be forgotten as soon as the bishop leaves, but would be inscribed on their hearts and retold to hundreds and thousands of others. Thus by working together with the priests, the bishop could achieve, so far as humanly possible, the goals of his calling.

But what are things like now?

Heavenly Father! What can be more humiliating, more disgraceful, more inhuman than the way the bishop treats the priests in general and rural priests in particular? Anyone who has been at the bishop's residence during the hours set for receiving petitions has no doubt seen that priests, even those with gray hair, shamefully hang about in the vestibule with sacristans and peasants, and are not even permitted to come into an antechamber to wait; there, in the entryway, they sit on the stairways, waiting until the bishop comes out. It does not matter if it is in the depths of severe cold weather, with temperatures as low as 25 degrees below zero: the bishop makes them wait two or three hours. If some aristocratic lady comes, then the wait can be up to five hours; then, after such a wait, the bishop passes on the order to announce that he is not receiving petitioners today and they should appear tomorrow. Now there is an example of how merciful and available to priests the bishops are. But that example is still too trivial: what goes on here?

I do not intend, however, to describe *everything* about the way bishops treat rural priests: it would require too much paper, and besides, it is too depressing to write such things. Besides, what good would it do? To put it briefly, bishops not only do not want to see the priests as servitors of the Heavenly Father, as their co-workers in the great cause of pastorship, or even as human beings. They keep them outside the doors of their entrance hall, like dogs; they hail them for a few minutes to submit a request or give some explanation that is required; and then they try to send them packing from their reception room as quickly as possible. Far from favoring the priest with a long discussion, the bishop does not even want to get close to him, and extends his hand through the doorway to receive the petitions. In a word, if anyone should care to observe Asiatic obsequiousness in all its glory, in all its magnificence (from the subordinate pounding his head on the floor to the figure of his superior expressing clearly an infinite, insatiable pride), just let him spend a few days at the bishop's residence. Have him consider, dispassionately and attentively, the relationship between the bishop and his subordinates. . . .[74]

What are the consequences of such a relationship? They are quite predictable. In the same entryway, along with priests, one finds sacristans and peasants standing about; the bishop looks with equal contempt upon a priest and upon the lowliest sacristan, guard, or soldier. Will anyone respect the unfortunate priest after this? Are sacristans not right when they insult their priest in the most insolent way and say (as they always do): "Phoo— who are you anyway? You are no better than I am; does the bishop treat you any differently from us?" Is it not true that when the servitor himself is held in universal contempt, his service suffers the same fate? Our Saviour! They fill the Apostolic positions only with learned types, who have a doctorate or master's degree in theology; but where is their Apostolic spirit, Your spirit, which

74. Pogodin also deleted the following offensive passage from the original manuscript:

The sole exception to all the bishops known to me was Gavriil of Tver, who received everyone warmly, cheerfully, and in a truly paternal manner. Unfortunately, few had the time to get to know him. Accustomed to quivering at the mere word "bishop," the priests (especially rural ones) appeared before him only in cases of exceptional necessity and were neither candid nor trusting toward him. This behavior profoundly offended the good bishop.

"But they are not guilty—they are just frightened and downtrodden," I once told him, in justification of the clergy's distant attitude that was so offensive to him.

"Alas, that's true," he answered. "It is terrible to see what things have come to: I have been here eight years and still have not managed to get a priest to speak with me calmly, without trembling. . . ."

Indeed, the good fruits of Grigorii's reign as bishop will not disappear for eighty years, I thought, even if all bishops are not so well meaning as Gavriil. And in Tver the clergy, as it were, still alive; in other dioceses they have completely abandoned hope and tremble before the police chief, bailiff, even before a stranger if he is not a peasant. [OR GBL, f. 231/II, k. 1, d. 66, l. 5]

embraces in miraculous love all mankind, from the first to the last sinner in the world, from Your friend John to Peter, who tempted You so many times, even the ingrate Judas? Through an act of ineffable condescension You made the miraculous sacrifice of Your flesh and blood; it is You Who has placed these priests so highly, indeed in such a lofty position that the angels themselves look on with reverence and trembling when the priests perform the sacraments. But bishops not only do not wish to see these priests as Your Servitors—they do not want even to see them as people, and regard them as filthy dogs!! Do the bishops really believe in You, in the reality of Your miraculous sacrifice? If they did, they would not reject with such undeserved contempt those who bear Your sacrifice [during the sacrament of communion]. . . .

And the priest, oppressed by such treatment, uses every possible means to avoid meeting with his bishop. Not a single rural priest who chances to be in the provincial capital on business would dare simply to visit the bishop, to receive his blessing and hear his words of instruction and counsel. Only the most urgent necessity compels him to overcome his fear and appear before the bishop. Here, if you could only see what is taking place in the cleric's soul, you would be overwhelmed by indignation at such a state of affairs and by compassion for the unfortunate priest. Whether standing or sitting, he feels a cold shiver run down his entire body. Would you care to verify the justness of my description? Just have any rural priest preparing to present himself to the bishop write or sign something; you will see what terrible convulsions cause his hands to shake. . . . He ponders how and what he should say to the bishop. But all around him the bishop's roguish aides—from the clerks to the lackey—are constantly scurrying about, and find it necessary to bump into him and interrupt his train of thought with a lackey's rude tone: "Hey, you, what are doing here?" It is a well-known axiom that the lackey reflects his master! So the priest moves to a different spot; but no matter where he sits or stands, there is no room here for the likes of him. Everywhere they abuse him and drive him off with curses; he still has not seen the bishop but has already

[171]

and half forgotten what he must talk about. Suddenly a whisper sweeps through the crowd of petitioners: "His Grace is coming!" The priest no longer feels the ground under his feet. It would be easier for him if, instead of these words, they had said that the roof was caving in! I swear by the Living God that this is the absolute truth; just ask any rural priest what happens to him when he is presented to the bishop: each will confirm what I have said, and perhaps only one in a hundred will want to boast of some fantastic courage. The bishop takes his petition and asks the priest:

"What do you need?"

"I need to speak with Your Grace."

"No doubt some kind of dispute—you are forever involved in such things."

After these words, uttered with such rudeness, severity, and annoyance, the priest completely loses his composure. His thoughts become muddled; he mutters something incoherent, senseless, unintelligible; he cannot understand where he is or what is happening to him. The bishop fails to make out what the priest said and, without waiting to the end, turns his back on the priest and of course on his version of things, although the tranquillity and even fate of the priest's whole life and his family often depends on this meeting with the bishop. One word, just one word of greeting and approval, could soothe the priest's anxious soul; then he could explain clearly and intelligently why he had come. But such words do not pass through the lips of bishops, just as their very glance never expresses either mercy or indulgence. These very same satraps in cassocks always give nobles this appraisal of rural priests: "What asses these rural priests [*popy*] are! You will never get an intelligent word out of them. I am amazed that you tolerate them and admit them to your presence (!!!)." Truly, is this recommendation not the very epitome of good intentions, intelligence, and episcopacy!? This is the unconscionable, inhumane way they trample an entire social estate into the ground, and they do so in the presence of people whose whole life has one goal—to trample everything underfoot. It is as though to say: "We have completely trampled the priests—you do the

[172]

same. They are all asses, who deserve nothing better. . . ." This could be done only by the *humble* bishops of Orthodox Rus'! . . .

During his visitation in the diocese the bishop acts no differently from the way he does in his inaccessible and terrifying residence. He does not stop to spend the night in the home of a poor priest, but makes inquiries beforehand to learn where the squires live. Thus he plans his route through their estates in hopes of passing the night there. He stops at these estates and commands the local priest to appear before him. They come and wait in the servants' quarters for several hours, until His Grace has finished talking with everyone else and deigns to receive them. His kind words leave them dismayed: "I hear that all the rural priests are drunkards and rowdy, and oppress the parishioners in everything; watch out—if I hear such things about you, do not expect any mercy." Then he dismisses them. After such words try to find respect for the hapless priest received thus by the bishop—not to say among nobles, but even among servants and peasant parishioners.[75]

Old Believers

The schism is one of the strangest, most inexplicable phenomena in the Russian church. Is it really possible that a Russian— with his common sense, with his ability to tolerate and endure various adversities in life—on such a simple issue as the correction of church books decided to tear asunder any union with the church, came to hate its authorities, forgot the sanctity of relics and miraculous icons, and rejected its age-old customs?

75. Here, too, Pogodin excised a case from Tver, in which one squire took offense at the bishops' mistreatment of their subordinate priests: "The squire [after one incident] did not once receive the bishop; he made an exception only for Gavriil, after learning that he is the sole exception among bishops in his treatment of the white clergy." Pogodin also struck out here another anecdote about Grigorii, who lost his temper in church when a priest forgot to bow to him and shouted out for all to hear, "You fool" (ibid., ll. 6 ob.–7).

That, however, in fact did happen. What caused this schism in the church?

This phenomenon is hardly due to the reasons that are customarily offered as an explanation. It was not because of changes in the prayerbook [*trebnik*];[76] the Gospels themselves have been corrected dozens of times and have even been distorted by copyists in the most ludicrous fashion. Yet that did not provoke rebellion in the church. With literacy at a minimal level, Russians very calmly prayed according to manuscript books, hardly guessing that they contain the coarsest mistakes. Then, all of a sudden, they show an amazing fervor for the letter, for each word!

No, something is awry here. But it is not appropriate here for me to express all my thoughts on this matter.[77]

The evil grew. It was all the more terrible that the people— who previously had only a weak and hazy comprehension of the true foundations of the faith, but who felt an irresistible need for such knowledge—took it into their heads to devise these foundations or to seek teachers of the faith from their own midst, no longer trusting a single member of the church. One can imagine what light was shed on the faith by such teachers, who are guided only by ignorance and evil intentions. Filled with bitterness, they launched an attack on the church and the Orthodox faith using debauchery of the most vulgar, shameful, and disgusting sort. . . .

What is now being done to convert the schismatics? The same thing as before: harsh, severe measures. But all these measures, it seems, have a single goal: to make it possible for these poor people to be robbed by anyone who has some relationship to

---

76. The *trebnik* is a prayerbook containing the order of services for all religious rites except the Eucharist and the ordination of priests.

77. Pogodin deleted from the text a passage flatly attributing the schism to monasticism:

> The idea of separating from the church developed simultaneously with the development of monasticism in Russia, and with the strengthening of the monks' power. This idea, circulating mutely among the people and sometimes finding expression in a few individuals, suddenly became a reality when the monks' authority reached its apogee in the person of [Patriarch] Nikon. [OR GBL, f. 231/III, k. 1, d. 66, ll. 7 ob.–8]

them. Schismatics are mercilessly and horribly robbed by their city and rural police, the provincial government, and . . . and . . . Is the priest to lag behind everyone else? As far as possible he takes his share too: the rural priest gets 10 rubles, the urban priest several times that sum, the archpriest counts his into the hundreds of rubles. It sometimes happens that schismatics become indignant at all these outrages, but the authorities have special means to deal with such cases. Can one think of anything more likely to intensify the schism and the schismatics' alienation from the church? Such treatment can only irritate them and annoy them to the point where they see each Orthodox person—from the most illustrious bishop to the lowliest clerk in the provincial chancellery or the local court—as a cruel, irreconcilable enemy, prepared to rob them and have them sent to prison. They have little faith in the most well-intentioned, honest priest; if they sometimes do draw close to a priest, it is only after a long, strict observation and after they are fully convinced that he does not intend to plunder them. How else should they look upon rural priests, or at least the majority of them? They ply them with food and drink; give them money and presents; and despise them in the most profound fashion. After observing the schismatics, Orthodox people also abandon the church: every year conversions from Orthodoxy to the schism are taking place.

Yes, I reiterate: *the schism is not diminishing, but rather is increasing with every year. That is true notwithstanding the fact that each year bishops report to the Synod: "In matters of faith everything is excellent— there were no conversions to the schism; on the contrary, such-and-such a number converted to Orthodoxy. . . ."*[78]

Converted! . . . This is the kind of conversions that took place. A young schismatic peasant (or merchant or petty townsman— it doesn't matter which) needs to get married, because a flagrant violation of marital law is permissible only for the squire and merchant millionaire; it is strictly forbidden for someone who is

78. Belliustin is correct about an increase in the number of schismatics, the tenor of many diocesan reports, and the unreliability of official statistics.

not wealthy.[79] So he goes to an Orthodox priest and asks him to conduct the marriage ceremony. He refuses; so the schismatic pays him money. The priest puts him down as converted, takes him to the church, and if all this was witnessed by others, actually performs the marriage ceremony. More often, if there were no witnesses about, he sings something and releases him. The schismatics then marry again under their own rules and perform some form of penance, usually prostrations and money [to expiate the sinful marriage by an Orthodox priest]; they are no closer to the church after the marriage than they were before. The priest lists both the man and his wife in the confessional registers as Orthodox; so long as they are punctual in making payments, he puts them down as having made confession or as absent because they were away from the parish. But if the schismatic forgets to give the priest his annual tax, the priest will inform the head of the district police office that N. has reconverted to the schism. The policeman comes and converts him to Orthodoxy, that is, plunders for himself and the priest as he pleases; the schismatic becomes still more stubborn and embittered. *The consistory and the bishop know all this.* But that parish provides bountiful support for the priest, and the consistory especially prizes such priests: their incomes are good, they have amassed much through illegal means; hence one could always bring them to trial, with excellent chances of making a great profit. But the priest does not let it come to that: he pays off the consistory generously, long before it comes to a formal inquiry. That is why the annual report declares that *"everything is in superb condition!"* All that I have said here about conversions is based on a multitude of cases in local and district courts where I myself was a witness and involuntarily had to listen.

In many villages where for two decades schismatics were counted as no more than a few dozen, half or two-thirds are now

79. The manuscript contained a footnote naming a rich merchant who had wives in separate districts and lived with them both with impunity, even though his case was known to both the local governor and the bishop (OR GBL, f. 231/III, k. 1, d. 66, l. 9).

schismatics. I know this for a fact, having heard it from priests and especially from the schismatics themselves.[80]

When and how will this ulcer be healed? When our *entire* clergy have been radically transformed, when they understand their high calling and break free from the impenetrable darkness in which they now stumble about; when the government itself understands that their conversion requires a policy that is the absolute opposite of the present one; when city governors, district police officials, and those in still higher positions cease to plunder schismatics. In a word, it seems, never!! . . .

Finally, I do not think it is superfluous to add the following remarks:

1. Of late not one bishop, consistory, or district board has converted a single schismatic to Orthodoxy, although each year they summon hundreds of them in an attempt to convert them to Orthodoxy.

2. Conversions are rare, nominal, and false, based on cold calculations (for example, to retain the legal status of merchant, which is impossible for schismatics) and without the slightest qualms. The schismatic, like the Jew, under present circumstances in no way will really join the church and will sunder ties with it at the first opportunity. I know that firsthand from the schismatics themselves, both "converted" and "unconverted." I say this with every assurance, because in such an important matter they have neither incentive nor need to lie.

3. The construction of churches in which services are performed according to the old style will not diminish the evil and may even increase it.[81] It is thought that such a concession will draw them closer to the church. What a gross error, which

80. A manuscript footnote claims that eight hundred people had converted to the Old Belief in nearby Rzhev in the past three years (ibid., l. 9 ob.).
81. Here Belliustin is speaking of the *edinoverie,* a policy initiated in the late eighteenth century in an attempt to rejoin Old Believers to the church; according to rules formally promulgated in 1800, Old Believers who agreed to rejoin the Orthodox church were allowed to celebrate religious rites according to the traditional liturgical books and customs in their own separate churches, with priests installed by the official church.

demonstrates a total ignorance of the schismatics' mentality! Thus a church was built in Moscow (in Rogozhskaia); the prelate of Moscow rejoiced over this great event and expressed his joy in a charter. Probably hoping to draw as close as possible to them, he wrote the charter completely in their spirit, even spelling Jesus Christ as they do—a practice against which he once inveighed so passionately.[82] But did he attain his goal? No, no, no!!! I say that with complete conviction. Does he know that the schismatics are literally following the canon of some church council—*curse the bishop who installs the priest in heresy?* Does he know that they compel their priest to curse the very same bishop who ordained him?

THE PRIEST AND SERVICE

Rural Priests as Preachers in City Cathedrals

It is a marvelous goal to have rural priests preach the Word of God in city cathedrals. For one thing, the Word of God should be proclaimed each holiday in the cathedral; then, too, at least once a year rural priests will reinvigorate their minds by reflecting and composing formal sermons and by appearing in a place where the truths of the Gospel absolutely must be proclaimed. But this goal, too, like everything else with the clergy, is transformed into a source of income.

The position of censor for sermons is never given to that priest in the town who is distinguished by his intelligence, exemplary conduct, and understanding of how to preach the Gospel, but rather to the person who will pay the most. Having paid for his position, he seeks to recover his expenses and make a profit as well. This profit is the censor's sole concern, the focus of all his efforts; the sermons themselves are the last thing on earth he is

82. That is, Filaret used the spelling Iисус (not Иисус, the form used in the Orthodox church after the mid-seventeenth-century reforms, which had led to the schism).

worried about. That is the way most rural priests understand this system. If he pays his quitrent [*obrok*] on time, he can rest easy. Thus the "marvelous goal" is achieved: priests pay, censors take, and in turn they pay those who appointed them!

Besides, what can one reasonably demand from the majority of rural priests? After living ten or twenty years in the country, they become so unaccustomed to intellectual activity that it becomes an intolerable burden for them to write a simple note or letter, let alone a sermon. It happens that some of the vain ones, especially the younger priests, still want to show off their abilities and appear with sermons. What kind of drivel and nonsense is this? Ordinarily it is a compilation of several sermons from the last century, which the priest splices together, adding his own explanations here and there in the text. The least he could do, one might think, would be to copy from modern preachers and not dare change a single word! But no, how could they do that? It would be immediately said that he *copied* it; if he selects carefully, however, then everyone will say it is his own work, his very own work!!

Just let the urban parishioners listen and receive edification from these truly amazing sermons! It goes without saying that most of the listeners flee from the church at the very beginning of the sermon; those who remain wait for the end with irritation, boredom, and disgust for the priest and his sermon. What is the result of all this? Afterward another fifty such priests come to preach. Then comes the fifty-first—but this time with a real sermon, expressed directly from his soul, filled with the warmth of his faith, with a firmness of conviction, with a most sincere desire to convey his conviction to the parishioners. But they flee from him; or they listen absent-mindedly, inattentively. "What is there to hear? *They all* talk nonsense." Such is the usual reply of parishioners when they are reproved for their inattention.[83]

Sometimes things get much worse. Among those who step to the pulpit are priests who only a week or month earlier were seen

83. Belliustin's sketch, sardonic as it is, was grimly realistic; see, for example, a very similar assessment by L. Milovzorov, "Ot sel'skogo sviashchennika: Neskol'ko zamechanii," *Pravoslavnoe obozrenie*, 1862, no. 7 (zametki), pp. 83–85.

in a drinking house or tavern in the same town. And it can get even worse: they show up at the church straight from some liquor shop, and, half-drunk, with impure lips, they dare to pronounce the Word of God. Satisfied beforehand, the censors regard such matters as something quite ordinary and themselves offer a cup or two of spirits *for the sake of boldness.* They file reports only against those who for some reason either do not bring money or offer too little. If one presents an excellent sermon without a bribe, the work is sure to be splattered with filth, with the censor's most absurd, inane comments.

No, that is certainly not the way all this should be handled. With the elimination of evil (that is, the present censors) and with the selection of suitable and worthy ones, it is important to issue the following orders as well:

1. Admit to the pulpit only those priests who are known for their good life.

2. Permit them to deliver only sermons that can interest, touch, and convince listeners.

3. Give the priest two or three hours' instruction on how to deliver a sermon, so that he clearly enunciates and does not mumble his sermon (as the sacristan does when he babbles "Lord have mercy upon us!"). Have such preachers give sermons no more than ten times a year; that is better than hundreds who just compile sermons and thousands of half-drunk preachers.

4. Present all such sermons at the end of the year to the bishop, so that he can reliably and unerringly judge the level of education in his diocese, so that he knows the better priests, so that he can reward the most active and entrust official posts to the most capable, and so that he can check on the censor's performance.

It is essential, however, that the bishop do all this himself and that he absolutely not appoint some committee to attend to this matter. For the surest way to do something in the most miserable way is to establish a committee and give it the responsibility for some task. Committees have been created to supervise instruction and explanations of catechism.[84] After two or three years of work

---

84. Catechization was supposed to follow broad outlines established by the Synod, but the final plan and execution remained the responsibility of the individual priest, operating under the supervision of a diocesan committee.

by these communities (which are filled with the most incompetent, vapid, jealous priests and archpriests), those catechists who could not—or would not—add some money to their talks have ceased to send in their homilies, while others have abandoned this activity altogether. Why bother sending them when you know beforehand that envy and ignorance will cancel everything out, will blot out and trample into the dirt the most zealous, best-intentioned work? Why bother when the bishop, on the basis of these evaluations, will issue the most insulting reprimand, the most degrading remarks?

But in order to choose the most capable and worthy censors possible, summon the archpriests and priests of each town in turn to the provincial capital and have them deliver a sermon, after having collected beforehand precise data on their conduct. Should a simple priest rather than an archpriest prove most worthy of the censor's post, appoint him to the position, because the whole point is not rank but knowledge of the matter at hand.

Here, as in everything, the main task is to eliminate bribery. Preaching is an important matter, one of the most important in the Christian church; however, this duty must be performed honestly, irreproachably. Only under that condition will God's Word be preached with hope of success.

Honors and Awards

It is an axiom that useful work demands a reward. This axiom, however, is observed everywhere except among the clergy, or—to be more precise—among the unfortunate priests who serve in villages and district towns. The reason is that the bishops and their satellites try with all their might to see that the axiom applies to them alone, that it is a problem only for the poor white clergy. When one begins to speak of awards for the poor white clergy, our omniscient bishops usually reply: "What is one to reward them for? They are *obliged* to toil, and *they do nothing particularly extraordinary.*" My God! But are you [bishops] not *obliged* to work? Why do you so hunger for promotions to better dioceses and for awards? Well, what is so *particularly extraordinary* about what you

[181]

do for the faith and the Orthodox church, at least so far as the great majority of you are concerned? You perform liturgies no more often than rural priests; you attend to your duties with greater or lesser zeal. Well, a priest serves too and can be good or bad in performing his work. Do not both of you have the same rights to awards, albeit different ones?

Unfortunate priests! You are even denied the right to awards. Copyists and clerks, expelled from the lowest classes of schools for lack of ability, for drunkenness, or for rowdiness, have the *right* to official rank, to medals for irreproachable service, to the Order of St. Vladimir, given for thirty-five years of service. You priests alone are denied this!

"What do you mean denied? The lower clergy receive awards."

To be sure, they do receive them—but *they do not have the right to receive them.* Whenever one has the *right,* his superiors do not dare to deny the awards, whatever they may be. When specific periods have been fixed for earning these honors, once the period is up, the servitor has no need to implore or pay money to be nominated for the award: he can demand it. Is that what now exists in the clergy? Are specific terms set for receiving awards? Does the priest at least know that after a certain number of years of honest, irreproachable service he will probably receive some kind of award, without any action on his own part? No, the clergy have nothing of the sort. As in everything else, this matter too is governed by the total arbitrariness of the consistory, which can punish or reward as it sees fit. As a result, awards for the priest turn into something sold at auction. Of late, in fact, they are selling the epigonation [*nabedrennik*] at especially low prices—three to five rubles; hence almost all the younger priests, after just two or three years' service, are covered with them, whereas previously one had to serve fifteen years or more.[85] But if a priest should make bold to demand what he has earned, they will give him such a dressing down that for years to come he will forbid his grandchildren even to think of anything of the sort.

---

85. Belliustin's vexation is understandable: he himself was required to serve for ten strenuous years before he finally received the epigonation, in 1849.

"But a priest serves the Heavenly God: why does he need temporal awards—from people? He shall receive his reward in Heaven, from God."

That is true. But the priest, especially the priest, is human: would it be logical to deny him those human desires and ambitions that are not harmful to either his office or his work? Moreover, for holy and celestial purposes, he does serve people: why then should he be denied rewards from people? People have no reason to reward an anchorite, the greatest anchorite; he is concerned only about himself; the goal of all his deeds is personal benefit. But the priest must attend to the salvation of hundreds of people. Should not people encourage his work and concerns with rewards? Then, too, if rewards are already introduced, why not fix definite periods for conferring them, why not determine everything by law, why not prohibit their sale by auction?

"The rural priest does nothing extraordinary."

But is it really not something extraordinary if he, fettered by great needs, immersed in the most revolting, fetid mire of life, does not lose his way and fall? Is it not a great deed, the greatest feat, to remain honest and pure in a plague-infested atmosphere—amidst the sacristans, amidst the Orthodox people? The challenges for any anchorite are infinitely easier than those facing the priest: the former has two enemies (the devil and the flesh), while the priest has, beyond these two, millions of others that the anchorite knows only through hearsay. One anchorite, after forty years of amazing feats, suffered a terrible fall when, for just one night, they left him near a girl whom he had just cured; thus the first encounter with a person from the real world brought the downfall of the elder, who had seemed to have outlived passion and emotion. What must be the condition of the priest, who from morning to night encounters all kinds of people from the real world? What must be the condition of his spirit, when at confession they tell him things that chill him to the bone, that make his hair stand on end, that cause the blood in his veins to stand still? If the priest maintains his purity amidst all this, is this not something extraordinary?

Terrible indeed are the deprivations to which the priest—and

[183]

his wife and children—are condemned after infinite toil. If he endures all these things with patience and good humor, all this— in the opinion of you sagacious, well-meaning bishops—is not a real feat, but only because you did not experience them yourself, because you have not the slightest comprehension of them. Is it your place to judge their significance? Oh, it would be infinitely better if, instead of the academy (which merely makes you arrogant), they forced you to be a rural priest for at least ten years! Then you would be more humble, more accessible, more knowledgeable about the affairs of rural priests—who now seem insignificant to you. And you would understand your own work much better!

"They do nothing extraordinary."

Well, what about some archimandrite, decorated with two orders—what did he do that was so exceptional? Just the fact that he invented a method to run through 10,000 rubles a year (not counting the basic necessities, which were already provided to him in kind)? And even though he is completely alone and gave nothing to the poor and orphans! Or just because he plundered his monastery, which he regards as his private estate? Or just because he serves the liturgy once a week and devotes his nights to intimate talks with wellborn ladies, after locking himself into his study? True, those are great and important accomplishments, far transcending the priest's onerous work, which is so full of suffering and torment! What a comparison! One lives like a sybarite; the best chef has difficulty satisfying his capricious taste with the most elegant dishes and expensive wines; for his delicate limbs no pillow is too soft, no rug is too springy; and his eyes can endure only the sight of silver and diamonds. Who is this? Who! A sacristan's son, fed on radishes and watery cabbage soup and raised amidst indescribable filth. Oh, Horace![86] What next! Where

---

86. The text reads Getrocha, evidently a corruption of Goratsii—that is, Horace (65–8 B.C.), the great Latin lyric poet, who wrote of his plebeian origins. The manuscript has a further passage here, noting that earlier aristocrats had entered the monastery to lead an ascetic life, but that now "the dregs of society enter the monastery and make themselves into aristocrats: *o mores!*" (OR GBL, f. 231/III, k. 1, d. 66, l. 14).

will it all end? He has eyes only for silver and diamonds; his activity goes no further than reading a newspaper or magazine; in the summer he varies this regimen with an outing in his carriage to the nearest grove, or by repaying the nocturnal visits of well-born ladies, etc. Meanwhile, the priest obtains his sustenance by the sweat of his own brow; he must be content with the same support as that of an ordinary peasant, despite the fact that he must satisfy the endless demands of his parishioners, often quite capricious and senseless. In storms, blizzards, in the middle of the night, in temperatures of 25 degrees below zero, he must ride a nag to a village three to six miles away, often after a whole day of the most murderous work, etc., etc. How can one not reward the archimandrite? *He lives extremely well!* Why give awards to the priest? *He does nothing extraordinary!*

"But how else can one comfort a monk," responded one famous bishop when asked why he permits his suffragan bishop to ride about on prize trotters from Orel. "How else can one comfort a monk, if not with a fine table or even Orel trotters?" A monk!! And such comforts!!! Such a reply is not surprising, however, when it comes from the lips of a bishop who permits his aide comforts that go well beyond this. . . .

"A priest has his family to enjoy," declared this same bishop, "but a monk after all has neither a wife nor children." Does he not? No! But for a priest it is wonderful entertainment when he has neither the means nor the opportunity to educate his children the way he would like, that is, to make something of them and not just rural priests or, God help us, monks! It is no accident that such pleasure often brings tears to his eyes, the full sorrow of which all the doctors of theology are in no position to understand.

"But this archimandrite was at the *academy,* whereas the priest is a mere seminary graduate." It is truly an eternal deed to have been at the academy and to have received a master's degree! It is a great blessing for Orthodoxy to memorize some homemade courses in philosophy and other learned matters, to make compilations, even simple translations, under the ponderous rubric of "reflections," and upon leaving the academy to rest on your

[185]

laurels in the monasteries with an income of several thousand rubles a year. A miraculous achievement, worthy of every honor! "He studied at the academy."

But just what was the special service he rendered to the church as repayment for consuming its bread and wearing its clothes? For attending the academy he receives a master's cross on a chain and full support: for four years of cramming, he receives room and board for life. Amazing! Not a single university in the world gives such a luxurious reward! What else could one want? "He studied at the academy." Well, prove by word, deed, or written work that you have really savored the wisdom of academe. What could be easier? You have every opportunity to do so! Not like some priest, who at times does not even have the money to purchase paper. If you prove the worth of your degree, then God be with you, take your honors and medals (even if thousands of rubles in income are a lot for just that). But what of the others, who only know how to sign their name and add "archimandrite" and the title of their honorary order! What perfect nonsense there is in all this, just as in all the institutions of the Orthodox clergy! Someone who holds a master's or doctor's degree from the university can die of starvation if he does not have a family estate, or if he does not apply his brains to some hard work; moreover, only after twenty-five years of toil can a professor at the university provide for his old age. But just anyone with a master's degree from the academy, usually the most uneducated creature in the world, immediately upon graduation is provided with full room and board for the rest of his life. Indeed, the master's degree itself is usually given for entering monasticism; if it is not given then, it means that the student was actually good. And five or ten years after leaving the academy, the monk receives a farm [a monastery] that often has the income that not a single doctor or *triusys juris*[87] or whatever could see in his entire life, and gives himself up to all the pleasures of life without the slightest fear that he will expose himself to punishment. The reason is that the monastic

87. *Triusys juris* is corrupted Latin (the first word has a Greek ending), but evidently signifies a high legal officer, analagous to the Russian *iuris-konsultant*.

bishop in the Synod is the very same monk, and he will always rescue from trouble his fellow man in black robe, unless the monk perpetrated something that no black mantle can conceal. . . . Oh, Rus', Rus', Rus'!! Only here can such miracles take place!

"But rural priests behave so badly that they do not deserve awards." If you like, I will agree with that. Some *do* receive awards, however, but precisely which priests receive them? Just those in rich villages or those who have no children. What is their special achievement that raises them above the poor and large-familied priest? It is one thing: they have surplus money! "They do not earn awards?!" you ask. The ones who do receive honors are precisely the ones who least deserve them; the worthy receive nothing, for they do not seek or pay to receive them.

I shall not repeat why—and through whose fault—so many unworthy priests are now in villages. But just introduce a strict, irreproachably honest system for conferring honors and medals, and this alone will force many disorderly priests to turn to a good life. At present, everyone knows that even if he is supremely deserving, he will never receive anything in all his life—except what he pays for; if he is supremely unworthy (and probably makes a sizable payment), he will receive excellent awards. As a result, the former lets himself go to seed; the latter makes no attempt to correct himself. Bestow honors only on the worthy, free from levies and demands, and then you will see what a change takes place in our rural priests. If not a consciousness of duty, then at least pride will force many to come to their senses, and behave and act in a way that befits a priest. It is a great thing to encourage that which is just and intelligent. A weak person will grow strong; in a word, he can often perform miracles. But you [bishops], who are so insanely generous with punishments, want to use neither this means nor any other to improve the rural clergy, and then you complain that you lack the strength to do so! . . . And you dare to complain and confer awards on some superintendent, a most inveterate scoundrel—that is, you encourage him (and others like him) in everything foul!! My God! Lord!

If by some miracle they bestow an award on some poor priest, it is actually more of a punishment than an honor for him. In all

other institutions awards are sent to the recipient's residence; in
the church, however, the archpriest is summoned to the bishop
[to receive his]. Why? To pay off the swine at the consistory and
on the bishop's staff. God help him if he pays too little, even if
it is because he is unable to give more (they pay no heed to that:
borrow or steal wherever you can, but pay generously). Having
received his reward, he endures at the consistory such shameless,
barnyard cursing and hears so many threats that he is ready to
curse the award itself. The threats are not empty words; at the
first opportunity they are acted on. Thus, because of some utterly
trivial matter, he must endure the most merciless abuse and even
punishment; all this would never have happened if he had not
had the misfortune to come to the consistory to receive his award.[88]

88. The manuscript offers an elaborate, revealing proposal on clerical awards:
   1. The first, most important step is to fix a strict order for distributing
awards, and to set the time required for receiving each award. At the same
time give the priest the right to appeal if the consistory fails to nominate him
for an award without legal cause. This will help in some measure to eliminate
the auctioning of awards.
   2. The time required for each award should be identical to that for each
rank among civil servants. If civil service ranks receive an award every three
or four years, then why offend the dignity of priests [by rewarding them less
regularly]? . . .
   3. The time set for receiving awards should also accord with the rules
existing in the civil service. In both the civil and ecclesiastical domains, the
briefest terms should exist for those who hold a doctor's degree, a master's
degree, or a first-division ranking in the seminary's graduating class. The
time required for seminary graduates in the second and third divisions of
their class should be longer. . . . After the second award, all should have
equal status in their right to awards, whether a priest in a cathedral or one
in the worst village. That time should be the same for all because they are
all toiling. I would even go further and say that a rural priest toils a thousand
times more than a priest in a cathedral where there is no parish, where the
entire work consists of nothing more than one week of service in an entire
month.
   4. Nominations for awards for outstanding service must be carefully ver-
ified by the Synod (since the consistory invents such miraculous feats as the
nominee never even dreamed of).
   5. Special awards should be conferred on those who teach religion in state
schools, who serve as exhorters in prison, who hold the office of superintendent, or who act as the ecclesiastical deputy to secular courts. The award
should indicate the position held, just as the color and cut of collars for civil
servants define their rank and position.
   6. Some will say: "Where is one to obtain so many awards for the priest

CONCLUSION

Enough! It would take an eternity to describe *everything*.

I have written all this with intolerable pain in my heart. More than once, as I described *the existing state of affairs,* the pen slipped from my hands, though as far as possible I have tried throughout to soften the bitter truth. I took up this work only after a terrible internal struggle that lasted two years. On the one hand, my soul has always been outraged by the condition into which the clergy, especially the lower clergy, has fallen. Indeed, what true Christian would not be enraged? What could be lower, more shameful, than this condition? Everywhere, from the most resplendent drawing rooms to smoky peasant huts, people disparage the clergy with the most vicious mockery, with words of the most profound scorn and infinite disgust. Even the most understanding people speak of the clergy with pity, or fall silent when it is caricatured by others. The clergy's condition is terrible!

In thinking about the clergy's condition, I have always wished with all my heart that the clergy would somehow free itself from this condition; that it would comprehend the wondrous, lofty goal for which it was created on earth; that it would strive to attain this goal as far as its strength and possibilities permit; in brief, that it would become what it is supposed to be. This dream

---

when those specifically created for the clergy number only four: the epigonation [*nabedrennik*], the priest's skullcap [*skuf'ia*], the kamelaukion [*kamilavka*], and the pectoral cross [*napersnyi krest*]." My God, is it really so difficult to devise forty, even four hundred of them? Besides, what kind of award is the skullcap, which only disfigures a person? The most suitable award for a priest, and the most visible honor, is a cross; just have a cross serve as the basis of all awards, issued in various forms, with various degrees, and made of various metals.

7. Priests who have been fined [for misconduct] should not receive these marks of meritorious service, and those subjected to censure should have any previous awards confiscated. These measures alone would work a miracle on the clergy! [OR GBL, f. 231/III, k. 1, d. 66, ll. 15 ob.–18]

After concluding with a request that the clergy be eligible for the civil service awards that confer noble rank, Belliustin appended a direct appeal to the emperor: "I shall hope that the existing order—that is, one with the most terrible disorders, inadmissible in any well-ordered society—will be eliminated in the reign of Alexander II, who has promised so much for the organization, the happiness, and consequently the glory of Russia! . . ."

has compelled me to describe, if not all, then the greatest part of the evil that afflicts the clergy, and to point out its causes and the means that (in my sincere belief) could in some degree overcome these evils. On the other hand, I was forever held back by the fear: will they understand, that is, will they want to understand the purpose of my note? Will it not annoy those who, consciously or not, have brought the clergy to this condition? Consequently, instead of helping the clergy, will it not cause even more harm for it? Will it not fall victim to the most cruel, heartless vengeance that will destroy it once and for all?

No, I finally told myself, there is still some goodness on earth: people of goodwill, in the highest meaning of that term, still exist on earth; otherwise, the world would perish, like five unfortunate cities.[89] Without doubt, those who recognize themselves in my description will call my words slander, absurdities, an ill-intentioned pamphlet. And against me, if the Lord permits, "they will stir up the people and the elders and the doctors of the law, and having set upon and seized me, will bring me before the council. They will produce false witnesses, who will say that this man is forever saying things against this holy place [the consistory] and the law."[90] Yes, they will certainly say: Having dared to speak the truth about the consistory, he undermines the faith and law at their very foundations; the synagogue and law, the consistory and the faith, in the opinion of Pharisees and doctors of law of all times, are a single inseparable whole; and all that is done in the consistory, whatever it may be, is done in the name of the faith and the law of Christ. . . . The consistory and faith! Oh, what two mutually exclusive words those are! They are as different as light and darkness, paradise and hell, Christ and Belial!! . . .[91]

89. The phrase "five unfortunate cities" seems to be neither classical nor biblical, and apparently represents a corruption in the text.

90. Belliustin's text suddenly inserts this passage in Slavonic, taken (without attribution) from Acts 6:12–13 and modified to fit his own purposes. The original text reads: "And they stirred up the people, and the elders, and the scribes, and came upon him, and caught him, and brought him to the council. And they set up false witnesses, which said, This man ceaseth not to speak blasphemous words against this holy place, and the law."

91. Belial is a biblical variant of Satan (2 Cor. 6:15).

"Hearing what he said (how it is necessary to destroy this place and to alter the customs handed down to us from ancient times), they were touched to the quick and gnashed their teeth in fury. And they gave a great shout and stopped up their ears. Then they made one great attack on me and, flinging me out of town (as a terrifying example for others!), punished me."[92]

That is what will happen if my note falls into their hands. Will the Lord really allow my note to come within their grasp, seeing the all-consuming love in my soul for the Orthodox church, for all that can serve its well-being and glory? But perhaps it will chance to come into the hands of good people? Oh, then my note will bring at least some good fruits! Without prejudice, without malice, they will read my essay; they will dispassionately check everything that I have said here, if they have not already heard or seen it for themselves (which is unlikely, however). And they will not pass up, and perhaps will even seek, an opportunity to help our lower clergy. . . .

A radical transformation for the *entire* clergy is essential. I hope that anyone who has had the patience to read my memoir will agree. But can this transformation be achieved only by some powerful hand? Yes, it can be done only by the Sovereign himself. Does the clergy deserve to move his hand to act? That is, is it so useful and essential to the state that the Sovereign will deign to turn his attention to this matter? *That is the question!!!* Upon his decision depends the whole future fate of the clergy, that is, will it arise again to a new, joyous, and beneficial life, or will it rot in some putrid swamp? . . .

I shall not dare to give a full answer to this question. I shall, however, make bold to express just one idea.

One of two propositions is true: either the clergy is necessary for the state or it is not. Not necessary? Then eliminate it, and

92. These passages, in Church Slavonic, are taken in modified form from the book of Acts: "For we heard him say, that this Jesus of Nazareth shall destroy this place, and shall change the customs which Moses delivered us" (6:14); "When they heard these things, they were cut to the heart, and they gnashed on him [Stephen] with their teeth" (7:54); "Then they cried out with a loud voice, and stopped their ears, and ran upon him with one accord" (7:57); "And cast him out of the city, and stoned him" (7:58).

I. S. Belliustin

the sooner the better. In society, as in the human organism, anything superfluous is harmful; consequently, in order for the organism to be healthy and for society to be constructed on firm
foundations and flourish, everything harmful should be expelled
and eliminated. Is the clergy necessary? Then determine the mag-
nitude and degree of its usefulness; fix the conditions for its existence—clearly, precisely, explicitly; free it completely from human
arbitrariness; give it the means and possibility to attain the goal
for which it is admitted into the state. After all this, strictly demand
that it deviate not one step from this goal. It is essential, however,
that all this be done immediately: evil is not like good—it grows
and develops quickly. We have seen the terrible dimensions it
has attained in the clergy. Should one really wait until its fatal
atmosphere has contaminated everyone and everything? In physical diseases it often happens that an hour can make the difference
between life and death for someone who is sick. Something similar exists in the case of moral diseases. They, too, as it were,
reach a crisis; if a beneficial hand does not come in time, all is
lost; no kind of effort, no kind of power can recall to life someone
who has perished morally, be it a single individual or thousands
of individuals (that is, a whole estate) or millions of individuals
(that is, a whole nation).

I think it is necessary once again to explain that in describing
the rural clergy I had in mind only the majority of priests, but by
no means all. You can find priests who are completely worthy of
their calling, who in no way correspond to my description. There
are also some who correspond in only certain respects. And,
unfortunately, there are those who are worse than those in my
description, who are beyond any description. Let's describe these
four categories in numbers (to be sure, approximately): of one
hundred priests, I have described seventy; five are better, twenty
are bad in some respects, and five are worse.
"The field was full of human bones. . . . And they were
extremely dry."[93]

93. A Slavonic passage taken (in modified form and without attribution) from
Ezekiel (37:1–2): "The hand of the Lord was upon me, and carried me out in the

We dare to ask Thee, Lord! Will these bones come to life?[94]

Can we expect to know the bright, miraculous joy that with the lips of Christ You will say to these bones: "Here I shall put the living spirit in you. And my spirit came into you, and you will live and you will know that I am the Lord.[95]

Oh, we believe, we believe without question, that this will come to pass! God's Annointed "will speak to these corpses and the spirit of life will enter them and they will come to life and rise to their feet, a mighty host. . . ."[96]

And a mighty host, called to life, will dedicate all of its most fervent prayers to the life-giving, divinely annointed Sovereign, to all his family and realm.

And this mighty host, there in the land of eternal life, before the throne of the King of Kings, with a powerful voice will cry out the name of that tsar of the Russian land who achieved what has not been done since the time of Prince Vladimir, the equal to the Apostles: he has brought out from the darkness of the netherworld those who are to lead others to the celestial world. . . .

---

spirit of the Lord, and set me down in the midst of the valley which was full of bones, and caused me to pass by them round about: and behold, there are very many in the open valley; and lo, they were very dry."

94. A Slavonic passage taken (in modified form and without attribution) from Ezekiel (37:3): "And he said to me, Son of Man, can these bones live? And I answered, O Lord God, thou knowest."

95. A Slavonic passage taken (in modified form and without attribution) from Ezekiel (37:5–6): "Thus saith the Lord God unto these bones; Behold, I will cause breath to enter into you, and ye shall live: And I will lay sinews upon you, and will bring up flesh upon you, and cover you with skin, and put breath in you, and ye shall live; and ye shall know that I am the Lord."

96. A Slavonic passage taken (in modified form and without attribution) from Ezekiel (37:10): "So I prophesied as he commanded me, and the breath came into them, and they lived, and stood up upon their feet, an exceedingly great army."

Priests in District Towns

The condition of priests in district towns, with very few exceptions, is even worse than that of rural priests. The merchant or townsman is identical to the peasant in his level of thought and comprehension, yet makes demands that are even more absurd and shameless than those of noble landlords in the countryside. The peasant *forgets himself* before the priest; the merchant *always regards the priest* as something between a servant and a beggar (I say this without the slightest exaggeration) and treats him accordingly. On the one hand, the merchant is shameless and insolent in demanding of the priest every service, quite often illegal ones; on the other hand, it is with indignation and contempt that he tosses the priest some petty sum, or even transmits it through a servant. Thus the priest in the town is more oppressed and down-trodden than a priest in the village. True, he does not face back-breaking toil; yet anyone will agree that any toil whatever is easier than making up to every petty townsman or clerk, groveling before merchants. True, he does live in greater cleanliness than rural priests do. This is probably why our omniscient, attentive bishops think that the priests of rural towns are all rich. Rich! Look at the wealth by whose grace an urban priest quite often cannot purchase two or three poods of rye flour at a time for lack of money. Rather, he suffers still more need and deprivation than other clergy because the cost of living is so high in towns.

But in terms of morality, he does stand much higher than the rural priest. The necessity of almost daily liturgies forces him to stay sober. The desire to have at least some influence on the parishioners often forces him to deliver sermons; hence he devotes much of his time to reading and reflection. Broadly speaking, the city priest given to coarse vices is a rare phenomenon.

But his relationship to the bishop, consistory, and so on is exactly the same as in the case of rural priests.

It is even more important, more urgent than in the case of rural priests that the urban priest be freed so far as possible from the shameless intolerable despotism of parishioners, that he be provided at least with the main necessities of life, so that he need not stand for an entire hour bareheaded before a parishioner for the sake of a pood of flour or a pound of candle wax. That is particularly the case if he is unfortunate enough to have a large family. Commerce and trade are declining rapidly in absolutely all towns; millionaires, men of capital, are a legend that do not merit belief. Consequently, those means that priests used earlier, those means that they acquired with great effort and humiliation, are declining with each passing year. But the impudence and shamelessness of the parishioners grow in proportion to the impoverishment of the priest. "If we do not give you anything, you will starve to death like a dog," some merchant will often say, as he demands something that is positively prohibited for an honest priest (to marry people who are closely related or under-aged, for instance). What happens? The prospect of dying of hunger, which would really be inescapable since the urban priest has absolutely no support other than emoluments, forces him to do this base act, which he would otherwise not do if he had at least the bare necessities of life, secure and independent of these vandals.

Oh, poverty, poverty! How many worthy priests have you ruined!

One thing is unclear: why did the project for the improvement of the clergy's material condition overlook precisely those who are the most important of all—the priests in rural towns: half paupers and ready to sink into total destitution?

A Few More Words on Seminary Education*

Seminary studies, as we have seen, turn young minds from all fundamental and useful knowledge and impart only external, superficial halfknowledge of subjects that are utterly useless in

*Taken from a memoir that I have specially prepared on current education in the seminary and how it should be reordered to achieve its proper objective—namely, the training of worthy priests.

real life. At the same time, they also inspire desires that are wholly inconsistent with that position in society which the students are to occupy when they leave the seminary. As a consequence, through a long series of unrealizable hopes, they lead fervent souls to despair, petty souls to the coarsest vices, and ordinary souls to base strivings and groveling. People who have greater determination and who do not belong to one of these pathetic categories require long, onerous lessons of real life to atone for the delusions spawned by the wondrous, vapid studies that make up our so-called education at the seminary. Without the slightest exaggeration, one can say that a student graduating from the seminary requires many years to unlearn all the false ideas, to purge the most absurd prejudices, and to reject the ridiculous pretensions that he has acquired from his teachers in the seminary. They sought not so much to make him into a person as to satisfy their professorial vanity, to create superficial polish and the most horrendous pride.

Such a system of education was understandable in the seventeenth century, when education had to provide only external brilliance, that is, some means to separate yourself from the common people. At that time they fully achieved this goal. In the course of ten to fifteen years a pupil at the seminary has achieved the ability to compose—in the language of Horace and Virgil—the most ridiculous syllabic verses [*virshi*], to discuss—in the language of Cicero—*de omni re scibili*,[97] without knowing a single one properly, *et quibusdam aliis*;[98] he was regarded as a miracle of learning, as one who had aspired to all human wisdom and had mastered all fields of learning. . . . But left unchanged from the seventeenth century to the present time, such an education is either the most monumental insanity or the most terrible evil, perpetrated by those who control this great cause of the church.

How can anyone possibly not realize that the present age demands that learning be not mere polish but substance, not flowers, but fruits? How can anyone not understand when every-

97. "[Concerning] all things known."
98. "And certain other things."

one else does; how can anyone not cry aloud for all to hear that a civilized society requires true, real learning that can be applied to life, learning that prepares a person to live not at the expense of others, not to be a burden on society, but to find himself the strength and means to satisfy all the requirements of life? The Lord has given everyone the capacity for such learning. To develop this capacity and to direct it toward goodness—that is what true education is all about![99]

A Salary for Priests

I am convinced that anyone who has had the patience to read my memoir will agree that the clergy need a salary. Indeed, they need it so badly that without a salary no other measure will enable them to fulfill the purpose for which they were created. But just what salary should be set for priests in district towns and villages? How can it be set so that it is neither too large nor too small? That is, so that it will not tempt the clergy to the excesses that abundance can engender and not force them (as earlier) to resort to the emoluments that deserve the imprecation of all honorable people? First let's see how this salary is arranged in other countries:

The Catholic clergy in France at the present time receive a salary, which varies according to the place of service and the position that the individual holds in the hierarchy: simple priests in large towns receive 385 silver rubles per annum, others 300 silver rubles; rural priests draw 212 silver rubles and in addition earn from 25 to 38 rubles as emoluments for performing various rites. Hence the condition of the lower clergy in France is far from brilliant.*

Their condition is not brilliant! But after all, they have no families; they do not need to educate sons, to arrange for the marriage of

99. The manuscript contains three pages of vitriolic attack on the curriculum, primarily against the prominence accorded the "dead" classical languages (OR GBL, f. 231/III, k. 1, d. 66, ll. 22 ob.–23 ob.).
*Ekonomicheskii ukazatel' [Economic index], 1858, no. 10, p. 240.

daughters, and the like. They also enjoy free housing; the consistory, local superintendent, and others do not plunder them. If the condition of the French clergy is "not brilliant," then how would you describe the condition of our lower clergy?

To be sure, there have been proposals in Russia too to provide the clergy with salaries, and in some provinces that in fact has already been done. I recently visited one of these provinces, and— I dare to speak the whole truth—I do not find that this has changed the relationship between priest and parishioner: the same abominable extortion still exists, the same spiritual gap separates pastor and flock as before. But why has this new support failed to achieve its goal?

The salary for the rural clergy is fixed according to the number of souls in the parish, and ranges from 100 to 200 rubles. What can one say about this method of determining salaries? Above all, it could only have been devised by monks. Only they, who have imbibed all human wisdom, could have such a total lack of common sense, such a complete lack of comprehension of the necessities of life, such a profound ignorance of the economic geography of the Russian expanse. A peasant who has any brains about him at all could arrange this matter a million times more intelligently and efficaciously. At the same time, this matter graphically illustrates something found throughout the church: that ridiculous self-reliance, that senseless vanity which does not permit the monks to turn for advice to those who are directly affected— and for whom they deem all their judgments infallible.

Is it not true that anyone with ordinary common sense will tell you that in the setting of salaries for priests (or officials or whomever you wish), the local conditions must first be taken into account? Do 100 rubles have the same value in internal provinces, in the eastern provinces, in the Ukraine, in Belorussia, in Siberia? In one area the cost of living is extremely low, permitting a life of abundance; in others, where the cost of living is high, what do these 100 rubles mean—as, for example, in such provinces as Tver, Vladimir, and (especially) Smolensk?

The distribution of salaries according to the number of souls in the parish seems at first glance to show more common sense: the priest who has more work (that is, rites) receives more salary. In reality, however, here too one finds little justice. Everyone is obliged to work; as the righteous Job said, "man is born to work."[100] If this dictum applies to anyone, it is to the priest. His specific goal is work. Consequently, it is irrelevant whether his parish is large or small; in either case the priest must devote all his time to the parishioners. In a small parish the quality must compensate for the lesser quantity of labor; that equalizes the work of all priests. Moreover, salary is not a reward for labor, but support to free the priest from the necessity of seeking his sustenance, from the need to resort to means that bring his service into disgrace. Toil for public benefit should receive its rewards, but not a piece of bread. Otherwise, the priest will be nothing more or less than a hired laborer; indeed, he will be the lowest form of hired laborer—one who works for his keep. No, the salary must be fixed according to the size of the priest's family: priests without children should receive one amount, those with small families another, and those with a large family still another. All that will satisfy the demands of common sense and reason, and—in a word—will be entirely just.

But is it possible to do this? Does it mean that each family must receive a particular salary? It is not at all so difficult as it seems. In November of each year the superintendent presents information to the consistory on the current number of priests and their families. The consistory, according to a tariff previously fixed, sends him the entire sum: that is all there is to it. Some might object: Is it not necessary each year to make a special designation of sums from the government for each province? Not in the least. The number of registered priests is already fixed; consequently, it will always remain unchanged. The number of their children are more in some years, less in others; consequently, the general calculation should (here as in everything else) be prepared for a ten-year period. But to those who still consider this impossible after what I have said, I would cite the example of solders' rations, which are dispensed to retired soldiers and their wives and children, and the whole operation is run in an orderly fashion. Actually, in this case the task is even more difficult, because the

100. No single passage in the book of Job corresponds to this quote.

objects dispensed are of diverse character. So why is it impossible for the church just to dispense money?

This measure, which is more just than any other, would yield many consequences of the most salutary sort. Envy, which so shamefully divides priests, would be eliminated. All of them, so far as possible, will be made equal; there will be nothing to envy. At present, priests often race from one position to another, some from dire necessity, others from simple whim; after this reform, there will be neither cause nor need to run from one place to another. Such running about, moreover, renders the priests' work useless: they do not manage to learn either the needs of their parishes or the means to satisfy them. At the same time, authorities will be spared the superfluous administrative work that is due to the transfers, etc., etc.

The monks have determined that the priest, whatever his family status may be, should be satisfied with 100 to 200 rubles. This makes it obvious that, besides all the monks' other faults, they were also evil and ungrateful children who ruined their parents and ate them out of house and home. Not once did they stop to consider or ponder what it costs for each of them to receive an education in the district school and seminary; not once did they turn a conscientious, well-meaning, filial glance to see all the needs, all the privations in which their families lived. No doubt, each time as they set out for the seminary they were concerned only to extract as much as possible from their parents; but to the question of how, on what means, their parents (now stripped to the bone) are to live they gave not the slightest thought. That is exactly the way it was; just examine the conscience of each about his past. Otherwise, they would not dare (and would be ashamed) to say and rule that a priest with a large family could live satisfactorily on 100 to 200 rubles a year.

For the benefit of their clever minds, let me offer a model budget of a priest's cost of living. I shall take a family with a typical number of members—that is, a priest, his wife, three sons, and three daughters—a total of eight persons. Such a family, moreover, requires a house servant, making a total of nine persons. Here I shall list only the most essential items of expenditure, with the needs and costs set at a minimum:

Description of the Clergy in Rural Russia

Item	Rubles	Kopecks
1. Rye flour (60 poods)	27	00
2. Wheat flour, 2nd class (15 poods)	18	00
3. Groats, salt, malt, etc.	20	00
4. Meat, butter, eggs, etc.	15	00
5. Candles, lamp oil, soap, etc.	15	00
6. Firewood (15 *sazhen'* at 2.50 rubles per *sazhen'*)	37	50
7. Upkeep of house, stoves, dishes, furniture	25	00
8. Priest's clothing: one outer cassock, one undercassock, two pairs of boots, one pair of gloves, one hat, etc.*	30	00
9. Wife's clothing: one coat, two dresses, two pairs of shoes, scarves, etc., etc.	30	00
10. Clothes, shoes, etc. for three daughters	60	00
11. Wages for female house servant	15	00
12. Clothes and footwear for house servant	10	00
13. Purchase price and forage for one cow	25	00
14. Expenditures for the unforeseen (which one cannot calculate precisely): medicine, paper, alms, payment to gravediggers, fees for those who maintain ice holes on the river in winter [for water], etc., etc. Individually, all this is trivial, but altogether comes to at least:	20	00
15. I shall add the costs of tea, sugar, vodka (not for daily use, but in the event someone is ill; or if someone comes in soaking wet and chilled; and for guests)	10	00
Total	357	50

For sons, two of whom are studying at the seminary:

1. For room and board, at 4 rubles per month each, for 10 school months:	80	00
2. Frock coat, overcoat, footwear, etc., etc., 40 rubles each per annum. Both:	80	00
3. For travel back and forth to school	25	00
4. For petty expenses (books, paper, pens, etc.)	8	00

*Cassocks and the like are not worn out in one year's time, but warm clothing is needed for both the priest and his wife. Thus each year one must buy a major article of clothing [of one or another type].

[201]

Item	Rubles	Kopecks
For one son, who is studying at the district school:		
1. Room and board, etc., for 10 school months	20	00
2. Frock coat, sheepskin overcoat, boots, pants, peaked cap, etc., etc.	15	00
3. For travel back and forth to school	10	00
4. For books, paper, pencils, etc. (I shall not even include the cost of "presents" for the bandits who teach)	4	00
5. Unforeseen expenditures for all three sons (e.g., costs incurred in case of illness)	8	00
Total	250	00
Amount needed for the entire family:	647	50[101]

A total of 647.50 rubles! What priest, even the most sagacious and experienced, could balance his accounts with the present salary? Can a salary of 100 or 150 or 200 rubles cover all his needs?

Those who are well fed, like sheep being fattened for slaughter, may call some items of expenditure here absolutely superfluous—luxuries, which under no circumstances should be permitted in the life of the clergy. I concur. The priest is no monk; he can do without cabbage soup, porridge, and meat pies on holidays, and indeed every other kind of luxury as well. So I shall strike out items 2, 3, and 4 (net reduction: 53 rubles). "The priest is no monk, who requires five or ten rooms; he can get by with a mere hut," you say. Agreed; so let's reduce the firewood by a third (net savings: 12.50 rubles). One can also eliminate items 13 and 15, which also smack of luxury (net reduction: 35 rubles).

It seems, however, that there is nothing left to eliminate: what remains would not satisfy a peasant's hired laborer. What then is the annual budget that remains? 547 rubles. Take away 100 rubles from the sons (they are not monks' children: they can

101. Belliustin's total of 647.50 rubles tallies as a sum of the individual items; his subtotals for the two parts of the budget (397.50 rubles for the first part, 350.50 rubles for the second) are erroneous and have been corrected here.

become half beggars at an early age); that leaves 447 rubles. Still, how is the priest supposed to make ends meet with his present salary? How is he to stretch his income? Involuntarily and sorrowfully, he resorts to extortions, even though he realizes all the baseness this entails. Hence the salary is in no sense consistent with the priest's needs; it can never eliminate the extortions. What is such a small salary good for? What is the use of such half-measures?

To be absolutely fair, authorities should designate the following amount, as a minimum salary, to satisfy the most pressing needs of the priests and their families in the internal provinces.

The priest should receive 100 rubles, his wife 80 rubles. I hope that these figures will not seem unduly great; a good hired laborer earns 60 rubles a year, plus room and board. I have set 20 to 25 rubles more for the priest than for an unskilled worker; that is not too much, it seems to me.

Sons should receive 50 rubles, daughters 30 rubles a year from the time of birth. Of course, while they are children one does not have to spend so much. But that sum will just suffice for the sons when they are enrolled at the district school; at the seminary they will need twice that amount. Thus during childhood a sufficient amount will be saved up to supplement the deficits encountered later at the seminary. Similarly, during the childhood of daughters it will be possible to save up a sum that is necessary as dowry for arranging their marriages.

But where is one to obtain so much money?

Once they want to do this, they will find the money. If, however, the government does not want to increase the sums already determined and allocated, then why not introduce here what already exists in France—that is, that the parishes make up the deficiencies (once a year, absolutely not in the form of emoluments for confession, communion, etc.)? It is even more convenient to do that here than anywhere else. Just give the peasants the land now used by the priests; in exchange they are to pay—which would be easier even if they paid in kind (for example, 30 liters of one type of grain or another, 1,638 kg. of hay, straw, etc., etc.).

[203]

A Necessary Explanation

   Throughout this note, wherever I have spoken of monks, my comments have been somewhat harsh. I therefore have cause to fear that others may sharply condemn me for disrespect toward monasticism. In addition, a more substantial vengeance may rain down upon me, despite the fact that I did not dare express my views publicly (indeed, who would hear and listen to me!), but rather just confided them to paper, which no one is likely to read anyway. However, I think it is appropriate here to add a small explanatory note.

   In expressing my ideas about monks, I had in mind only *some,* certainly not *all,* monks—still less *monasticism* itself. Lord have mercy and save us! With all my soul and heart, I have the most profound respect for monasticism—perhaps still more than most of those who decorate themselves with this name. I respect true monks; I hold in veneration the names of Serafim and other ascetics of the Sarov Monastery.[102] When I read the letters of Svjatogorets, Umanets, and others, I am grateful to the Lord that righteous men still abound in our time, with their miraculous superhuman feats reminding us of the ascetics of the Lybian monasteries, of Egypt, etc.[103] And it is with feelings of love that I inscribe into my notebook (a poor legacy for my children, intended for their memory and edification) the names of those monks who are close to me. They are unknown to the general populace and known only to God: a true monk always hides away in some poor monastery and flees from the most prestigious, richest monasteries. They perfect themselves here in feats of purity and sanctity; they eagerly use every chance to capture and note the special characteristics of their ascetic life, to hear the words of salvation, attained not from courses in rhetoric or philosophy but from

102. Serafim Sarovskii (1760–1833), the most famous ascetic monk of the early nineteenth century, was canonized in 1903.
103. Sviatogorets was the literary name for Sergei (Vesnin), 1814–1853, a monk and popular religious writer. A. Umanets was another religious writer, known mainly for his travel accounts about the Orthodox East (*Poezdka na Sinai s priobshcheniem otryvkov o Egipte i Sviatoi zemle,* 2 pts. [St. Petersburg, 1850]).

sleepless nights devoted to prayer, from days onerous for human flesh and passed in the most cruel self-mortification.

But I lack the strength to speak dispassionately about a monk who has no sense of calling, who has purely human aims, who is a monk in name only—not at all in his way of life.[104] Nor can I write calmly about an archimandrite who seeks to become a bishop, about a bishop who seeks medals and better dioceses regardless of the costs, or about a monk, whoever he may be, who seeks to give himself the airs of an aristocrat and magnate. What is left then of the vows he gave upon entering monasticism? Is the vow a mere toy, a flimsy web that he can tear up at will? Nor can I write with detachment about a monk who, under the specious excuse of governing the church, claims and holds on with all his strength to the unfounded right to intervene in all the affairs of the white clergy! As if its salvation were otherwise impossible! Oh, Heavenly Father, forgive me! I lack the strength to speak calmly about such monks. . . .

Some will say: "Even at the height of all the bishop's honors, it is nevertheless possible for him to remain a monk." But did anyone deny this? I, even I, have entered the names of two or three such bishops in my notebook; I deem it my irrevocable duty each day to pray to the Lord to preserve them on the slippery path of honors and wealth. But I am firmly convinced that they did not seek elevation; in fact, they feel burdened by all this, and at the first opportunity would abandon all things of this world in order to toil for the Lord alone in a silent cell, undisturbed by the squabbles that are inescapable in diocesan affairs. But how many such bishops are there???

"Learned people cannot be mere monks." Well, for heaven's sake, why did you accept this high, angelic rank? To corrupt the souls of others? If you felt an inclination for scholarly life, you should have just become a professor! "But the professor's salary

104. The manuscript contains a further passage, deleted by Pogodin: "A rector of the seminary, an archimandrite, had the impudence and shamelessness to pronounce in front of a class of one hundred pupils: 'We are scholars, not monks; we are also officials, and the cassock is our uniform' " (OR GBL, f. 231/III, k. 1, d. 66, l. 28).

is too small, and his status is too modest and humble." So that's why! But after this I have every right to doubt that you have a true calling for the scholarly life. For a person with such a calling, salary and demands of human vanity are the least concerns; they think and worry about themselves least of all; they love scholarship for its own sake, not because in time it provides them an opportunity to ride about behind two pairs of Orel trotters, to have the best chef, etc., etc. The truly learned, said [Francis] Bacon, make the general welfare their goal, not their own happiness and greatness; they live with the conviction that they must always render accounts before God, king, and fatherland.

In general, the monk who rules the white clergy is—to say the least—a strange phenomenon. In a well-ordered society each person must be true to his calling and must never transgress its limits and meddle in any sphere (whatever it may be) that is alien to him. Thus the monk ought to know his cell, the church—and nothing else. All worldly matters should be absolutely alien to him, because he has voluntarily ceased to live for them: he has voluntarily and irrevocably taken vows of seclusion, silence, denial of material wealth, etc. It is simply not his affair to govern things outside the walls of the monastery; others besides him can be found to run the church. This is not the fifteenth to eighteenth centuries, when learning was concentrated solely in the monasteries; among the white clergy there are now many who are no less (if not more) learned, intelligent, and educated than any monk. Then, too, one does not need vast erudition to administer a diocese (indeed, they are now governed by some who have very little education); more important than a doctorate is conscientiousness, prudent sternness, knowledge of the life of those governed—the most important quality of all.

We can find superb examples of administration by priests, administration that is truly paternal and Christian, in the person of the two chief priests [*ober-sviashchenniki*].[105] We see, hear, and know how benevolently they treat their subordinates; how attentive they are to their needs (that is hardly surprising: they

---

105. *Ober-sviashchennik* was the formal title of the chief chaplains of the army and guards' regiments, both of whom were members of the Synod and one of whom, V. B. Bazhanov, had direct ties to Belliustin.

themselves are family men and—unlike monks—understand a family's material life and needs); how they support, encourage, and reward worthy priests; how they *themselves* (they have no den of thieves surrounding them) examine all the misdeeds of unworthy priests and strictly discuss not only the *actions* but also the *causes* of such behavior (that is not surprising: they know the world and its temptations) and judge accordingly. . . . Thanks to their compassion, their flock of subordinate priests are provided with a salary, room, and board; their families are provided for; even for bribes of 100 to 200 rubles, the rogues employed at the consistory or bishop's chancellery do not dare to deprive priests of their positions or even to lay a finger on them. . . .

Knowing all this, we ask: My Lord, why are we [ordinary priests] so unfortunate?! We serve still more than army chaplains, and we suffer so much while they lead a life easy for their conscience, so peaceful, fearing neither the consistory secretary nor others; even the superintendents do not rob them and they submit their confessional lists without the slightest bribes, etc., etc. Why, Lord, why? What are our sins? And how long shall we priests endure such trials and tribulations? Has the time really not yet come for us to be a *necessary* link in the state, not something merely tolerated; are we not needed to transmit the faith, devotion to the church and throne, among the lower classes of society? *The Tsar is as strong as the spirit of his people; it is not the official or the police but the priest who has the power to uplift the people's spirit.* Give them the means, give them the possibility, and—above all—save them from those who hold them in darkness and isolation, and you will see what will happen! . . .

One thing, I dare to say, must be changed: the term *ober* [used in *ober-sviashchenniki*], which is foreign and sounds alien to the ear of Orthodox Russians. Here it is better to use the term *protopresvitery*. Indeed, in the words of the Apostles: "A bishop should have one wife" (I Timothy 3:2). Hence they have every right to be called *bishops*.[106]

106. The full text of I Timothy 3:2 actually reads: "A bishop then must be blameless, the husband of one wife, vigilant, sober, of good behaviour, given to hospitality, apt to teach." The biblical term "bishop" has the generalized meaning of "leader" and was applied to men who assumed responsibility for spiritual affairs.

We put our trust in You, Lord,and we are not ashamed to do so.

A NOTE FROM THE PUBLISHER

Those who wish to participate in the publication of Russkii zagranichnyi sbornik [A Russian miscellany abroad] may address the undersigned, who pledges to include all that concerns literature, politics, and religion, with the condition, however, that the work contributed include nothing contrary to the Christian faith, the foundations of morality, legitimate authority, all of which are so precious to the Russian heart. I hereby declare this to the [empire's] crowned representative, the more willingly because I find in him a monarch who desires to govern his subjects by justice alone and to lead them along the path of peace toward further brilliant ends.

A. Frank
Paris, rue Richelieu 67

GLOSSARY

academy (*akademiia*) a higher educational institution of the Orthodox church, formally equal to a university

archbishop (*arkhiepiskop*) second highest rank in the hierarchy of Russian bishops

archimandrite (*arkhimandrit*) abbot, head of a monastery

archpriest (*protoierei*) personal title, in the mid-nineteenth century limited to a dozen or so priests in each diocese

bishop (*episkop*) lowest rank in the hierarchy of the Russian episcopate

black clergy (*chernoe dukhovenstvo*) monastic (celibate) clergy

cathedral (*sobor*) a major urban church, with or without parishioners

chief procurator (*ober-prokuror*) chief lay official of the Russian Orthodox Church, appointed by the emperor as his personal overseer

consistory (*konsistoriia*) diocesan board of clergy, which assisted the bishop in the conduct of diocesan affairs

diachok (pl. *diachki*) upper sacristan rank, with the right to wear a surplice

diocese (*eparkhiia*) the main administrative unit of the Orthodox church, directly subordinate to the Synod and usually identical to the province in civil administration

district (*uezd*) a subdivision of a diocese and province

district board (*dukhovnoe pravlenie*) an intermediate unit of diocesan administration, composed of two to three clergy and responsible for one to four districts

district school (*dukhovnoe uchilishche*) four-year elementary school for the clergy's sons

gymnasium (*gimnasium*) a public secondary school that prepared students to enter a university

hierarchy (*ierarkhiia*) the episcopate, consisting of metropolitan, archbishop, and bishop, in descending order

inspector (*inspektor*) second-ranking officer of the seminary, bearing primary responsibility for the conduct and moral education of students

[209]

metropolitan (*mitropolit*) highest title in the Russian episcopate, normally granted only to bishops appointed to the sees of St. Petersburg, Moscow, and Kiev

Old Belief (*staroobriadchestvo*) a religious sect of Orthodox dissenters who rejected the liturgical reforms of the seventeenth century

pomoch' parish assistance to the local clergy in the cultivation of their land

ponomar (pl. *ponomari*) lower sacristan rank, inferior to *diachok* and without the right to wear a surplice

rector (*rektor*) head of a seminary (always a monk) or district school (usually a monk, sometimes an archpriest)

sacristan (*tserkovnosluzhitel'*) an unordained member of the clergy holding the rank of *diachok* or *ponomar*, without the right to administer sacraments

schism (*raskol*) official term for the Old Belief

seminary (*seminariia*) a six-year church school midway between the district school and the academy, formally equivalent to a gymnasium

superintendent (*blagochinnyi*) a local supervisor of the clergy, usually with responsibility for overseeing ten to fifteen parishes

white clergy (*beloe dukhovenstvo*) parish clergy, consisting of both ordained clergy (archpriests, priests, deacons) and sacristans (*diachki* and *ponomari*)

zapiska memoir

SELECTED BIBLIOGRAPHY

For a convenient introduction to literature on the prerevolutionary church, see the bibliographies assembled in Theofanis Stavrou and Robert Nichols, eds., *Russian Orthodoxy under the Old Regime* (Minneapolis, 1978), pp. 205–237. Specialized bibliographies are to be found in A. P. Dobroklonskii, *Rukovodstvo po istorii russkoi tserkvi*, 4. vols. (Riazin and Moscow, 1886–93); G. V. Florovskii, *Puti russkogo bogosloviia* (Paris, 1937), pp. 527–574; G. L. Freeze, *The Parish Clergy in Nineteenth-Century Russia: Crisis, Reform, Counterreform* (Princeton, 1983), pp. 477–496; and Igor Smolitsch, *Geschichte der russischen Kirche* (Leiden, 1964), pp. xv–liii.

MAIN WORKS OF I. S. BELLIUSTIN

"Chto sdelano po voprosu o dukhovenstve." *Beseda*, 1871, no. 3, pp. 134–157; no. 11, pp. 61–82; 1872, no. 2, pp. 179–210.
"Dukhovenstvo i zemstvo." *Dukh khristianina*, 4 (1865), no. 9: 467–484.
"Dukhovno-obshchestvennye voprosy." *Sbornik "Nedeli": russkie obshchestvennye voprosy* (St. Petersburg, 1872), pp. 404–417.
"Dva i poslednie slova o narodnom obrazovanii." *Zhurnal Ministerstva narodnogo obrazovaniia*, 109 (1861), otd. 1: 141–148.
"Etnograficheskie ocherki (Kaliazinskogo uezda)." *Zhurnal zemlevladel'tsev*, 1 (1858), pt. 6: 11–54.
Iz tserkovnoi besedy. St. Petersburg, 1872.
"Iz zametok o perezhitom." *Tserkovno-obshchestvennyi vestnik*, 1882, nos. 18, 33, 36, 39, 43, 47, 54, 59.
"K voprosu o raskole." *Tserkovno-obshchestvennyi vestnik*, 1879, nos. 43–44.
Liturgiia: Iz pisem o tserkovnom bogosluzhennii. St. Petersburg, 1886.
Nauka: put' k tsarstvu vechnomu. Iz tserkovnykh pouchenii. St. Petersburg, 1867.

[211]

"Nravstvennoe znachenie monastyrei." *Beseda*, 1872, no. 9.

Opisanie sel'skogo dukhovenstva. Paris [Leipzig], 1858.

O tserkovnom bogosluzhenii. St. Petersburg, 1862. 2nd ed., 1865.

"O vrachakh dlia krest'ian." *Zhurnal zemlevladel'tsev*, 1 (1858), pt. 7: 59–67.

"Po voprosu o bespriiutnykh sirotakh-devitsakh dukhovnogo zvaniia." *Pravoslavnoe obozrenie*, 1862, no. 6 (zametki), pp. 50–53.

"Prikhodskie uchitelia." *Zhurnal Ministerstva narodnogo prosveshcheniia*, 110 (1861), otd. 1: 1–30.

Put' uskii i shirokii. St. Petersburg, 1870.

Sel'skoe dukhovenstvo vo Frantsii. St. Petersburg, 1871.

"Sem'ia." *Zhurnal zemlevladel'tsev*, 4 (1858), otd. 2: 93–120; 5 (1858), otd. 2: 41–80.

Strastnaia nedelia. Moscow, 1869.

Vechernie besedy s krest'ianami. St. Petersburg, 1865. 2d ed., 1886.

PRIMARY SOURCES

Barsov, I. I. "Vospominaniia protoiereia." *Russkaia starina*, 105 (1901): 283–304, 521–558; 106 (1901): 53–75, 277–306, 497–522; 107 (1901): 77–96, 241–266, 531–554; 108 (1901): 85–100, 271–291, 533–560.

Barsov, S. T. *Sbornik deistvuiushchikh i rukovodstvennykh tserkovnykh i tserkovno-grazhdanskikh postanovlenii po vedomstvu pravoslavnogo ispovedaniia*. St. Petersburg, 1885.

Elagin, N. V. *Beloe dukhovenstvo i ego interesy*. St. Petersburg, 1881.

——. *Ruskoe dukhovenstvo*. Berlin, 1859.

Giliarov-Platonov, N. P. *Iz perezhitogo*. 2 vols. Moscow, 1886.

Golovine, I. G. *Mémoires d'un prêtre russe, ou La Russie religieuse*. Paris, 1849.

Griaznov, E. *Iz shkol'nykh vospominanii byvshego seminarista Vologodskoi seminarii*. Vologda, 1903.

Ismailov, F. *Vzgliad na sobstvennuiu proshedshuiu zhizn'*. Moscow, 1860.

Izo dnia v den': Zapiski sel'skogo sviashchennika. St. Petersburg, 1878.

Livanov, F. V. *Zhizn' sel'skogo dukhovenstva*. 3 pts. Moscow, 1877.

M. V. *Shkol'nye i semeinye vospominaniia*. 2 pts. St. Petersburg–Petrograd, 1911–15.

Malein, I. M. *Moi vospominaniia*. Tver, 1910.

Nikitin, I. S. "Dnevnik seminarista." In *Sochineniia*, 4 vols., 4:7–130. Moscow, 1959–61.

Pevnitskii, V. F. *Moi vospominaniia*. 2 vols. Kiev, 1910–11.

Pomyalovsky, N. G. *Seminary Sketches*. Trans. Alfred R. Kuhn. Ithaca, 1973.

Selected Bibliography

Popov, A. *Vospominaniia prichetnicheskogo syna*. Vologda, 1913.

Rostislavov, D. I. "Nashi monastyri." *Beseda*, 1872, nos. 3–8, 10–11.

———. *Ob ustroistve dukhovnykh uchilishch v Rossii*. 2 vols. Leipzig, 1863.

———. *O pravoslavnom belom i chernom dukhovenstve*. 2 vols. Leipzig, 1866.

———. *Opyt issledovanii ob imushchestvakh i dokhodakh nashikh monastyrei*. St. Petersburg, 1876.

———. "Peterburgskaia dukhovnaia akademiia do gr. Protasova: Vospominaniia." *Vestnik evropy*, 1872, nos. 7–9.

———. "Peterburgskaia dukhovnaia akademiia pri gr. Protasove, 1836–1855." *Vestnik evropy*, 1883, nos. 7–9.

———. "Zapiski." *Russkii arkhiv*, 27 (1880), nos. 1, 3–4; 28 (1880), nos. 5–7; 33 (1882), no. 11; 34 (1882), no. 6; 42 (1884), no. 6; 43 (1884), nos. 7–8; 56 (1887), no. 11; 57 (1887), no. 1; 59 (1888), no. 7; 76 (1892), no. 12; 77 (1893), nos. 1–3; 78 (1893), no. 4; 79 (1893), no. 9; 80 (1893), no. 10; 81 (1894), no. 6; 82 (1894), nos. 9, 12; 83 (1895), nos. 3–4, 6.

[Rozanov, A. I.] *Zapiski sel'skogo sviaschchennika*. St. Petersburg, 1882.

Savva (Tikhomirov). *Khronika moei zhizni: Avtobiograficheskie zapiski*. 9 vols. St. Petersburg, 1897–1911.

Vladislavlev, V. F. *Avtobiograficheskie zapiski*. Tver, 1906.

SECONDARY SOURCES

Becker, Christopher B. "The Church School in Tsarist Social and Educational Policy from Peter to the Great Reforms." Ph.D. dissertation, Harvard University, 1964

Blagovidov, F. V. *Deiatel'nost' russkogo dukhovenstva v otnoshenii k narodnomu obrazovaniiu v tsarstvovanie imp. Aleksandra II*. Kazan, 1891.

Bryner, Erich. *Der geistliche Stand in Russland: Sozialgeschichtliche Untersuchungen zu Episkopat und Gemeindegeistlichkeit der russischen orthodoxen Kirche im 18. Jahrhundert*. Göttingen, 1982.

Clayton, Dennis R. "Parish or Publish: The Kiev Ecclesiastical Academy, 1819–1869." Ph.D. dissertation, University of Minnesota, 1978.

D'iakonov, K. *Dukhovnye shkoly v tsarstvovanie Nikolaia I-ogo*. Sergiev–Posad, 1907.

Edwards, D. W. "Orthodoxy during the Reign of Tsar Nicholas I: A Study in Church–State Relations." Ph.D. dissertation, Kansas State University, 1967.

Felmy, K.-Ch. *Predigt im orthodoxen Russland: Untersuchungen zu Inhalt und Eigenart der russischen Predigt in der zweiten Hälfte des 19. Jahrhunderts*. Göttingen, 1972.

Florovskii, G. V. *Puti russkogo bogosloviia*. Paris, 1937.

Freeze, Gregory L. "A Case of Stunted Anticlericalism: Clergy and Society in Imperial Russia." *European Studies Review*, 13 (1983): 177–200.

——. "Caste and Emancipation: The Changing Status of Clerical Families in the Great Reforms." In *The Family in Imperial Russia*, ed. David L. Ransel, pp. 124–150. Urbana, Ill., 1978.

——. *The Parish Clergy in Nineteenth-Century Russia: Crisis, Reform, Counter-reform.* Princeton, 1983.

——. "Revolt from Below: A Priest's Manifesto on the Crisis in Russian Orthodoxy." In *Russian Orthodoxy under the Old Regime*, ed. Theofanis Stavrou and Robert Nichols, pp. 90–124. Minneapolis, 1978.

——. *The Russian Levites: Parish Clergy in the Eighteenth Century.* Cambridge, Mass., 1977.

Gagarin, Jean [Ivan]. *Le Clergé russe.* Brussels, 1871. Translated as *The Russian Clergy.* London, 1872.

Nichols, Robert L. "Metropolitan Filaret and the Awakening of Orthodoxy." Ph.D. dissertation, University of Washington, 1972.

Oswalt, Julia. *Kirchliche Gemeinde und Bauernbefreiung: Soziales Reformdenken in der orthodoxen Gemeindegeistlichkeit Russlands in der Ära Alexanders II.* Göttingen, 1975.

Papkov, A. A. *Tserkov' i obshchestvo v epokhu Tsaria-Osvoboditelia (1855–1870 gg.).* St. Petersburg, 1902.

Preobrazhenskii, I. V. *Otechestvennaia tserkov' po statisticheskim dannym s 1840–41 po 1890–91 gg.* 2d ed. St. Petersburg, 1901.

Runovskii, N. *Tserkovno-grazhdanskoe zakonopolozhenie otnositel'no pravoslavnogo dukhovenstva v tsarstvovanie Imp. Aleksandra II.* Kazan, 1898.

Smolitsch, Igor. *Geschichte der russischen Kirche.* Vol. 1. Leiden,1964.

——. *Russisches Mönchtum: Entstehung, Entwicklung, und Wesen, 988–1917.* Würzburg, 1953.

Stavrou, Theofanis, and Robert Nichols, eds. *Russian Orthodoxy under the Old Regime.* Minneapolis, 1978.

Stupperich, Robert, ed. *Die Russische Orthodoxe Kirche in Leben und Lehren.* Wittenberg, 1966.

Titlinov, B. V. *Dukhovnaia shkola v Rossii v XIX st.* 2 vols. Vilna, 1908–9.

Znamenskii, P. V. *Prikhodskoe dukhovenstvo v Rossii so vremeni Petra Velikogo.* Kazan, 1873.